INTRODUCING BAKHTIN

MANCHESTER
UNIVERSITY PRESS

FOR MY PARENTS

SUE VICE

INTRODUCING BAKHTIN

MANCHESTER UNIVERSITY PRESS

MANCHESTER AND NEW YORK

distributed exclusively in the USA by St. Martin's Press

Published by Manchester University Press
Oxford Road, Manchester M13 9NR, UK
and Room 400, 175 Fifth Avenue, New York, NY 10010, USA

Distributed exclusively in the USA by
St. Martin's Press, Inc., 175 Fifth Avenue, New York,
NY 10010, USA

British Library Cataloging-in-Publication Data
A catalogue record for this book is available from the British Library

Library of Congress Cataloging-in-Publication Data
Vice, Sue, 1961–
Introducing Bakhtin/Sue Vice
    p.   cm.
Includes bibliographical references and index.
ISBN 0-7190-4327-1 (cloth; ak. paper). – ISBN 0-7190-4328-X (pbk.;
alk. paper)
1. Bakhtin, M. M. (Mikhail Mikhailovitch), 1895–1975.
2. Criticism. I. Title.
PN81.V46 1997
801'.95'092—dc21

ISBN   0 7190 4327 1 *hardback*
       0 7190 4328 x *paperback*

First published in 1997
01 00 99 98   10 9 8 7 6 5 4 3 2

Typeset by Action Typesetting Ltd, Gloucester
Printed in Great Britain
by Bell & Bain Ltd, Glasgow

CONTENTS

ACKNOWLEDGEMENTS

I am grateful to the following for all kinds of help throughout this study: Carol Adlam, Rachel Armstrong, John Banks, Rachel Falconer, Alex George, John Haffenden, Ken Hirschkop, Agnes McAuley, Ian MacKillop, Gemma Marren, Alastair Renfrew, Neil Roberts, Anita Roy, Erica Sheen, Stephanie Sloan, other members of Manchester University Press's staff, and my family. Thanks also to St Andrews University Library, which was invaluable during two summers, and to the *Guardian* for permission to reproduce Pass Note no. 839, 'The Gay Gene', 24 June 1996.

ABBREVIATIONS

Abbreviations of titles of the works of the Bakhtin circle appear before page numbers in the text, and in the notes, except where extended discussion makes clear which work is meant. All phrasing, italics, and so on are Bakhtin's own except where signalled otherwise (ellipses of the kind '[...]' are mine). Full publication details are to be found in the bibliography.

AA   *Art and Answerability: Early Philosophical Essays by M. M. Bakhtin*

AH   'Author and Hero in Aesthetic Activity' in AA

B   'The Bildungsroman and Its Significance in the History of Realism (Toward a Historical Typology of the Novel)', in SG

DI   *The Dialogic Imagination*

DN   'Discourse in the Novel', in DI

EN   *Epic and Novel*, in DI

F   *Freudianism: A Critical Sketch*

FM   *The Formal Method in Literary Scholarship: A Critical Introduction to Sociological Poetics*

FPND   'From the Prehistory of Novelistic Discourse', in DI

FTC   'Forms of Time and Chronotope in the Novel', in DI

MPL   *Marxism and the Philosophy of Language*

PDP   *Problems of Dostoevsky's Poetics*

PND   'From the Prehistory of Novelistic Discourse', in DI

PSG   'The Problem of Speech Genres', in SG

PT   'The Problem of the Text in Linguistics, Philology and the Human Sciences: An Experiment in Philosophical Analysis', in SG

RW   *Rabelais and His World*

RQ   'Response to a Question from the *Novy Mir* Editorial Staff', in SG

SG   *Speech Genres and Other Late Essays*

TPA   *Toward a Philosophy of the Act*

TRDB   'Toward a Reworking of the Dostoevsky Book', in PDP

Introduction

The scope of this work

This book was inspired by the perception that there was no basic introductory guide to Bakhtin's works and theories which could be recommended to students: that is, humanities students who probably know no Russian, although they are familiar with literary criticism and theory. The works available on Bakhtin tend to fall into two camps: high-level texts which presuppose a knowledge of Bakhtinian terminology and familiarity with his writings; and critical collections of his works, which juxtapose short introductory sections with edited selections from the writings of the Bakhtin circle. Neither mode is quite right as a general, literary introduction.[1]

I have concentrated in this study on those of Bakhtin's terms which are of most interest to such students, and other readers – these are heteroglossia, dialogism, polyphony, carnival and the grotesque, and the chronotope – and, on a smaller scale, on Bakhtin's attitude to poetry, epic, and drama. Of course, different categories could have been isolated; Carol Adlam, for instance, gives a list which ranges from the broad to the particular: 'dialogism; openendedness; chronotopes; genre; great time'. Anthony Wall and Clive Thomson have a slightly different list of concerns: chronotope, carnival and becoming, memory, and language in the everyday. Gary Saul Morson and Caryl Emerson's 'three global concepts' in *Mikhail Bakhtin: Creation of a Prosaics* are: prosaics, unfinalizability, and dialogue.[2] As well as trying to work out what Bakhtin meant, by using his own phraseology as much as possible, I have done what many Bakhtinian critics do, which is to extend the implications of his arguments to fields or purposes he did not have in mind. Hence the appearance of his ideas in film, post-structuralist, post-colonial and queer theory, following the route mapped out by feminist extensions of his work. This is just to list the literary homes Bakhtin's work has found; his concepts also appear in works on fine art, architecture, and social geography.[3]

The habit of concentrating on Bakhtin's literary writings, rather than his more philosophical ones, is continued here. This primarily Western focus is largely the consequence of the history of translating Bakhtin's writings from Russian into other languages, which has been, as Ruth Ginsburg notes, 'both piecemeal and non-chronological'.[4] Continuing this habit goes against the arguments of writers, both Russian and anglophone, who see the proper role of any discussion of Bakhtin's work as, in the words of Paul de Man, the use of the 'poetics of novelistic discourse [to] gain access to the power of a hermeneutics'.[5] That is, literary examples are there to help the critic construct a more general interpretative structure. However, for students and critics in many humanities disciplines, de Man's phrase may work best the other way round: Bakhtinian hermeneutics may be used to gain access to the specifics of the novel. It is true that Bakhtin saw himself as a philosopher, rather than a literary critic. His disciple and executor Sergey Bocharov, who was one of the students responsible for bringing Bakhtin into the limelight in the 1960s, mentions the 'grimace' with which Bakhtin used the phrase 'merely literary criticism' to describe the first chapter of *Problems of Dostoevsky's Poetics*.[6] However, Bakhtin was interested in literary texts as a testing-ground for his ethical and philosophical concerns; and, according to Bakhtin's own categories, his philosophical bias does not mean that some approaches to Bakhtin are valid – the Russian, Russian-speaking, or hermeneutic, for example – and some not – those which seek to 'imitate' or 'apply' his work, as de Man rather disdainfully puts it.[7] Anthony Wall and Clive Thomson observe that 'what one says about Bakhtin is never what Bakhtin himself says [...] no study of Bakhtin's work can ever function "within Bakhtin" or even "from within Bakhtin's thought"',[8] and this is the 'alibi' for the approach I have taken in this work. Bakhtin writes on value-laden under-standing, and in his article 'Response to a Question from the *Novy Mir* Editorial Staff' he argues that, '[c]*reative understanding* does not renounce itself, its own place in time, its own culture [...] it is immensely important for the person who understands to be *located outside* the object of his or her creative understanding – in time, in space, in culture' (RQ 7).

Specific points are exemplified in the present work with the help of textual examples, either my own or Bakhtin's. Such is the lure of producing Bakhtinian readings of individual texts, texts which often surge into new meaning when reconsidered in terms of polyphony or the chronotope, that I am sometimes conscious of getting carried away with the examples, as if they are the point of the investigation. This is a common problem in literary Bakhtin studies: does the literary text serve to clarify and complicate Bakhtin's terms, do those terms produce a new reading of the text, or is there a dialogic mixture of two voices, one critical, one fictional? Can one avoid simply trainspotting occurrences of, say, words with a loophole, and go on to make something more out of their presence? Bakhtin says, of his own attention to nineteenth-century novelistic versions of the carnivalesque, that his interest is in 'the discourse of a *language*, and not its *individual use* in a particular *unrepeatable context*, although, of course, the one cannot exist without the other' (PDP 159). David Lodge describes his interest in dialogism in terms of increased flexibility and a widening of options:

> Instead of trying desperately to defend the notion that individual utterances, or texts, have a fixed, original meaning which it is the business of criticism to recover, we can locate meaning in the dialogic process of interaction between speaking subjects, between texts and readers, between texts themselves.[9]

Much has been written on the 'Bakhtin industry', and the reasons for Bakhtin's popularity in the West today – Robert Crawford, for example, calls Bakhtin *the* critic for the 1990s, as one who has much to offer those interested 'in the construction of regional and national territorial voices in literature'; and much has been said on the differences between the Russian and the Western Bakhtin.[10] Bakhtin's style, familiar to Western readers in translation, is infamously repetitive and unsystematic. Further, Bakhtin's use of central concepts may shift according to context, or he may attempt to include within individual concepts incompatible ideas, as he does for example in the case of both dialogism and heteroglossia. Caryl Emerson rather acidly describes the style of *Rabelais and His World* as an alternation between 'naive ecstatics and ploddingly dull academic prose'; Sergey Bocharov, on the other hand, quotes the Russian scholar M. L. Gasparov's comment that Bakhtin's style is '"*provocatively* imprecise"'.[11] None the less, much of Bakhtin's writing is accessible and lively, peppered with soundbites and concrete analogies for the abstractions he is discussing.

As I have remarked, Bakhtin's writing has been read alongside contemporary post-structuralist theory, and, particularly, in relation to feminist theory.[12] Critics have pointed out both the implicit patriarchal bias, and yet also the potential for reappropriation, offered to feminist criticism by Bakhtin's theories. Nancy Glazener has usefully summarized what Bakhtin can do for feminism. First, Bakhtin's notion of novelistic discourse as a struggle among socio-ideological languages 'unsettles the patriarchal myth that there could be a language of truth transcending relations of power and desire'; and second, gender must have a shaping influence on discourse as it is a very clear instance of social differentiation within language (albeit not one mentioned by Bakhtin). As Jane Miller puts it, 'It is not surprising that certain feminist writers have turned to Bakhtin's and Volosinov's work on language, given its emphasis on speakers of language rather than on language as an abstraction and on literature's place within such a view of language'.[13] I have tried to extend a gender-aware analysis to Bakhtin's other categories, such as the chronotope and 'outsideness', as well as the more well-trodden area of Rabelaisian grotesque realism. Bakhtin's orientation, as he would say, was towards a more traditional model of the human subject, and of the author, than critics in the post-structuralist era may be accustomed to, and for this reason it seemed unnecessary here to go far into juxtaposing or combining his theories with those of, say, the psychoanalyst Jacques Lacan, although I have compared Julia Kristeva with Bakhtin. Several critics have pointed out that the overlap in Lacan's and Bakhtin's terminology – Bakhtin detects an 'other' in language, Lacan in the psyche – elides an important distinction. While Bakhtin's other is social, Lacan's is psychological.[14] Interesting work could be done comparing Lacan's model of self–other relations, and his interest in language and the subject, with Bakhtin's, as Ann Jefferson has achieved in her comparison of Barthes and Sartre with Bakhtin. A comparison between Bakhtin and Julia Kristeva is a different matter, as the influence Bakhtin has had on her theories, and her connections, as a Russian-speaking Bulgarian émigrée, with the culture he came from, make linking her work with his 'interilluminating' in an introductory study of Bakhtin.

A general problem that Bakhtin's own chronotopic moment raises is his preference for the term 'author' over 'narrator'. Most readers will be accustomed to using the latter much more frequently, and 'author' only for the particular historical personage or her or his implied variants. Ken Hirschkop argues that Bakhtin uses the term 'author' to refer to 'the structure of the artistic work as a whole, its formal dimension', so that we can make a distinction in Bakhtin's writing between the author of the work and 'the actual "person" who wrote it'. Hirschkop continues, 'If the narrator appears within the work as an identifiable voice, then it is no longer equivalent to the author insofar as it has itself become an "image", another voice shaped by the authorial structure'.[15]

I have started this introductory work with a chapter on heteroglossia, as it is this concept of the many 'different languages' which make up social life that underlies all Bakhtin's other concepts. Bakhtin, rather confusingly, also claims that some languages may be more heteroglot than others, an argument which, taken to its logical conclusion, would mean that a particular language might equally be *mono*glot. It is important to recognize this kind of confusion in Bakhtin's work, of the specific instance with the general principle, but it need not prevent one from using 'heteroglossia' as a critical tool. In this chapter, the central textual example is Henry Roth's 1934 novel *Call It Sleep*, in which images of heteroglot variety and interaction abound. Although the novel's characters are multilingual, their utterances are represented in English, making it a perfect example of Bakhtin's argument that heteroglossia, transposed into a literary text, appears in artistic form, and not as literal samples. *Call It Sleep* also offers specific challenges to parts of Bakhtin's discussion of heteroglossia: its images of an authoritative, monoglot language – in this case Biblical Hebrew – are brought into contact and conflict with the surrounding everyday languages. More relativization takes place than Bakhtin allows for.

Dialogism, the subject of Chapter 2, is Bakhtin's central concept. It refers to the ceaselessly shifting power relations between words, their sensitivity to each other, and the relativizing force of their historically motivated clashes and temporary resolutions. Again, Bakhtin treats this category in a manner which confuses the historical with the normative: he argues that dialogism is both a universal property of language and a specific property to be found only in certain instances of language. After discussing examples of the dialogic construction of meaning from a medium dear to Bakhtin's heart, the newspaper, I go on to give a detailed dialogic reading of two novels. Helen Zahavi's *Dirty Weekend* (1991) wears its dialogism on its sleeve: the battle between different meanings within single utterances is very clear here, and a Bakhtinian approach can make linguistic and political sense out of this strategy. The second novelistic example, James Kelman's *How Late It Was, How Late* (1994), presents a particular narrative problem. As both narrator and character speak the same Glaswegian dialect, it is often difficult to distinguish between them; indeed, it is not clear if there *is* any difference between them. This difficulty is the strength of Kelman's novel, and Volosinov's discussion of the varieties and history of reported speech, from *Marxism and the Philosophy of Language*, can help to establish how and why such a textual blurring works.

Bakhtin's concept of polyphony, the subject of Chapter 3, is deceptively simple; so much so that many critics have assumed the term is synonymous with heteroglossia or dialogism. In fact, it refers to the 'many-voicedness' of texts in which characters and narrator speak on equal terms. The narrator does not speak over the characters' heads, giving the reader privileged moral or physical information; the characters narrate themselves, and the narrator never knows more than they do. The textual example here is that of Malcolm Lowry's revisions to his 1947 novel *Under the Volcano*, made over a period of ten years. These revisions consisted largely of converting an obtrusive, omniscient narrator into a narrator whose voice is simply one among others within a polyphonic text. For Lowry, such alteration was equivalent to 'writing better'; it is as if he had hit accidentally upon Bakhtin's notion of polyphony, and examination of specific changes in the drafts shows the notion being enacted. At the same time, Lowry progressively added various heteroglot and intertextual layers to his novel, multiplying the number of languages among which dialogic friction could occur. The case of *Under the Volcano* shows in action the relations between the three categories of heteroglossia, dialogism, and polyphony. I conclude this chapter with a consideration of how a film can be polyphonic, or double-voiced, if one credits it with a narratorial presence.

Bakhtin's notion of carnival is appealingly based on the historical carnivals of the Middle Ages, which, he says, have survived in certain kinds of writing: the disruptive, profane, grotesquely realistic. This is discussed in Chapter 4. Critics have raised various objections to Bakhtin's uncomplicatedly liberatory model of carnival. Despite, or because of, the fact that Julia Kristeva's project and intellectual heritage are different from Bakhtin's in important respects, while overlapping in others, I have found it useful to consider these problems by comparing Bakhtin's discussion of the features and functions of the grotesque body with Kristeva's psychoanalytic view of the same phenomena, which she calls 'the abject'. The textual example I have used, as well as discussing the way in which Bakhtin uses Rabelais as his grotesque exemplar, is

Jenefer Shute's *Life-size* (1992), a dark carnivalesque novel about the anorexic body.

The last category I consider, in Chapter 5, is the chronotope, Bakhtin's term for the specific 'time-space' co-ordinates which shape every novel. Bakhtin uses the road narrative as an example of a textual device where time and space are clearly interwoven: time passed means space travelled. I have taken up this idea, and argue that a chrontopically aware reading of Ridley Scott's film *Thelma and Louise* (1991) can both increase the spectator's appreciation of that film and show the potential for Bakhtin's theory to be extended to include categories, such as gender, which he does not consider. Ida Fink's fictionalized autobiography, *The Journey* (1992), set during the years of the Holocaust, shows in a different way the workings of Bakhtin's concept. In this novel, the chronotopic layers of history, memory, and narrative chronology are very starkly inter-connected.

It may be helpful, before going any further, to consider two interrelated debates which will strike anyone starting to read in or about Bakhtin. The first is the 'authorship debate'; the second concerns Saussure.

The problem of the canon

Three works regularly included in the Bakhtin canon are published under names other than his. *Freudianism* and *Marxism and the Philosophy of Language* are by V. N. Volosinov, while *The Formal Method in Literary Scholarship* is credited to M. M. Bakhtin/P. M. Medvedev (although it was first published, and in some editions continues to be published, under the name of Medvedev alone). Are these '"deuterocanonical"' texts[16] really by Bakhtin himself, writing under the protective covering of the names of others? (Rather arbitrarily, I have chosen to discuss *Marxism and the Philosophy of Language* in the present work, in the chapter on dialogism, because of Volosinov's insights into the double-voiced phenomenon of reported speech, but not *The Formal Method*.)

Critics have a variety of voices in the authorship debate. The editors and translators of Volosinov's works say, understandably, that the historical Valentin Volosinov was indeed responsible for the best part of the works which bear his name. The translator of *Freudianism*, I. R. Titunik, thinks Volosinov has been given short shrift, and offers an account of the genesis of the authorship problem to explain why this is so. A note to a 1973 article on

Bakhtin by the Soviet linguist Viacheslav V. Ivanov claimed that works signed by Volosinov or Medvedev were in fact written by Bakhtin. Ivanov offered no proof for his claim, and Bakhtin, who was alive until 1975, made no statement on the matter at the time; but this attribution 'was immediately widely accepted'. At the same time, details about the Bakhtin circle, the group of young scholars surrounding Bakhtin in the 1920s, began to come to light. This inspired some commentators, including Albert J. Wehrle, translator of *The Formal Method*, to speculate about how far collaboration might have gone in the circle: did each text have only one author, or were they collaborative works?[17] It has become accepted practice to get around the authorship problem by saying that all these works are the product of 'the Bakhtin circle' or 'school'.

As Ladislav Matejka and Titunik add in the translators' introduction to *Marxism and the Philosophy of Language*, Volosinov and Medvedev differ from Bakhtin in their particular kinds of expertise, the technical aspects of which are very clear in their respective books. The matter is further complicated by 'the explicitly espoused and implemented Marxist orientation of the writings signed by Volosinov and Medvedev and the conspicuous absence of any such orientation in the writings signed by Baxtin [*sic*]', although, as we will see, not everyone agrees with this assessment of the two as card-carrying Marxist critics.[18]

As Titunik points out in the translator's introduction to *Freudianism*, opinions on the authorship debate generally line up with particular views on Bakhtin's Marxist leanings. This is because Marxist discourse and terminology are much more prominent in those books not published under Bakhtin's name. Put briefly, the three positions are: first, that Bakhtin's Marxism is just 'window-dressing'; second, that it is a genuine element of his works; third, that we should keep an open mind on the issue. It is easier to argue that Bakhtin was not a Marxist if he is *not* thought to be responsible for Volosinov and Medvedev's works, but, if it is claimed that he was, then the 'window-dressing' argument can be applied to them too.

Titunik describes the first position in the authorship debate, one of denying the troublesome Marxist content of Bakhtin's works. Titunik interprets silence on the matter of Bakhtin's 'Marxist credentials' from scholars in the then Soviet Union as implicit denial of these credentials. These scholars include, Titunik argues, Bocharov, Ivanov, and V. Kozhinov – leader of the student group who helped rehabilitate Bakhtin's reputation.[19] Titunik describes the majority view of Western critics, that any apparent Marxist leanings in Bakhtin's work are to be ascribed to '"expedience and "disguise", as a necessary but ultimately meaningless pretence undertaken for the sake of making those works acceptable for the Soviet press'. It is thus possible to claim that Bakhtin was responsible for the works currently under Volosinov and Medvedev's names, in which any Marxist elements are also just 'window-dressing'. Titunik says Michael Holquist is the main proponent of this view, that Bakhtin is the author of all the disputed works, and that their veneer of Marxist commitment can easily be explained away. In his introduction to *The Dialogic Imagination*, Holquist declares that he believes 'ninety percent of the three books' are the work of Bakhtin.[20] On the other hand, some Marxist scholars, who endorse the clear and 'genuine' Marxism of Volosinov's and Medvedev's works, in contrast to the absence of such an approach in Bakhtin's, have concluded that Bakhtin could not possibly have been responsible for them. As an example of this view, Titunik cites the work of Helmut Glück, who translated Medvedev's *The Formal Method* into German. Ken Hirschkop takes issue with any such clear-cut assessment of Volosinov and Medvedev's Marxist credentials: 'They are Marxist only in so far as they theorize superstructural practices in a socially materialist fashion, leaving aside [...] the vexed relation to the base'.[21]

The second view is that Bakhtin's signed works *do* exhibit such unmistakable Marxist commitment that he must be the author of Volosinov's and Medvedev's works as well. There is no window-dressing here. Titunik names as subscribers to this view Fredric Jameson and Marina Yaguello, the French translator of *Marxism and the Philosophy of Language*. No one, of whatever persuasion, has yet tried to argue that all the other works published under the names of Volosinov and Medvedev were really by Bakhtin, suggesting a hypothetical variant of the second position: all three writers were Marxists, and each wrote their own books which separately support this fact. Titunik, however, lists all of Volosinov and Medvedev's works in his discussion of the authorship problem, and, while he admits that no attempt has been made to attribute these other writings to Bakhtin, he claims that 'they comprise a single set with respect to the argument over attribution'.[22]

A third, more agnostic, view, held by critics such as Todorov, is that it would be preferable to be able to hold to the idea of a unified body of work written by Bakhtin alone, but that the 'ideological discrepancy' between his works and those of the other two writers presents a significant stumbling block. Sergey Bocharov argues that, if incontrovertible proof is what readers are after in the authorship debate, they will never reach any resolution. However, he quotes an impressive array of witnesses, ranging from Volosinov's widow ('"These books were written by Mikhail Mikhaylovich"', she apparently said of *Freudianism* and *Marxism and the Philosophy of Language*) to I. I. Kanaev (who wrote that Bakhtin was short of money in 1925, so wrote an article entitled 'Contemporary Vitalism' from books provided by Kanaev, which was published under Kanaev's name) to Bakhtin himself. Bocharov argues that there is a 'conceptual rather than textual unity' among the works of Bakhtin, Volosinov, and Medvedev.[23] This enables him to answer the knotty question, 'What do we do with *Marxism and the Philosophy of Language*, that monster title from which Bakhtin distanced himself with a grimace?' The Marxism of the disputed works is only superficial: 'The attentive reader will notice that the required phraseology does not affect the specifically Bakhtinian core of the work[s] and can easily be distinguished as a separate layer'. As Titunik points out, Bocharov's own position is easy to fit into the pattern of the authorship debate; he is of the Holquist subset of the window–dressing school. Titunik discusses various unanswered questions about the debate in an article revealingly entitled, 'Bakhtin &/or Volosinov &/or Medvedev: Dialogue &/or Doubletalk?'.

Bocharov, like Morson and Emerson, extends the problem into one of authorship and textual practice in general. He cites Bakhtin's observation that 'he did not write as he would have written under his own name; he wrote in a half mask'. As Bocharov argues, the names of Volosinov and Medvedev 'constitute parts of the texts', and should therefore remain.[24] Morson and Emerson suggest that, dialogically, the influences in the Bakhtin circle must have worked both ways:

> Once one begins to think in terms of dialogue and influence, rather than identity and pseudonymy, other possiblities come into view. If Bakhtin influenced Voloshinov [*sic*] and Medvedev, why could they not have influenced him? [...] Is it not possible that strong Marxist renditions of his own ideas provoked the change [to a sociological emphasis]?[25]

Saussure

Ferdinand de Saussure, and his extremely influential linguistic theory, is the object of some explicit, and much more implicit, polemic in Bakhtin's work. An understanding of the differences between the two writers is necessary to appreciate Bakhtin's innovations, and the latter's insistence that conventional linguistics cannot account for precisely the textual effects he is interested in. Put simply, Bakhtin was impressed by Saussure's innovatory work in linguistics, but sought to replace the latter's 'neutral' formalism with a socio-ideologically aware linguistic theory which could take account of language's value-laden nature.[26] The issue at stake is Saussure's division of language into two dimensions: *langue* and *parole*. The first refers to language as a system of rules which are called upon every time a speaker uses that language. Each specific utterance is an instance of 'parole'. The infinite variability of parole makes it unsuitable as an object of inquiry, according to Saussure, whose linguistics concentrates instead on the general structure of language.[27] As Terence Hawkes points out, Saussure's own example of the game of chess is helpful in considering the difference between langue and parole: knowing the rules of chess allows the players to embark on an individual game (parole), even though all the rules (langue) will not be called upon during each game.[28] Bakhtin's interest is in each specific game of chess, and not in the rules, which are what interest Saussure. As Bakhtin says of his own approach, '[w]e are taking language not as a system of abstract grammatical categories, but rather language conceived as ideologically saturated' with the tones of the moment (DN 354).

Saussure is mentioned only once by name in 'Discourse in the Novel', where Bakhtin cites him as the inspiration for critics who replace analysis of novelistic style with a description of the language of the novel (263). Style here 'is understood in the spirit of Saussure: as an individualization of the general language'. Saussurean linguistics is an instance of the sort of poetics which cannot adequately describe the novel, according to Bakhtin's polemic, nor, indeed, genre itself.[29] Saussure's approach presupposes both a 'unity of language' and 'the unity of an individual person realizing himself in this language' (DN 264). The Bakhtinian novel, however, is a only a 'unity' in so far as it is constructed out of 'heteroglot, multi-voiced, multi-styled and often multi-languaged elements'. Volosinov has rather more to say about Saussurean linguistics, and its widespread influence on Russian linguistics in the 1920s, in *Marxism and the Philosophy of Language*. He argues that attempting to construct a mathematical science of signs implies interest only 'in the *inner logic of the system of signs itself*, taken, as in algebra, completely independently of the ideological meanings that give the signs their content' (MPL 58).[30] Volosinov also emphasizes the dependence of the utterance on its context, and on both speaker and listener, elements which do not form part of the Saussurean agenda; as he puts it, the utterance 'will always be determined by the real conditions of its uttering, and foremost by the nearest social situation' (MPL 101).

Volosinov implicitly takes issue with other elements of Saussurean linguistics. These include the latter's argument that the two elements of the linguistic sign, signifier and signified, are linked only in an arbitrary and unmotivated way. There is no essential connection between the signifier 'dog', for instance, and the concept we have learned to associate with it. Meaning is therefore relational and not substantive; it comes about not in isolation but through the relation of different terms to each other (we understand 'dog', for instance, because it is neither 'hog' nor 'pup'). The implications of this highly influential view include the idea that language is a closed, and not a referential, system with its own rules; and that reality does not pre-exist language, but is constituted by it: in the famous example, words for colours in different national languages cannot necessarily be precisely translated.[31] Hirschkop suggests that Volosinov takes the Saussurean sign and makes it 'the space for the conflicts of parole'.[32] Although he acknowledges the importance of Volosinov's work for Marxist criticism, Raymond Williams describes Volosinov's linguistics as *deceptively* radical, since, despite his interest in history, and in dialectical processes – in contrast to Saussure's ahistoricism and allegiance to the rigidly dual structure of signifier and signified – he keeps the concept of the 'binary' sign. For Volosinov,

> [t]he relation within the sign between the formal element [the signifier] and the meaning which this element carries [the signified] is thus inevitably conventional (thus far agreeing with orthodox semiotic theory), but it is *not* arbitrary and, crucially, it is not fixed. On the contrary the fusion of formal element and meaning [...] is the result of a real process of social development.[33]

Volosinov argues that 'various different classes will use one and the same language. As a result, differently oriented accents intersect in every ideological sign. Sign becomes an arena of class struggle' (MPL 23). Toril Moi explores the feminist potential in the recognition that the 'power struggle intersects in the sign'; battles for the meaning of words like 'witch' and 'shrew' reveal that 'there is no inherent sexist essence in the English language, since it shows itself appropriable for feminist purposes'.[34] The question Volosinov puts at the end of the first chapter of *Marxism and the Philosophy of Language* can clearly have only one answer: 'what is the real mode of existence of language: unceasing creative generation or inert immutability of self-identical norms?' (63).

Finally, as Bakhtin would not say, a word on the attraction of Bakhtin for contemporary criticism. David Lodge singles out Bakhtin's interest in the novel in its own right as the reason why he finds Bakhtin's approach so fruitful. Bakhtin makes the novel central to his aesthetic and critical project, not a poor relation to poetry.[35] (This is true even of Bakhtin's ethical and philosophical writings, where the novel can function as a space in which to test out ideas.[36]) The centrality of the novel is also implicit in Morson and Emerson's choice of subheading for their explication of Bakhtin: *Creation of a Prosaics*. Rather than trying to fit novelistic discourse into poetic categories, the novel should have an aesthetic of its own, which also acknowledges its connections with the 'particularities of everyday life (the prosaic)'.[37] Other critics have adopted the term 'dialogic criticism', as a more generic and less author-focused way of approaching texts with Bakhtinian notions in mind. Clive Thomson says this critical approach can include awareness of both the wider historical context and the internal polyphonic heterogeneity, within a text.[38]

Notes

1 See Hirschkop's 'Bibliographical Essay', in Ken Hirschkop and David Shepherd, eds, *Bakhtin and Cultural Theory*, Manchester University Press, Manchester 1989, pp. 195–212; Anthony Wall and Clive Thomson's summary of recent work in their review of G. S. Morson and C. Emerson, *Mikhail Bakhtin: The Creation of a Prosaics*, Stanford University Press, Stanford, California 1990: 'Cleaning Up Bakhtin's Carnival Act', *Diacritics* 23 (2), summer 1993, pp. 47–70, p. 47; Carol Adlam's overview, 'In the Name of Bakhtin: Appropriation and Expropriation in Recent Russian and Western Bakhtin Studies', in A. Renfrew and Graham Roberts, eds, *Exploiting Bakhtin*, Strathclyde Modern Language Studies, 2, 1996. Partial exceptions to this binary opposition of edited readers and high-level monographs are Lynne Pearce's *Reading Dialogics*, Edward Arnold, London 1994, and David K. Danow, *The Thought of Mikhail Bakhtin: From Word to Culture*, Macmillan, London 1991.

2 Adlam, 'In the Name of Bakhtin', p. 81; Wall and Thomson, 'Cleaning Up Bakhtin's Carnival Act', p. 50; Morson and Emerson, *Mikhail Bakhtin*, pp. 10–11.

3 See, for instance, on Bakhtin and feminist criticism Nancy Glazener, 'Dialogic Subversion: Bakhtin, the Novel and Gertrude Stein', in Hirschkop and Shepherd, eds, *Bakhtin and Cultural Theory*, pp. 109–29; Carol Adlam, 'Ethics of Difference: Bakhtin's Early Writings and Feminist Theories', in C. Adlam, R. Falconer, V. Makhlin and A. Renfrew, eds, *Face to Face: Bakhtin in Russia and the West*, Sheffield Academic Press, Sheffield 1997; Dale M. Bauer and S. Jaret McKinstry, eds, *Feminism, Bakhtin, and the Dialogic*, State University of New York Press, Albany, NY 1991; Karen Hohne and Helen Wussow, eds, *A Dialogue of Voices: Feminist Literary Theory and Bakhtin*, University of Minnesota Press, Minneapolis, Minnesota 1994. On art and architecture, D. J. Haynes, *Bakhtin and the Visual Arts*, Cambridge University Press, Cambridge 1995; and on social geography, Peter Jackson, 'Street Life: The Politics of Carnival', *Society and Space* 6, 1988, pp. 213–27. Queer theory is an area where Bakhtin's influence is just beginning to register; see for instance Ed Cohen's discussion of 'the novel of trial' in relation to Oscar Wilde, and grotesque realism in relation to press coverage of 'non-standard sexual practices' using '"low"' cultural forms to do so (*Talk on the Wilde Side*, Routledge, London 1993, pp. 129, 249 n. 59); and David Bergman's discussion of overlaps and differences between camp and carnival (*Gaiety Transfigured: Gay Self-Representation in American Literature*, University of Wisconsin Press, Madison, Wisconsin 1991, pp. 111–13); and Paul Tyrer, 'Indecent Acts: Parodying Homophobic Evangelism', forthcoming; I am grateful to Paul Tyrer for these references.

4 Ruth Ginsburg, 'Bakhtin Criticism in Israel: A Short Story of Non-Reception', *Le Bulletin Bakhtine/The Bakhtin Newsletter* 5, 1996, *Special Issue: Bakhtin Around the World*, eds Scott Lee and Clive Thomson, p. 180.

5 Paul de Man, 'Dialogue and Dialogism', in Gary Saul Morson and Caryl Emerson, eds, *Rethinking Bakhtin: Extensions and Challenges*, Northwestern University Press, Evanston, Illinois 1989, p. 114.

6 Sergey Bocharov, 'Conversations with Bakhtin', *PMLA* 109 (5), October 1994, p. 1013.

7 De Man, 'Dialogue and Dialogism', p. 114; and Adlam, 'In the Name of Bakhtin', *passim*.

8 Wall and Thomson, 'Cleaning Up Bakhtin's Carnival Act', p. 48.

9 David Lodge, *After Bakhtin*, Routledge, London 1990, p. 86.

10 Robert Crawford, *Identifying Poets: Self and Territory in Twentieth-Century Poetry*, Edinburgh University Press, Edinburgh 1994, pp. 9, 5; Adlam notes that the combined number of entries on Bakhtin in Sheffield University's Bakhtin Centre on-line database, and the MLA database, is over 2000, 'In the Name', n. 1; and there are two collections of essays, as well as Caryl Emerson's 'Preface' (to Mikhail K. Ryklin, 'Bodies of Terror: Theses Toward a Logic of Violence', *NLH* 24 (1), winter 1993), on the Russian versus the Western Bakhtin: Adlam et al., eds, *Face to Face*, and Amy Mandelker, ed., *Bakhtin in Contexts: Across the Disciplines*, Northwestern

University Press, Evanston, Illinois 1995.

11 Emerson, 'Preface', p. 47; Bocharov, 'Conversations', p. 1018 (my italics).

12 In relation to post-structuralist thought, see, as a relatively random sample, Terry Eagleton, 'Wittgenstein's Friends', *New Left Review* 135, 1982, pp. 64–90; Dragon Kujundzic, 'Laughter as Otherness in Bakhtin and Derrida', in R. Barsky and M. Holquist, eds, *Discours Social/Social Discourse: Bakhtin and Otherness*, 3 (1–2), spring–summer 1990, pp. 271–93; Barry Rutland, 'Bakhtinian Categories and the Discourse of Postmodernism', in Clive Thomson, ed., *Mikhail Bakhtin and the Epistemology of Discourse*, *Critical Studies* 2 (1/2), 1990, pp. 123–35; as well as de Man, 'Dialogue and Dialogism'.

In relation to feminism, see n. 3 above; Myriam Diaz-Diocaretz, 'Bakhtin, Discourse, and Feminist Theories', in M. Diaz-Diocaretz, ed., *The Bakhtin Circle Today: Critical Studies* 1 (2) 1989, pp. 212–39, and Clive Thomson, 'Mikhail Bakhtin and Contemporary Anglo-American Feminist Theory', in ibid., pp. 141–61; the section entitled 'Feminism' in David Shepherd, ed., *Bakhtin, Carnival and Other Subjects*, *Critical Studies* 3 (2)–4 (1/2), 1993; Maroussia Hajdukowski-Ahmed, 'Bakhtin and Feminism: Two Solitudes?', in Thomson, ed., *Mikhail Bakhtin and the Epistemology of Discourse*.

13 Glazener, 'Dialogic Subversion', pp. 109–10; Jane Miller, *Seductions: Studies in Reading and Culture*, Virago, London 1990, p. 149.

14 See William R. Handley, 'The Ethics of Subject Creation in Bakhtin and Lacan', in Shepherd, ed., *Bakhtin, Carnival and Other Subjects*, pp. 144–62.

15 Alastair Renfrew has pointed out that the rigid distinction drawn by Western critics between author and narrator, within which the concept of the author is frequently banished, is not one which Russian critics hold to in the same way. For the latter, it is rather the 'conditional' narratorial voice which may not necessarily be present. The importance of *skaz*, a kind of narration in which the form of an individual speaking voice is reproduced, in Bakhtin's writing is that it is an instance where the narrator *is* clearly present (personal communication).

16 'Deuterocanonical' is S. S. Averintsev's term, quoted in Bocharov, 'Conversations', p. 1013; although *The Formal Method in Literary Scholarship* is usually referred to as a work by Medvedev, it is published as being by M. M. Bakhtin/P. M. Medvedev; Tzvetan Todorov, in *Mikhail Bakhtin*, University of Minnesota Press, Minneapolis, Minnesota 1984, refers to the author of *Marxism and the Philosophy of Language* as 'Bakhtin/Volosinov'.

17 F xvi, FM vii ff., respectively.

18 MPL x–xi, F xviii.

19 Biographical details from Bocharov, 'Conversations', and F xvii.

20 DN xxvi.

21 F xvii; Hirschkop, 'Bakhtin, Discourse and Democracy', *New Left Review* 160, November/December 1986, pp. 92–113.

22 Titunik lists Volosinov and Medvedev's other writings in 'Bakhtin &/or Volosinov &/or Medvedev: Dialogue &/or Doubletalk?', in Benjamin A. Stolz, I. R. Titunik and Lubomír Dolezel, eds, *Language and Literary Theory*, Papers in Slavic Philology 5, University of Michigan, Ann Arbor, Michigan

1984, pp. 536–7, and comments on this list, p. 561 n. 2. In the collection *Bakhtin School Papers* several articles by Volosinov and Medvedev appear in translation, although four of them have Bakhtin's name bracketed alongside the authors'. In the introduction to this collection, Ann Shukman, while observing that the problem is 'ultimately insoluble, given Bakhtin's writing habits', discusses the differences between the contested works and Bakhtin's 'own name' writings (*Bakhtin School Papers*, Russian Poetics in Translation vol. 10, RPT Publications, Oxford 1983, p. 2).

23 Bocharov, 'Conversations', pp. 1014, 1015–16.

24 *Ibid.*, pp. 1017, 1018. See Titunik, 'Bakhtin &/or Volosinov', on the reasoning behind the slash between Bakhtin and Medvedev; he quotes Wehrle likening it to the bar between signifier and signified, although who stands for the signifier in this case alters significantly; and Todorov, who argues that the slash can suggest collaboration, substitution or a two-way model of communication (p. 538).

25 Morson and Emerson, *Mikhail Bakhtin*, pp. 113–19.

26 See for instance, Hirschkop, 'Introduction', in Hirschkop and Shepherd, eds, *Bakhtin and Cultural Theory*, pp. 40–3; Morson and Emerson, *Mikhail Bakhtin*, pp. 123–5; Lodge, *After Bakhtin*, pp. 91 ff. The work in question by Ferdinand de Saussure is his *Course in General Linguistics*, Fontana, London 1974 [1916].

27 Todorov, *Mikhail Bakhtin*, p. 33; see also pp. 42–3.

28 Terence Hawkes, *Structuralism and Semiotics*, Methuen, London 1977, pp. 20–1. Individual games of chess, and the implications of the rules, as in chess problems, are discussed more often than the rules themselves.

29 Todorov, *Mikhail Bakhtin*, p. 57.

30 See Volosinov's extended discussion, MPL 57–61, including an account of what time Saussure *does* have for parole, pp. 60–1.

31 Louis Hjelmslev, *Prolegomena to a Theory of Language*, trs. Francis J. Whitfield, University of Wisconsin Press, Madison, Wisconsin, 1969; and Catherine Belsey, *Critical Practice*, Methuen, London 1980, pp. 39–40.

32 Hirschkop, 'Bakhtin, Discourse and Democracy', pp. 97 ('heteroglossia substitutes for langue'), 109; he notes that Bakhtin is indebted to Saussure, 'Introduction', p. 22, as Titunik notes of Volosinov, MPL 2–3; and, 'the contrast of historical becoming and static structure which organizes Bakhtin's thinking about language has its political complement in the contrast of vital social development and deadening attempts to structure social life from above', Hirschkop argues in 'Bakhtin, Discourse and Democracy', p. 104.

33 Raymond Williams, *Marxism and Literature*, Oxford University Press, Oxford 1977, p. 36; see the rest of his discussion, pp. 35–42; along with Kristeva's 'Word, Dialogue, and Novel', in *Desire in Language: A Semiotic Approach to Literature and Art*, Basil Blackwell, Oxford 1980, and Todorov's *Mikhail Bakhtin*, this account introduced Bakhtin's circle to the West.

34 Toril Moi, *Sexual/Textual Politics: Feminist Literary Theory*, Methuen, London 1985, p. 158.

35 Lodge, *After Bakhtin*, p. 90.

36 See Michael F. Bernard-Donals, 'Bakhtin, the Problem of Knowledge, and

Literary Studies', in *Mikhail Bakhtin: Between Phenomenology and Marxism*, Cambridge University Press, Cambridge 1994, pp. 159–78.

37 See Gary Saul Morson and Caryl Emerson's reply to Wall and Thomson, 'Imputations and Amputations: Reply to Wall and Thomson', *Diacritics* 23 (4), winter 1993, pp. 93–9, p. 98.

38 Adlam, 'In the Name of Bakhtin', p. 87; and see Pearce's discussion of 'dialogics' as a general critical term, *Reading Dialogics*, pp. 160–72.

Heteroglossia: 'I hear voices everywhere ...'

Introduction

Heteroglossia means 'differentiated speech', and has been called 'Bakhtin's key term for describing the complex stratification of language into genre, register, sociolect, dialect, and the mutual interanimation of these forms'.[1] This description of heteroglossia takes up terms from contemporary sociolinguistics, such as 'sociolect' (discourse determined by different social groups according to 'age, gender, economic position, kinship' and so on) and 'register' (discourse belonging to 'the lawyer, the doctor, the businessman, the politician' (DN 289)) which were unavailable to Bakhtin.[2] However, Bakhtin uses the term 'heteroglossia' to mean not simply the variety of different languages which occur in everyday life, but also their entry into literary texts. These languages bring with them their everyday associations, which can of course include literary ones, as well as making their own in the textual setting. Because all languages are related hierarchically, dialogic interaction will occur within textualized heteroglossia, with potentially position-altering effects.

It has been pointed out that Bakhtin's argument about heteroglossia relies on two conflicting methodologies: that of philosophy and that of empirical cultural analysis. In the light of the former, heteroglossia is a quality of language itself, which is necessarily various; in that of the latter, heteroglossia is a quality of *a* language at a particular historical moment, so that it would also be possible to speak of a language being monoglot instead. 'Heteroglossia, like most of Bakhtin's other concepts, is both historical and normative': it refers both to a variable state of affairs and to one which is constant.[3]

Bakhtin describes what happens when heteroglossia's varieties of language are transposed into the literary arena:

When heteroglossia enters the novel it becomes subject to an artistic reworking. The social and historical voices populating language, all its words and all its forms [...] are organized into a structured stylistic system that expresses the differentiated socio-ideological position of the author amid the heteroglossia of his epoch. (DN 300[4])

Heteroglossia takes two general forms: first, '"social languages" within a single *national* language'; and second, 'different national languages within the same *culture*' (275[5]). Within the novel, these forms of heteroglossia appear as, first, characters' dialogue and inner speech; second, the various kinds of 'speech genre' which exist within, say, English at a given moment (SG 114), languages of a profession, class, literary school, newspaper, and so on; and third, texts which reproduce a culture's various dialects and languages: this might be English and Scots in James Kelman's novels, Spanish and English in Malcolm Lowry's *Under the Volcano*, or Yiddish and English in Henry Roth's *Call It Sleep*. Even though Yiddish is rarely 'authentically' quoted in Roth's novel, while English is quoted alongside the Scots in Kelman's *How Late It Was, How Late* and Spanish in Lowry's novel, it still has a heteroglot role to play, as we will see. The way in which all three categories of language interact in a text is dialogic: they all know of each other's existence, are changed by and react to each other.

Once it enters the novel, heteroglossia does not simply consist of a neutral series of different languages; these languages are bound to conflict at the very least with the 'author's' language, with each other, and with any surrounding languages which do not necessarily appear in the text. If they appear in a character's mouth, they become '*another's speech in another's language*' (DN 324), expressing the author's intentions but in a refracted way.[6] Heteroglossia is thus a double-voiced discourse, as it 'serves two speakers at the same time and expresses simultaneously two different intentions: the direct intention of the character who is speaking, and the refracted intention of the author'. As Allon White puts it, 'because languages are socially unequal, heteroglossia implies dialogic interaction in which the prestige languages try to extend their control and subordinated languages try to avoid, negotiate, or subvert that control'. Paradoxically, 'speech diversity in class society indexes actual inequality'. Although such speech diversity is a good thing for the novel, it is the consequence, White argues, of 'an increasing division of labour'.[7]

Heteroglossia in the text

Bakhtin gives an example of double-voiced heteroglossia from Turgenev's *Virgin Soil* (1877): 'But Kallomyetsev deliberately stuck his round eyeglasses between his nose and his eyebrow, and stared at the [snit of a] *student who dared not share* his "apprehensions." [*Virgin Soil*, ch. 7]' (DN 318). As Bakhtin points out, this quotation is composed of two accents: 'the author's ironic transmission, and a mimicking of the irritation of the character'. Kallomyetsev's tone is used to render the 'snit of a student' and what he sees as the student's timorousness: he 'dared not share ...'. The whole utterance is 'permeated with the ironic intonation of the author'.

The task of the critic is to separate out the period-bound or internal heteroglot layers within an utterance, as Bakhtin says in 'Discourse in the Novel': 'It is possible to give a concrete and detailed analysis of any utterance, once having exposed it as contradiction-ridden, tension-filled unity of two embattled tendencies in the life of language' (272). Real-life heteroglossia – informal and varied languages, dialects and speech genres[8] – is implicated in the origins of the novel, as Bakhtin describes:

> At the time when poetry was accomplishing the task of cultural, national and political centralization of the verbal-ideological world in the higher official socio-ideological levels, on the lower levels, on the stages of local fairs and at buffoon spectacles, the heteroglossia of the clown sounded forth, ridiculing all 'languages' and dialects [...] there was to be found a lively play with the 'languages' of poets, scholars, monks, knights and others, where all 'languages' were masks and where no language could claim to be an authentic, incontestable face. (DN 273)

As Bakhtin's choice of such phrases as 'tension-filled', 'embattled', 'ridiculing' suggests, heteroglossia was already, in the mythic medieval scene he describes above, 'aimed sharply and polemically' at official languages. 'It was heteroglossia that had been dialogized'. It is important to note the precise relationship between heteroglossia and dialogism. Dialogism describes the way languages interact, while heteroglossia describes the languages themselves. Heteroglossia, whether it refers to a variable or a constant feature of language, is always dialogically arranged in a text, if that text can properly be called a novel, which makes it very hard to talk about either heteroglossia or dialogism without talking about the other as well. It is not only textually that dialogic interaction between languages occurs, as Bakhtin points out; all languages are 'shot through with intentions and accents', and there are no neutral words (DN 293), once these are in use. Bakhtin emphasizes that it is precisely in use that speakers of a language come to understand and repeat the 'inflections' of meaning which are absent from the dictionary.

As the quotation above also suggests, Bakhtin has in mind a model of heteroglossia as primarily informal, everyday kinds of language, which will at once conflict with the formal language of narration within a text. However, different kinds of literary discourse, or different kinds of everyday discourse – that is, languages on the same plane – can interact as dialogized heteroglossia. As Bakhtin also points out, literary language itself is heteroglot: it is just one among many 'professional' languages, and 'in its turn is also stratified into languages (generic, period-bound and others)' (DN 272). Once it enters a text, heteroglossia is automatically 'consciously opposed' to 'the linguistic center of the verbal-ideological life of the nation and the epoch' (DN 273). Novelization dialogizes heteroglossia.

Heteroglot difference can produce a variety of effects, related to time (the past), space (geography, nationality), class, and so on, as Bakhtin points out; heteroglossia

> represents the co-existence of socio-ideological contradictions between the present and the past, between differing epochs of the past, between different socio-ideological groups in the present, between tendencies, schools, circles, and so forth, all given a bodily form. (DN 291)

These languages may seem very separate, but Bakhtin argues that they can be juxtaposed as they are all 'specific points of view on the world' and will thus 'mutually supplement one another, contradict one another and be interrelated dialogically' (DN 292).

It is not only through characters or narrators that double-voiced construction occurs, since characters are only one of the ways in which heteroglossia can become novelized. Examples of other kinds of 'internally dialogized' heteroglot discourse within the novel include stylization, *skaz* or parody (DN 335); 'comic, ironic or parodic discourse, the refracting discourse of a narrator, refracting discourse in the language of a character, and finally the discourse of a whole incorporated genre' (DN 324). These 'incorporated genres' can range from the literary (poems or songs within a novel) to the non-literary (menus, telegrams, sermons, advertisements): 'in fact it is difficult to find any genres that have not at some point been incorporated into a novel by someone', as Bakhtin says (321). Some incorporated genres have a closer relationship to the novel and its history than others; these include 'the confession, the diary, travel notes, biography, the personal letter' (DN 321). They may branch out to 'determine the structure of a novel as a whole', in for instance the epistolary or confessional novel. In other words, whenever a second language is present in a text, or even implied, as is often the case in first-person narrative where a single language may be all that is formally represented, dialogized heteroglossia is present. The examples Bakhtin gives are simply the most obvious ways in which a second – or third – language might enter a novel.

Bakhtin is adopting the term *skaz* here, known best to western readers from its use in Russian Formalist criticism, as one of the forms in which heteroglossia can enter the novel. (The Russian Formalists, who were active in the 1920s, argued that literary language has its own forms and logic, and is not to be confused with everyday uses of language.) *Skaz* is a mode of narration that 'imitates the oral speech of an individualized narrator' (PDP 8, n. b). Bakhtin changes the Formalists' emphasis, which was on the oral element of *skaz*, and argues that the important thing about it is its double-voicedness, its 'orientation towards *someone else's speech*' (PDP 191). *Skaz* becomes double-voiced in the novel because it is a representation, so there are two voices present in it: the one represented, and the one representing. Bakhtin would call the representing voice the author's, while we would call it the narrator's. *Skaz* can be either 'simple' or 'parodic'; if it is the latter, like any parody, it will possess a 'semantic intention [...] directly opposed to the original one' (PDP 193). This is an example of oral narration from Dostoevsky's *Notes from Underground* (1864), quoted by Bakhtin to exemplify 'hidden polemic' as well:

> To live longer than forty years is bad manners; it is vulgar, immoral. Who does live beyond forty? Answer that, sincerely and honestly. I will tell you who: fools and worthless people do. I tell all old men to their face, all those respectable old men, all those silver-haired and reverend old men! I tell the whole world that to its face. I have a right to say so, for I'll go on living to sixty myself. I'll live till seventy! Till eighty! Wait, let me catch my breath. (quoted PDP 228)

The two voices Bakhtin perceives here are that of the author, although it is absent formally, and that of the first-person narrator, the Underground Man, which appears as *skaz*: its tone and structure are those of oral narration. Again, we would want to label the first of the two voices that of the narrator, and this too is formally absent, or at least indistinguishable from that of the character. The hidden polemic, that is, the narrator's address to an absent interlocutor, which is clear from the questions and 'abusive' tone here, makes this extract double-voiced in a different way as well. As Bakhtin says, hidden polemic, or 'the word with a sideward glance', is present in the barbs and digs which characterize our everyday discourse (PDP 196). The discourse of the Underground Man is constructed with another double-voiced, other-oriented device, that of 'a word with a loophole' (PDP 232). Bakhtin defines this structure:

> A loophole is the retention for oneself of the possibility for altering the ultimate, final meaning of one's own words. If a word retains such a loophole this must inevitably be reflected in its structure [...] it is only the penultimate word and places after itself only a conditional, not a final, period. (PDP 233)

In the case of the Underground Man, even his estimate of his own appearance is so dependent on the word of another that his discussion of it is characterized by a loophole. The Underground Man hopes for a 'sincere refutation' of his negative estimates of himself from the other: 'Condemning himself, he [...] demands that the other person dispute this self-definition, [but] he leaves himself a loophole in case the other person should suddenly in fact agree with him' (PDP 233). What the Underground Man really wants is refutation, but this is implicit only formally in his utterance. No one can point to the content of his words as evidence that he does not really believe he is sick and ugly; this is like a giant case of fishing for compliments. At the very least, he will gain the endorsement of agreement with his view. This is the Underground Man's word-with-a-loophole view of his own body: 'I happened to look at myself in the mirror. My harassed face struck me as extremely revolting, pale, spiteful, nasty, with disheveled hair. "No matter, I am glad of it", I thought; "I am glad that I shall seem revolting to [Liza]; I like that"' (PDP 236). Strictly speaking, this is a three-way address: while talking with 'himself, with another, with the world', the Underground Man 'simultaneously addresses a third party as well: he squints his eyes to the side, toward the listener, the witness, the judge'. The Underground Man can have no objective view of his discourse or body because he is both extremely dependent on, and extremely hostile to, the other's consciousness (PDP 230). An objective view of himself would be impossible, as it would demand the absence of words with a sideways glance or loophole. It is as if the Underground Man wishes his discourse did not have to be dialogic, and could 'free [him]self from the power of the other's consciousness'. He makes his discourse and appearance as ugly as possible in order to 'kill in himself any desire to appear the hero in others' eyes' (PDP 232). Freeing himself from the other's word is of course impossible, as all discourse is dialogic;[9] the word with a loophole, '[j]udged by its meaning alone, should be the final word about oneself [...] but in fact it is forever taking into account internally the responsive, contrary evaluation of oneself made by another' (PDP 233).

The Underground Man's discourse is heteroglot, as it consists of the oral narration of *skaz*, and it is on this level that one might analyse it in terms of its content; for instance, it possesses several traits Freud isolates in his discussion of the melancholic (Bakhtin himself notes that, unlike Devushkin in *Poor Folk* (1846), the Underground Man is an 'ideologist' (PDP 236), with strongly held views on society and the world).[10] His discourse is heteroglossia dialogically represented, as the double-voicedness of hidden polemic, the word with a loophole, and the *skaz* narration show.

The 'sideward glance' need not be aggressively oriented, but may rather be cringing or fearful: 'here belongs all self-deprecating overblown speech that repudiates itself in advance, speech with a thousand reservations, concessions, loopholes and the like' (PDP 196). The 'hidden polemic' in the quotation above consists of the Underground Man's reactions to implied words, treated antagonistically; while the whole is an example of *skaz*, its principal means of construction is the 'word with a sideward glance'. The following is an example of speech which 'literally cringes in the presence or the anticipation of someone else's word, reply, objection', from Dostoevsky's *Poor Folk*. This discourse, in a letter written by Makar Devushkin, is one which 'cringes with a timid and ashamed sideward glance at the other's possible response, yet contains a muffled challenge' (PDP 205). Again, it is *skaz* in the form of a word with a sideward glance, but this time a propitiating glance. In this extract, Devushkin's 'halting' style, constantly interrupted by reservations', has its eye on its reader, Varenka Dobroselova, whose imagined words determine how Devushkin will speak. As Devushkin, who has to sleep in the kitchen, 'is afraid she will think he is complaining, he tries in advance to destroy the impression that will be created by the news that he lives in the kitchen, he does not want to distress her, and so forth':

> Well, so that is my little corner. So don't you imagine, my darling, there is anything else about it, any mysterious significance in it: 'here he is living in the kitchen!' Well, if you like, I really am living in the kitchen, behind the partition, but that is nothing. I am quite private, apart from everyone, quiet and snug. (PDP 206)

As Bakhtin points out, this kind of double-directed discourse – hidden polemic or dialogue – gives some scope for active involvement to the second, absent voice, which 'actively influence[s] the author's speech, forcing it to alter itself accordingly under their influence and initiative' (PDP 197). In stylization or parody, the other person's discourse is 'completely passive'.[11]

Images of language

It may be hard to reverse the common-sense readerly view, that language in the novel is there to serve characters, but, as Bakhtin observes, it is indeed the other way round: '[c]haracteristic for the novel as a genre is not the image of a man in his own right, but a man who is precisely the *image of a language*' (DN 336). This is equally true of narratorial utterance and incorporated genres. They are all 'images of language', alternative forms for allowing as wide a range of different languages as possible into the novel. As Bakhtin says, 'The speaking person and his discourse in everyday speech [...] serves as a subject for the engaged, practical transmission of information, and not as a means of representation' (DN 340). When heteroglossia enters the novel in the form of such a speaking person, this is reversed and the character serves *only* as a 'means of representation'.

Bakhtin devotes a section of 'Discourse in the Novel' to a discussion of the impossibility of representing a character's 'ideological world' without representing his or her discourse (DN 335). He points out that 'a speaking person in the novel need not necessarily be incarnated in a character', and again it is important to note precisely which way round this relationship works. Heteroglot languages, many of which will possess the point of view which makes them a 'speaking person', may enter the novel, as we have seen, in the form of inserted genres, or stylizations such as *skaz* or parody. It is heteroglossia, in other words, which gives novelistic characters the opportunity to exist, and not the other way round.

This is of course equally true of novels where there is relatively little direct speech, for instance Malcolm Lowry's *Under the Volcano*, James Kelman's *How Late It Was, How Late*; the characters' discourse is still present, as various kinds of represented or narratorial speech. Again, Bakhtin insists on the importance of representation; the speaking person may have a very significant role in everyday life, as 'one of the main subjects of human speech is discourse itself' (DN 355), but this simply involves the 'transmission' of discourse (DN 340).

As with carnival, Bakhtin traces the history of this kind of representation back to a late medieval era where the 'devices [...] for constructing images of a language' and 'coupling discourse with the image of a particular kind of speaker' were literally acted out. This took place 'in the minor low genres, on the itinerant stage, in public squares on market day, in street songs and jokes' (DN 400); all such discourse was stylized to be 'socially typical [...] for a priest, a knight, a merchant, a peasant, a jurist, and so on', so that '[e]very discourse has its own selfish and biased proprietor'.

All the concrete examples mentioned – characters, parody and *skaz*, inserted genres – as means of creating an image of language in the novel fall under three formal headings, Bakhtin says: '(1) hybridizations, (2) the dialogized interrelation of languages and (3) pure dialogues' (DN 358). To go through these categories in order: we have seen the example from Turgenev as one of hybridization, in which two different voices coexist in the same utterance. These voices may be 'separated from one another by an epoch, by social differentiation or by some other factor'.

An example of the second category, 'dialogized interrelation of languages' as an image of language, is the following from Henry Roth's novel *Call It Sleep* (1934), about the childhood of David Schearl in a turn-of-the-century New York slum, where small boys are whispering together in English in their Hebrew class, despite the rabbi's warning that he does not want to hear a word of 'goyish' from them. The central character David asks his neighbour how Isaiah's mouth was burned by coal in the Bible, and receives the following reply: '"A lighten', yuh dope! A blitz! Kent'cha tuck Englitch? Ha! Ha! Sheor yerokos halaylo hazeh – Dat's two on dot! I wuz shooting chalk wid it. Somm bean shoodah! My fodder'll give your fodder soch a kick –"'[12] The unnamed boy's voice utters accented English, Yiddish (ironically, the word he offers David as evidence of the latter's inability to talk English is 'blitz', Yiddish for 'lightning'), and Hebrew ('"Sheor ..."'). The dialogic nature of these languages' interrelation is clear on various levels: the Biblical language is represented simply as sound, as the boys cannot yet translate it, and as an intrusion into the more important discussion about a pea-shooter. English itself does not appear here in a standard form, and thus has an implicit polemic directed against it. Both languages, authoritative in different ways, are made material, into images, and relativized, by the presence here of Yiddish-inflected American English.[13]

Hebrew in this novel, as a 'dead' Biblical language,[14] should be a prime example of the 'authoritative discourse' Bakhtin discusses, which is monoglottically separated from other neighbouring languages by various means including 'a special script'. In a footnote, Bakhtin refers to 'the phenomenon of foreign-language religious texts in most cultures' (DN 343 n. 29), which protects the authoritative word from the taint of dialogized heteroglossia. Such a language 'is incapable of being double-voiced; it cannot enter into hybrid constructions [...] it is not surrounded by an agitated and cacophonous dialogic life' (DN 344). However, as the above example shows, an 'authoritative discourse' can perfectly well take part in a hybrid construction, and is certainly surrounded by 'an agitated and cacophonous dialogic life'. In a reverse of Bakhtin's comment, and of its supposedly monologic status, Hebrew here is not transmitted but represented, which automatically makes it double-voiced.

The quotation from *Call It Sleep* could be described as 'hybridization', as well as 'dialogized interrelation of languages'; as Bakhtin observes, the three categories of the formal representation of heteroglossia are only artificially separable (DN 358). As we have seen, *any* artistic image of a language will by definition consist of two voices: one which represents and one represented. The second representing voice makes the difference between an image of language and a 'sample'. The phrase '"Kent'cha tuck Englitch?"' is a miniature version of dialogized heteroglossia in itself: a heavily accented, polylingual voice makes a paradoxical claim for its proficiency in the language of the gentile majority and the narrator. This claim is 'washed over' (DN 368) by narratorial irony, but it is an irony also directed at perfect English. The little boy's speech *is* a variety of English, and English in this text is forced to encompass and express languages alien to itself. As White puts it, 'even after a society has engaged with another language as a deeply important part of its own culture, monoglossia tends to reassert itself, one language attempts to gain hegemony, to incorporate the new'.[15]

Here, standard English represents an immigrant tongue which, by the time *Call It Sleep* was written in 1934, and even more so by the time it was reissued in 1963, was in the process of being 'incorporated' as its speakers 'assimilated'.[16] Its languages do not have to be literally present in order to be represented. Bakhtin's distinction between 'real-life' and novelistic heteroglossia in relation to artistic hybrids is relevant here:

> as distinct from the opaque mixing of languages in living utterances [...] the novelistic hybrid is an artistically organized system for bringing different languages in contact with one another, a system having as its goal the illumination of one language by means of another. (DN 363)

He concludes that '[t]he primary stylistic project of the novel as a genre is to create images of languages' (DN 366), not necessarily to reproduce those languages themselves.

Of 'pure dialogue', the third category in his list, Bakhtin says that, although it is compositionally central to the novel, it cannot be reduced to the 'pragmatically motivated dialogues of characters' (DN 364). Rather, it is a more general form of 'dialogue of languages', out of which every element of the novel is structured, as Bakhtin puts it: 'literary language becomes a dialogue of languages that both know about and understand each other' (DN 400).

Heteroglossia in Henry Roth's *Call It Sleep*

Henry Roth's *Call It Sleep* features characters who speak a variety of languages and dialects, the former ranging from Yiddish and Italian to Hebrew, the latter from standard American-English to English spoken with an Italian, Irish or Yiddish accent. All of the dialects are directly represented. The non-English languages, apart from most of the Hebrew, are rendered as English, so that although only the narrator, with a couple of small exceptions, 'speaks' standard English, more than three-quarters of the novel is *rendered* as standard. Both dialects and languages appear as images of language. The illusion that the discourse is actually being represented is more compelling in the case of the dialects, the fact that we are reading 'artistic images' clearer in the case of the languages. Bakhtin, in a passage contrasting poetry with fiction, has this to say about the acknowledgement of heteroglossia by the novel: 'Any way whatever of alluding to alien languages, to the possibility of another vocabulary, another semantics, other syntactic forms and so forth, to the possibility of other linguistic points of view, is equally foreign to poetic style' (DN 285). 'Any way whatever' in *Call It Sleep* turns out to be a means of not only alluding to but representing alien languages without actually changing vocabulary to do so. As an ostensibly monoglot novel, in which all the narration is in English, and nine-tenths of characters' discourse too, it is none the less made to represent 'other linguistic points of view'. As Bakhtin puts it, '[a]n image of language may be structured only from the point of view of another language, which is taken as the norm' (DN 359).

Roth's 'noisy' novel, which is about a small boy growing up in what Bakhtin might have described as 'one of the most sharply heteroglot eras' (DN 418), Lower East Side New York in the early twentieth century, exemplifies clearly Bakhtin's definition of the novel as a heteroglot 'system of *images* of languages' (DN 416).[17] Roth's method of representing Yiddish in particular, to an English-speaking readership, shows how much of an 'image' it is, and that it is neither a sample of a dialect nor an 'expounding' (DN 378) of characters' voices.

For instance, these are the two voices of one character, Mrs Mink:

> 'Hollo, Mrs Schearl! Hollo! Hollo! Comm een!' [Mrs Mink] scratched her lustreless, black hair excitedly.
> 'I hope you don't find my coming here untimely', his mother smiled apologetically.
> 'No, as I live!' Mrs Mink lapsed into Yiddish. 'You're wholly welcome! A guest – the rarest I have! [...] Do sit down.'[18]

Here, the 'maimed English and subtle Yiddish'[19] of recent immigrants is very clear. The discourse of Mrs Schearl throughout, and Mrs Mink, when she is not trying to speak English, is courtly and fluently grammatical. When Mrs Mink does try to speak English, it is fractured, accented, imperfect. When most of the characters *do* speak English, it is 'maimed', a dialect which relativizes the narratorial language. Fiedler's comment above would be more accurate if rephrased as 'the maimed English and subtle English' of the immigrants, where the 'subtle English' represents those moments when they are actually using their mother-tongue. Yiddish in this novel is thus clearly an 'image' and not a 'sample'; in general, its representation is artistic and not mimetic, although there are moments when it is closer to the latter, for instance:

'Albert' she said timidly, 'Albert'.
'Hm?'
'Gehen vir voinen du? In Nev York?'
'Nein. Bronzeville. Ich hud dir schoin geschriben.'[20]

Even here, however, Yiddish resists being represented entirely mimetically, as its alphabet is Hebrew-based, not Roman. Although it seems much more familiar because of its similarity to German, this representation of Yiddish uses the same method as the text's representation of Hebrew: it is transcribed and not translated.

The topsy-turvy effect of this fact, that the less able the characters are to speak English, the more their utterances are represented by perfect English, is shown most clearly in the case of David's mother.[21] Her English is even more mellifluous than the narrator's – she gives her son a glass of water and asks for a kiss: '"It is summer," she pointed to the window, "the weather grows warm. Whom will you refresh with the icy lips the water lent you?"'.[22] However, Mrs Schearl 'really' speaks English at a police station when David gets lost, and the contrast between her usually eloquent, poetic language and her failure to understand the policeman's questions, repeating simply, '"T-tanks so-so viel!"', is a shock to the reader. '"And how they must have laughed at my English!"' she says later – in perfect English.[23] As Bakhtin says,

> The more broadly and deeply the device of hybridization is employed in a novel – since it occurs not with one but with several languages – the more reified becomes the representing and illuminating language itself, until it finally is transformed into one more of the images of languages the novel contains. (DN 361)

Bakhtin distinguishes carefully between hybridization and 'internally dialogized interillumination of language systems'. In the latter case, which applies to *Call It Sleep*, 'there is no direct mixing of two languages within the boundaries of a single utterance – rather, only one language is actually present in the utterance, but it is rendered in the light of another language. The second language [...] remains outside the utterance' (DN 362). Internally dialogized mutual illumination of a language is clearest in 'stylization', Bakhtin argues, which is closer to the way in which Scots dialect is represented in Kelman's *How Late It Was, How Late*, although Bakhtin assumes more of a division between that dialect and its implied author than is the case here. He says that within a stylization the stylizer 'works exclusively with the raw material provided by the language he stylizes', and the intrusion of 'anachronistic' words or phrases would disrupt the stylization (DN 363). (Bakhtin assumes the distance between stylizer and stylized language is one of time; but, using his own chronotopic flexibility, it could just as easily be one of space, that is, geography, nationality, or class.)

The topsy-turvyness of the images of Yiddish in *Call It Sleep* is itself a manifestation of dialogized heteroglossia: within this text, the language of narration is enlisted to contribute to its own relativization. The language of immigrants manages to get inside the narrative itself and disrupt it, by overturning the usual hierarchy of languages in which standard English is best, broken English better than nothing, and Yiddish bad. The terms of this hierarchy are questioned in Roth's novel, although each of its main languages is still clearly 'value-laden'. In this text, Yiddish is the language of the home, and the older generation; it is rendered as perfect English. Hebrew is distinct from Yiddish in not being used for everyday communication, shown by the small boys' learning how to read the alphabet separately from learning how to translate. It is represented as an image of sound, in which individual words and their pronunciation are made clear. Bakhtin observes that '[d]istinctions between genres frequently coincide with dialectological distinctions (for example, the high – Church Slavonic – and the low – conversational genres of the eighteenth century)' (DN 294), but in this text it is hard to pin down which dialect is high and which low. Yiddish is shown to be refined and poetic; David thinks of Hebrew as the tongue in which one speaks to God, but it is rendered as untranslated words, which materializes and downgrades it, as does the context of the school – never a synagogue – in which it is uttered, offsetting its holy status.

English is the language of the street and the new generation; of the gentile world in general; and the language of the text. The best English in the novel is uttered by those who cannot speak it, qualifying its narratorial transparency. Polish appears as an image of an image of sound. Not a single Polish word, nor an image of how Polish might sound to an ear which cannot understand it, is represented; we read, 'he pried [...] among the gutturals and surds'.[24] It is the language of the past, of secrets and love, none of which the nine-year-old David can understand.

Each one of the languages relativizes the others; for instance, David thinks of Hebrew as being 'Not Yiddish', despite its Hebrew-based alphabet, and eagerly awaits the 'mica-glints' of Yiddish among the Polish when his mother talks to his aunt. Shifts

from Yiddish to English are sometimes quite apparent, as in this
dialogue between David and his aunt in her candy-store: '"Hea', I
giff you a pineepple vit' emmend. Do I speak English better?".'[25] By
contrast, in the following incident, the shift is clear only after David
has replied, that some words were not in his mother's tongue:

> 'Mama! Water doesn't burn when you throw a match in a puddle.'
> 'Puttle?' she repeated. 'What is puttle? Your Yiddish is more
> than one-half English now. I'm being left behind'.[26]

Bakhtin gives a skeleton description of this kind of 'critical
interanimation', which can occur in a single polyglottic consciousness or text, in relation to the infamous example of the peasant
living amidst different languages (DN 295–6); it fits *Call It Sleep*
almost perfectly:

> The language and world of prayer, the language and world of
> song, the language and world of labor and everyday life, the
> specific language and world of local authorities, the new language
> and world of the workers freshly immigrated to the city – all these
> languages and worlds sooner or later emerged from a state of
> peaceful and moribund equilibrium and revealed the speech diver-
> sity in each.

Hirschkop points out a flaw in this model of heteroglossia.
Although heteroglossia may result from the moment in which
'previously separated and independent social groups are thrown
together by the sudden onset of capitalism and its urban effects', an
obvious feature of 'advanced capitalist societies is the emergence of
homogenising public linguistic forms'.[27]

Although Roth does catch what Leo Braudy calls 'the dispossessed' at a historical moment when they had 'freshly immigrated'
and their language was still distinct from that of the surrounding
majority,[28] this accuracy is incidental.[29] As Bakhtin argues, the 'artistic image of a language' is always the main point in the novel, so
that

> the novelist makes no effort at all to achieve a linguistically (dialec-
> tologically) exact and complete reproduction of the empirical data
> of those alien languages he incorporates into his text – he attempts
> merely to achieve an artistic consistency among the images of these
> languages. (DN 366)

More important than exactness is the fact that the majority language
is made to recognize and represent the voices of the dispossessed.

In doing so, however, the uncomfortable historical truth of Yiddish's social status and inevitable decline is revealed: it has to be represented in English for it to have any intelligible heteroglot status.

Roth's method of representing Yiddish, which is distinct from, for instance, Leo Rosten's more conventional method,[30] also has a polyphonic role to play in *Call It Sleep*. As Walter Allen points out, there is 'an American truth [...] or the truth in English' about some of the novel's characters, including Mrs Mink, and the Hebrew teacher, Reb Yidel Pankower, a 'Dickensian' character who, from an external viewpoint, is '[d]irty, irascible, a petty sadist'.[31] The temptation for the narrator to yield to representing these characters' discourse, as well as their behaviour, as it would appear to an American, English-speaking audience, is firmly resisted in the text (although resisted more strongly on behalf of characters like Mrs Schearl than for Mrs Mink). Mrs Schearl is allowed her own voice for nearly the whole span of her appearance in the text, and the 'shock' the reader receives on hearing her speak in an alien tongue is based on the fact that it is the natural tongue of the reader, and of the text itself. The 'best' English turns out not to be English at all. The shock is an example of the relativizing moment which Bakhtin says can cast a sense of materiality over one's own language (DN 367), and a moment typical of the workings of any novel: 'The novel is the expression of a Galilean perception of language, one that denies the absolutism of a single and unitary language – that is, that refuses to acknowledge its own language as the sole verbal and semantic center of the ideological world' (DN 366).

The 'American' truth about Yiddish is that it is comic; the vocabulary and intonations of its speakers are a source of humour, both kind and unkind. In Roth's text, this American view is present alongside a European-based perspective. David's Aunt Bertha is more at the mercy of the narrator in this respect, and when she and her nephew go uptown to an art gallery David 'began to feel uneasy at his aunt's loud voice and Yiddish speech both of which seemed out of place here'. Lost in the gallery and following two people who seem to be heading for the exit ('"We must cleave to them like mire on a pig!"'), Bertha gives vent to 'typical'-sounding imprecations: '"Pheh!" she spat on the stairs as they went down. "May a bolt shatter you to bits! If I ever walk up these stairs again, I hope I give birth to a pair of pewter twins!"'[32] Although Bertha's utterances do sound rather like Bakhtin's description of '[v]ulgar, nonliterary discourse [...] saturated with low intentions and crude emotional expressions' (DN 384), and this is certainly how her brother-in-law hears her, her discourse is involved and articulate, and her intentions by no means always 'low'. None the less, 'everyday genres' of speech are introduced into the novel, 'not in order to "ennoble" them, [but ...] for the sake of their potential for introducing nonliterary language (or even dialects) into the novel' (DN 411).

However, the language of David's parents is represented more transparently, and their idioms and speech patterns are not ironized in this way. The mother's discourse represents a different pole of Yiddish, the sentimental and archaic, less often associated with this language in the American view of it than the comic, the emotional, and the excessive.

The representation of Bertha's position on the border between Yiddish and English also operates in a way different to that of the Schearls. Her forays into what she calls '"fency Engalish"' are all somewhat carnivalesque. She mispronounces the vanilla '"bum bonnies"' whose consumption means she must go to the dentist, an event which allows her to annoy her brother-in-law with some risqué bilingual puns, on 'kockin' and 'cocaine', and on 'molleh' and 'molar'. These puns are glossed for us by David: '"Kockin"', as David had learned long ago, was a Yiddish word meaning to sit on the toilet'; and 'David didn't know what "molleh" might mean in English. He did know that "molleh" in Yiddish had something to do with circumcision. Aunt Bertha was being reckless to-night ...' Bertha's Yiddish–English punning tends to the lower bodily stratum.[33]

The bilingual misunderstandings which occur among other characters are more akin to potential tragedy than this kind of comedy. They also reveal the dialogically opposed world-views behind the different languages in the novel. David is confused by a story of his mother's: '"What's a – what you said? Altar?" It was his turn to be puzzled. "Means old man?"'[34] This prepares us for the confusion David experiences overhearing his mother's tale of a secret romance with a gentile in the old country: 'A goy, Aunt Bertha had said, an "orghaneest". What was an "orghaneest"?'[35] In the street, the small boys' grapplings with English phrases effects a similar two-way conflict, relativizing both their English and the English itself, as ideologically central American institutions become transformed:

> 'Aaaaah! Ooooh!' he quavered, 'My country 'tis of dee! [...] Land where our fodders died!'

'I know somebody wod he hoided his hand on de Futt f'om Jillai
– wid a fiyah crecker.'

'Id ain' no Sendy Klaws, didja know?'[36]

The two-way dialogism of this heteroglossia, residing here in individual words and phrases, has a further productive sense; in the first
two instances above at least, the joke is not really at the expense of
the immigrant boys, but in their favour. It could, though, be a joke
at the expense of Yiddish, which is already becoming superfluous.
As Reb Pankower asks himself, 'What was going to become of
Yiddish youth? What would become of this new breed? These
Americans?'[37]

Perhaps the most extreme polemicizing with the American
view of the novel's characters occurs when David gets lost. The
incident lacks any finalizing perspective, and remains mysterious to
characters and readers alike. David tries to tell passers-by the name
of the street where home is, and his pronunciation of a word he
cannot spell causes chaos. The WASP woman he first encounters
interprets his '"Boddeh Stritt"' according to her own accent:
'"Why, you silly child, this is Potter Street! Now stop your crying!"
[...] "Id ain'd!" he moaned. "What isn't?' [...] "Id ain'd Boddeh
Stritt!" "Bodder! Bodder! Are you sure?" "Yeah!" his voice trailed
off. "Bodder, Bother, Botter, try and think!"'[38] When the woman
leads David to the police station, the variant pronunciations of the
mysterious 'Boddeh Street' become cacophonic in the mouths of
policemen with, respectively, an Irish and a New York accent:

> 'And Boddeh Street is the name and you can't spell it?
>   'N-no!'
>   'Mmm! Boddeh? Body Street, eh? Better look at the map [...]
> Know it?' he inquired of the helmeted one. 'Body Street – sounds
> like the morgue.'
>   'Near the school on Winston Place? Boddeh? Pother? Say, I
> know where he lives! Bahrdee Street! Sure, Bahrdee! That's near
> Parker and Oriol – Alex's beat. Ain't that it?'
>   'Y-yes.' Hope stirred faintly. The other names sounded
> familiar. 'Boddeh Stritt'.
>   'Bahrdee Street!' The helmeted one barked good-naturedly.
> 'Be-gob, he'll be havin' me talk like a Jew. Sure!'[39]

Because this is heard through David's ears, and his mother comes to
find him before the helmeted policeman's hypothesis is tested, we
can never be sure what the name of his street is, nor how to spell

it 'properly'. It is never monologically present. The irony of the scene lies partly in the fact that even the police, representatives of law and order, cannot establish either here. The apparently endless possibilities of pronunciation are irresolvable, and at the very moment when the Irish policeman tries to solve the mystery he is defeated by the inability of David's mother to understand his question or his language: '"he sure had us up a tree with his Pother an' Body an' Powther! Now you spell it bee-ay-" "T'anks so viel!" she repeated.'[40]

The 'consistency' Roth achieves among the images of the languages in *Call It Sleep* is constructed very clearly. For instance, the difference between the Catholic, 'Polish-American' (as he calls himself) Leo and Jewish David is signalled by their different pronunciations of the same phrases. David calls his aunt's shop a '"kendy staw"', while Leo calls it a '"canny staw"'; David's '"orghaneest"' is Leo's '"awginis"'.[41] In fact, rather than describing these phrases in terms of different pronunciation, it would be more accurate to say that the two boys are distinguished by the way their utterances are spelt. As we will see in relation to James Kelman's novel *How Late It Was, How Late*, 'graphological conventions are exploited impressionistically',[42] as we are in the realm of images of language, not everyday language itself. As Leo Rosten puts it, 'Nothing is more lame than a passage of mangled pronunciation recorded in accurate phonemes. Any yokel in the Ozarks can try to be a thigh-slapper by writing "We wuz shure suprized by Maw's coolinary conkokshun".'[43]

The basis for consistency in Roth's novel is the viewpoint of David, through whom all the action is focalized. This almost conforms to Bakhtin's description of 'a fundamental intersecting of languages in a single given consciousness, one that participates equally in several languages' (DN 367). However, David's relation to the text's languages is not as all-comprehending as this, and nor, significantly, is the narrator's or implied author's. Because Yiddish is David's mother tongue,[44] it sounds to him as natural and transparent as standard English to the text's reader (one formal reason why Yiddish is represented in this way); he cannot translate Hebrew, so it appears as transliterated syllables, as we saw above; he speaks and hears accented English in the street, as do we; and he understands no Polish, so when his mother and aunt lapse into that language there is a gap in the text. Not even its sounds are directly represented, although, significantly, this is a very literately expressed illiteracy:

'I could watch him then as he went by, follow with the others a little ways, stare at him unafraid, Love –'
    With the same suddenness as before, meaning scaled the horizon to another idiom, leaving David stranded on a sounding but empty shore. Words here and there, phrases shimmering like distant sails tantalized him, but never drew near.[45]

It is important to note that it is the artistic image of Yiddish as it interacts with other languages in Roth's novel which is an example of dialogized heteroglossia, not Yiddish itself.[46] Bakhtin claims that both language itself, and individual languages, such as that of a novel, are heteroglot. He thus characteristically describes heteroglossia in terms of 'both a "transcendental" or philosophical significance and an analytical or empirical meaning'. The paradox here is that if the latter is true, the former cannot be; if language is by definition heteroglot, it is hard to see how it can ever be monoglot.[47]

If any individual language were obviously heteroglot, that language is Yiddish. Benjamin Harshav describes it as 'a language of fusion', like English, but one which remained aware of and open to its composing languages as it lived with them, 'among Hebrew texts and German and Slavic neighbors'. Harshav shows that in Yiddish different, value-laden languages can co-exist within the same sentence or the same word,[48] which can relativize either Hebrew, the 'holy tongue',[49] or the local languages it comes into contact with. Harshav also points out that Yiddish was a stark contrast to the 'intellectual but detached or bureaucratic language used in post-Enlightenment western societies', lacking any high cultural or philosophical tradition, and with whole semantic fields missing: he mentions the absence of vocabulary relating to flora and fauna, military and courtly life.[50]

All this makes Yiddish sound like a heteroglot language with a carnivalesque function (and indeed Harshav uses Bakhtinian terminology, mostly implicitly and once explicitly, when using the chronotopic notion of 'social space' in Yiddish fiction).[51] However, as we have seen, we are not usually dealing with accurate linguistic 'samples' in a text. For our purposes, Yiddish becomes an internally dialogized element of heteroglossia when it enters a text, and inter-acts there with other languages. Yiddish itself is composed of a 'mixture of heterogeneous syntactic forms characteristic of language systems (forms that might take place in *organic* hybrids)' (DN 360). The novelistic hybrid, of which Yiddish is a part in Roth's novel, consists by contrast of 'two individualized language-intentions'.[52]

Some critics have pointed out that Bakhtin's model of the master–slave language relation may be too general, and too simplistic. There are occasions where the triumph of a unitary language can be seen as progressive; and many instances where the development of grammatical apparatus and official recognition of a language are part of a bid to escape colonial rule, as Harshav says of the early twentieth-century drive for a 'pure' Yiddish. Tony Crowley argues that Bakhtin's arguments in favour of heteroglossia are historically specific, and contrasts them with Antonio Gramsci's arguments for the freedom, in his political situation, of monoglossia:

> If Bakhtin, faced with the increasing centralisation and brutal forms of unity engendered by Stalinism, had argued for the importance of diversity and pluralism, Gramsci, faced with a divided and multi-factional national-popular mass, stressed the need for unity; [an argument] based on the difficulties of organising an illiterate mass in a society in which literacy was largely the prerogative of the governing class.[53]

As Crowley points out, by historical coincidence, Bakhtin's preference for heteroglossia 'is correct when analysing the formation of the "standard language" and its role in the cultural hegemony of Britain' and the USA. Bakhtin's allegiance to heteroglossia under his own circumstances is clear from such comments as 'It is necessary that heteroglossia wash over a culture's awareness of itself and its language, penetrate to its core, relativize the primary language system underlying its ideology and literature and deprive it of its naive absence of conflict' (DN 368). In the Italian context, Crowley argues that such a stance would actually be 'reactionary', as refusing to work for common forms in a culture where there is a hierarchy of languages, and certainly no 'naive absence of conflict', is 'tantamount to support for an unjust distribution of power'.[54] It is also important to remember that Bakhtin's emphasis is more usually literary than historical (although Crowley implies that the former is a cover for the latter), as the following makes clear: 'It is precisely thanks to the novel that languages are able to illuminate each other mutually; literary language becomes a dialogue of languages that both know about and understand each other' (DN 400).

As we have seen throughout this discussion of *Call It Sleep*, historical multilingualism may give the novel the *textual opportunity* for heteroglossia, but it will always deal with artistic images and not straightforward reproductions of language. It is true that Bakhtin analyses historically polyglot eras as especially fruitful for the development of the novel; he has this to say about trilingual ancient Rome and its languages of Greek, Oscan, and Roman:

> Lower Italy was the home of a specific kind of hybrid culture and hybrid literary forms. The rise of Roman literature is connected in a fundamental way with this trilingual cultural home; this literature was born in the interanimation of three languages – one that was indigenously its own, and two that were other but that were experienced as indigenous.[55] (PND 63)

Crowley's point is partly that Bakhtin's own circumstances gave him a particular model for literary history and language; had Gramsci formulated a model of the novel based on his circumstances, in modern Italy, it might have looked quite different.

Despite the heteroglossia of *Call It Sleep*, which is very obvious both within David's single consciousness and within his own community, there also exists a clear demarcation between language-worlds, and a 'deafness' to each other's languages, as David's not knowing the meaning of 'altar' and 'organist' suggests. The Polish-American Leo learns a Yiddish phrase, '"shine maidel"', 'pretty girl', only to aid in his seduction of one of David's cousins; and has problems with the word 'mezuzah', which he renders '"Miss oozer"': '"I busted it, an' cheez! It wuz all full o' Chinee on liddle terlit paper".'[56] However, this partial deafness of one interest group to the language of another serves to highlight the dialogic friction between them, a highlighting doomed to vanish with the more multicultural heteroglossia (and the bilingualism of different groups of immigrants) which Robert Stam sees as typifying New York at the end of the twentieth century.[57] Reb Pankower's disinclination for hearing 'goyish' spoken is destined not be indulged, as his perception of his charges as new Americans shows, which points to a future where the delineations of heteroglossia will be harder to perceive.

The situation is rather like that of folk humour, which Bakhtin discusses in *Rabelais and His World*; this kind of humour was at its height when divisions between standard and non-standard life, feudal and carnival existence, were rigidly established. Bakhtin says that the pious and the grotesque genres in the Middle Ages followed parallel lines which remained unmerged until the Renaissance (RW 96). Inevitably, these distinctions became fainter, with the accompanying loss of the ambivalence and renewal of folk humour, but, perhaps, with the gain of a more subtle appreciation of that

humour's continued, if less stark, presence: 'The walls between official and unofficial literature were inevitably to crumble, especially
because in the most important ideological sectors these walls also
served to separate languages – Latin from the vernacular' (RW 72).
The fact that Henry Roth himself, as implied hero of his own
Künstlerroman (that is, the story of how he came to be an artist), does
not write in his native tongue of Yiddish is testimony to this crum-
bling of walls between languages, as Bakhtin observes: '[t]he
adoption of the vernacular by literature and by certain ideological
spheres was to sweep away or at least weaken these boundaries'. As
we have observed, however, Roth's retrospective view of a past age
of clearly defined heteroglot interaction is simply one way of
presenting an 'artistic image' of the languages involved, not something which makes that heteroglossia anachronistic.

   Call It Sleep was published in 1934, a generation after the
period of 1907-10 in which it is set, and reissued in 1964; the second
time round, it was the first paperback to be reviewed on the front
page of the *New York Times Book Review*, and sold a million copies.[58]
Henry Roth reappeared on the literary scene in the early 1990s,
after sixty years' silence, with a projected sequence of six novels,
entitled *A Star Shines Over Mount Morris Park*, and a collection of
essays. His death soon after, in 1995, contributed to a second revival
of interest in his work. The increasing distance of generations of
readers from 1907 does not lessen the novel's heteroglot impact, as
it continues to perform as Bakhtin describes such a text: formally
rather than specifically. Its heteroglot force does not depend on the
author's presentation or the reader's knowledge of any particular
language or dialect (other than English), which is its paradoxical
heteroglot strength.

Notes

1 Allon White, 'Bakhtin, Sociolinguistics, Deconstruction', in *Carnival,
   Hysteria and Writing: Collected Essays and an Autobiography*, Oxford
   University Press, Oxford 1994, p. 136. Unlike 'chronotope' and 'polyphony', which are close to Bakhtin's Russian terms (*'khronotop'*,
   'polifoniya'), the Russian term is *'raznorecie'* (Holquist, 'Introduction', DN
   xix), or *'raznorechie'*, which literally means '"different-speech-ness"'
   (Graham Roberts, 'Glossary', in Pam Morris, ed., *The Bakhtin Reader:
   Selected Writings of Bakhtin, Medvedev, Voloshinov*, Edward Arnold, London
   1994, p. 248).
2 White, 'Bakhtin', p. 137.
3 Ken Hirschkop, 'Introduction', in *Bakhtin and Cultural Theory*, eds Ken

Hirschkop and David Shepherd, Manchester University Press 1989, pp. 4, 5.

4 As Bakhtin says in 'The Problem of the Text', 'Extraliterary utterances and their boundaries (rejoinders, letters, diaries, inner speech and so forth) transferred into a literary work (for example, into a novel). Here their total sense changes. The reverberations of other voices fall on them, and the voice of the author himself enters into them' (PT 114).

5 This quotation is explored further in Chapter 2.

6 Bakhtin's use of 'narrator' and 'author' is discussed in Chapter 3; David Lodge says of Bakhtin's pre-structuralist approach, 'Barthes says: because the author does not coincide with the language of the text, he does not exist. Bakhtin says, it is precisely because he does not so coincide that we must posit his existence', *After Bakhtin: Essays on Fiction and Criticism*, Routledge, London 1990, p. 99.

7 White, 'Bakhtin', pp 137, 156, 150.

8 Bakhtin defines speech genres in the following way: 'Each separate utterance is individual, of course, but each sphere in which language is used develops its own *relatively stable types* of these utterances. These we may call *speech genres* [...] Like Molière's Monsieur Jourdain who, when speaking in prose, had no idea that was what he was doing, we speak in diverse genres without suspecting that they exist' (PSG 60, 78).

9 Many critics have located the normative-descriptive paradox in Bakhtin's writing by pointing out that, if dialogism is a condition of all language, then it cannot be that some forms of language-use, such as some kinds of novel, are monologic. See Gary Saul Morson, 'Tolstoy's Absolute Language', *Critical Inquiry* 7, 1980–1, and Lodge, *After Bakhtin*.

10 See Sigmund Freud, 'Mourning and Melancholia', *Standard Edition of the Complete Psychological Works of Sigmund Freud*, ed. and trans. James Strachey, The Hogarth Press and the Institute of Psycho-Analysis, London 1953–73, vol. 14.

11 See Bakhtin's chart of varieties of double-voiced discourse, PDP 199.

12 Henry Roth, *Call It Sleep*, Bard Books, New York 1963 [1934], p. 230. Subsequent references are to this edition.

13 White discusses the disadvantages of 'simply' relativizing, and argues that Pynchon, for instance, instead 'produces a dialogic confrontation whereby power and authority are probed and ritually contested by [his] debunking vernaculars' ('Bakhtin', p. 148).

14 Benjamin Harshav points out that Hebrew was not dead but unspoken until its revival in Palestine in the late nineteenth century (*The Meaning of Yiddish*, University of California Press, Berkeley and Oxford 1990, p. 22).

15 White, 'Bakhtin', p. 150.

16 Neil Roberts, 'Epic and Novel in George Eliot', in C. Adlam, R. Falconer, V. Makhlin and A. Renfrew, eds, *Face to Face: Bakhtin in Russia and the West*, Sheffield Academic Press, Sheffield 1997.

17 Walter Allen, 'Afterword', in Roth, *Call It Sleep*, p. 418; Bakhtin points out that national literary languages may reflect 'the macrocosm not only of national heteroglossia, but of European heteroglossia as well', which is certainly the case here (DN 295).

18 Roth, *Call It Sleep*, p. 47.

19 Leslie Fiedler, Foreword, Henry Roth, *Call It Sleep*, Cooper Square Publishers, New York 1976.

20 Roth, *Call It Sleep*, p. 16; these words are uttered in the novel's Prologue, before David's focalization begins.

21 It is equally a shock to be presented with the fact that the father cannot speak standard English either, over four hundred pages into the book where it represents an unusual humility and acceptance of his paternity: '"My sawn. Mine. Yes. Awld eight. Eight en' – en' vun mawnt' (Roth, *Call It Sleep*, p. 437).

22 Roth, *Call It Sleep*, p. 18; the fact that what we are dealing with here is images and not samples of language is emphasized by the response David gets to looking inside his mother's parcel: '"Yes, as soon as we've *gotten* upstairs"', she replies (Roth, *Call It Sleep*, p. 172; my italics). At this point she is speaking Yiddish rendered in American English: a clear instance, especially for a non-American reader, that even the representing language is historically circumscribed and open to relativization.

23 Roth, *Call It Sleep*, pp. 106, 114.

24 *Ibid.*, p. 195.

25 *Ibid.*, pp. 213, 309.

26 *Ibid.*, p. 120. As we saw in n. 21, these shifts are usually strategic.

27 See Hirschkop's discussion of the peasant, 'Introduction', p. 19 and p. 18.

28 Harshav, *The Meaning of Yiddish*, p. 26.

29 *Ibid.*, p. 90.

30 See Leo Rosten's humorous stories, set in an adults' English class; the action centres on the egregious errors of the pupils, particularly the eponymous Mr Hyman Kaplan, focalized through the eyes of the English teacher and narrated by someone fond of such phrases as 'our shores'. This summary reveals the stories' lack of polyphony: we know better than the characters; however, despite his presence in an adult education class, Kaplan is unteachable and heteroglossia rules in the form of his 'maimed' English. Again we are at a moment just before assimilation has entirely taken place, but the dialogized heteroglot relativization in such *bon mots* as Kaplan's 'Gilbert and Solomon' (67) or 'Abram Lincohen' (9) is sacrificed to more general laughter. The clash of world-views implicit in the latter two renamings is not distinguished from the merely incorrect, such as 'Mr Kaplan had stated that Washington's Farewell Address was – Mount Vernon' (67), or simple manglings: 'Mr Kaplan [...] transformed a pencil sharpener into a "pantsil chopner"' (79) (all page references to Leo Rosten, *O Kaplan! My Kaplan!*, Constable, London 1979). Thanks to Lawrence Douglas for bibliographical assistance in investigating Mr Kaplan.

31 Allen in Roth, *Call It Sleep*, p. 445. The 'American viewpoint' is clearer now than it would have been then.

32 Roth, *Call It Sleep*, pp. 147, 149, 150.

33 *Ibid.*, pp. 162, 160.

34 *Ibid.*, p. 120.

35 *Ibid.*, p. 196.

36 *Ibid.*, pp. 62, 138, 141 respectively.

37 *Ibid.*, p. 374.

38 *Ibid.*, pp. 99–100.

39 *Ibid.*, p. 101.

40 *Ibid.*, p. 106.

41 *Ibid.*, pp. 303, 318, 319, 321.

42 Geoffrey Leech and Michael Short, *Style in Fiction*, Longman, London 1982, p. 132.

43 Rosten, *O Kaplan! My Kaplan!*, p. xv; it could be queried whether this is an 'accurate' transcription anyway, and Rosten's use of the term 'thigh-slapper' suggests this does not matter; it is after all not so different from Rosten placing such utterances as '"Ufcawss!"' in Kaplan's mouth.

44 As Harshav points out, Yiddish is traditionally associated with the realm of the mother, Hebrew with men (*The Meaning of Yiddish*, p. 23); Bakhtin says, 'The authoritative word is located in a distanced zone, organically connected with a past that is felt to be hierarchically higher. It is, so to speak, the word of the fathers' (DN 342). Again, this authoritativeness is qualified in *Call It Sleep*.

45 Roth, *Call It Sleep*, p. 197.

46 It may seem curious that Bakhtin never mentions Yiddish, although he spent much of his youth among the heteroglossia of Vilnius and Odessa, where, as Michael Holquist says, 'Yiddish and Hebrew were [...] in the air' (*Dialogism: Bakhtin and His World*, Methuen, London 1990, p. 1). After the First World War, Bakhtin lived in Nevel, an 'essentially Jewish town' at the time of the Russian Revolution, according to Holquist and Katerina Clark; Bakhtin's close friend was Matvei Kagan, a member of the Bakhtin circle, whose poor Jewish upbringing meant he spoke only Yiddish and no Russian as a young child; Vitebsk, where Bakhtin lived also after the war, was 'half-Jewish', and Marc Chagall founded the Art Academy there (*Mikhail Bakhtin*, Harvard University Press, Cambridge, Mass. 1984, pp. 41, 47). Carol Adlam has unearthed and translated the following fascinating extract from a 1973 interview with Bakhtin:

> – And your marriage?
> – Our marriage took place in 1921.
> – She was local [from Vitebsk], your wife?
> – She wasn't completely local. Her father was a very distinguished, prominent official of the province, before the Revolution, and they also had a small estate near Polotskii. I lived there, I stayed there with them for two or three summers (her parents were still alive). She was born in this estate near Polotskii. It's also just a stone's throw from Vitebsk.
> – What is the name, patronym, and surname of your wife?
> – Elena Aleksandrovna Okolovich, Bersh-Okolovich.
> – Bersh? What's that, Jewish?
> – 'Bersh' is like 'von' or 'de'. 'Bersh' was added by the nobility. Bersh-Okolovich ... I can't even remember very well now ... she was of Bulgarian extraction. But this Bulgarian extraction is very old, and both her mother and father were completely Russian.

(From M. M. Bakhtin and V. D. Duvakin, 'Razgovory s M.M. Bakhtinym: Nevel'. Vitebsk' ('Conversations with M. M. Bakhtin: Nevel'. Vitebsk'), *Chelovek* 1 (1994), p. 173.)

Despite all this, and the assumption made by the interviewer, Yiddish is an absent voice in Bakhtin's work.

47 Hirschkop, 'Introduction', p. 4; cf. p. 5.

48 Harshav, *The Meaning of Yiddish*, pp. 26, 32.

49 As Harshav points out, Hebrew is not always used exclusively as a holy language-component of Yiddish, and he quotes coarse Hebrew vocabulary, 'perhaps coming from the language of the underworld, where Hebrew was used to conceal messages from the Gentiles' (*ibid.*, p. 40).

50 *Ibid.*, p. 94; in an echo of Bakhtin's comments on metalinguistics, Harshav points out that linguistics alone cannot account for the meaning of Yiddish utterances: 'In a statistical count of Yiddish lexemes, the phrase ['scattered and dispersed'] would be registered only for its German components, but its actual subtext is Hebrew and its semantic substance is specifically Jewish' (p. 37); pp. 90, 44.

51 *Ibid.*, p. 153.

52 *Ibid.*, pp. 360, 361.

53 Tony Crowley, 'Bakhtin and the History of the Language', in Hirschkop and Shepherd, eds, *Bakhtin and Cultural Theory*, p. 84. This analysis presupposes a particular kind of (Western) Marxist politics; and the hegemony of an entropic 'heteroglossia' may be 'the most insidious and powerful of "official" discourses', Roberts, 'Epic and Novel in George Eliot', p. 308.

54 Crowley, 'Bakhtin and the History of the Language', p. 85.

55 See White, 'Bakhtin', pp. 143–4; and EN 11–12.

56 Roth, *Call It Sleep* pp. 342, 306.

57 Robert Stam, *Subversive Pleasures: Bakhtin, Cultural Criticism and Film*, Johns Hopkins University Press, Baltimore, Maryland 1989, p. 32.

58 Jason Cowley, 'Rip Van Winkle Wakes in Albuquerque', *Independent on Sunday*, 6 February 1994, p. 44.

2

Dialogism: '... and conflict between them'

Introduction

The term 'dialogism' means 'double-voicedness',[1] rather than 'relating to dialogue', although Bakhtin is keen to point out analogies between the wider linguistic phenomenon and this everyday interchange of utterance (DN 280). Bakhtin's discussion of the term 'dialogism' is ambiguous, however, as it is both linguistic and novelistic. He uses it to refer to particular instances of language, perceptible in novels and popular speech; and also to refer to a defining quality of language itself, and its most fundamental sense-making capacities.[2] In the case of the former, dialogism refers to the presence of two distinct voices in one utterance. When this sense is joined by the wider one, of a property of all language, then dialogism takes on its more precise characteristics, such as 'the mixing of intentions of speaker and listener', the creation of meaning out of past utterance, and the constant need for utterances to position themselves in relation to one another.[3] Hirschkop points out that contemporary critical debate over the meaning of dialogism arises from Bakhtin's own ambiguity over 'whether it is a relation among utterances or styles, or whether it is a relation between any two intentions or an "authorial" and a "heroic" one'. A third possibility is that it may mean the intersection of two or more 'contexts' in an utterance, that is, the interaction of the social and historical contexts of heteroglossia.[4] Kristeva suggests that the two senses of dialogism are connected, and perceiving 'dialogical relationships' within a text is possible only 'because dialogism is inherent in language itself', and that Menippean satire and Socratic dialogue both serve to 'reveal language's dialogism'.[5] For her, the slippage in Bakhtin's discussion between a normative and a historical dialogism is not problematically ambiguous but an obvious way of 'linking structural models to cultural (historical) environment'.[6] This implies that it would be surprising if language exhibited multi-voiced

45

tendencies and literary language did not; and this position underlies the objection that, if Bakhtin is right, and language is necessarily dialogic, how could any example of language-use be monologic?

If we think of language itself as dialogic, then we can see that, as we live among the many languages of social heteroglossia, dialogism is necessarily the way in which we construct meaning. The language we use in personal or textual discourse is itself composed of many languages, which have all been used before. At any moment, our discourse will be synchronically informed by the contemporary languages we live among, and diachronically informed by their historical roles and the future roles we anticipate for them. Each utterance, whether it takes the form of a conversation in the street or a novel, consists of the unique orchestration of well-worn words. As in an everyday dialogue, all these languages will interact with each other, jockey for position, compromise, effect a temporary stabilization, before moving on to the next construction of meaning.

It has been suggested that Bakhtin's use of the term may be subdivided into three, any or all of which may be perceptible in a particular textual utterance. Carol Adlam summarizes the Russian critic L. Chernets's argument that, first, 'in his theory of genre and style Bakhtin proposes an intertextual dialogic relation', that is, the intersecting voices are those of different texts, and response and anticipation takes place within 'the chain of culture' as a whole. Second, 'in the concept of addressivity and the alien word Bakhtin anticipates the reader's response in dialogic understanding'. Third, 'in the analysis of the interaction between author and hero undertaken in the studies of Dostoevsky and the essay "Author and Hero", Bakhtin discusses specifically intratextual dialogic relations', that is, intersections within the text itself. These three categories can be perceived in any single text.[7]

Dialogism in newspaper and novel

The following are two examples of the necessary dialogization of heteroglossia in the everyday and literary textual worlds. The first shows different elements of dialogism from the second; it is a newspaper headline, used of the British Labour Party campaign to win recruits in mid-1996. Its emphasis is on the second category of dialogism, reliance on the reader's understanding of the interaction between text and context, combined with the intertextuality of the first category which goes to make up the 'context': 'New Labour, new sandpies, as Big John fights them on the beaches'.[8] For many newspaper readers, on this particular day, unravelling and understanding the interaction of synchronic and diachronic levels of dialogism in this headline might take a moment, but no more than that. The phrase 'New Labour, new sandpies' is a deliberate misquotation of the Conservative anti-Labour slogan, 'New Labour, New Danger': this is the synchronic level of dialogized heteroglossia, as the two voices here require a precise recognition of words with a particular, and probably very short-lived, history. The 'sandpie' element is literally seasonally limited, referring to Labour's summer campaign to canvass voters at the seaside. The diachronic element of this headline is the 'quotation' with a more stable history, one which will not be only 'of the day', as Bakhtin says of newspaper discourse. '[F]ights them on the beaches' is a 'reduced' echo of Winston Churchill's wartime speech, rallying faith in Britain's ability to repel the threat of German invasion. This is a phrase with a very chequered and widespread history of usage, and its first – rather than original – context is still one of the voices to be heard in every subsequent usage. As Bakhtin says, 'The life of the word is contained in its transfer from one mouth to another, from one context to another context, from one social collective to another, from generation to another generation' (PDP 202).

Finally, even the phrase 'Big John' carries traces of other contexts, as it is a nod towards both John Wayne, and Little John, hero of English folk myth and sidekick to Robin Hood, who robbed the rich to give to the poor. Here dialogic friction increases – 'big' John Prescott (at this time Deputy Leader of the Labour Party) bears little resemblance to the Hollywood cowboy, and he may or may not be a similar sidekick to 'new' Labour leader Tony Blair, who may or may not be robbing and giving in the same way as Robin Hood. This marshalling of varied and rather crudely used echoes of meaning is endemic in journalism, particularly headline writing, but it calls upon the same structure as any manifestation of dialogism. Words, phrases, utterances in general, place themselves side by side in such a manner that their past contexts come together and interact in a momentary spark of meaning.[9] The unrepeatability of this moment is very clear in the case of a newspaper, which is literally a throwaway utterance, many of its local heteroglot threads to be lost or forgotten by the next day. As Tzvetan Todorov says, the implication of Bakhtin's discussions of dialogism is that 'culture consists in the discourses retained by collective memory (the commonplaces and stereotypes just as much as the exceptional words), discourses in relation to which every uttering subject must situate himself or herself'.[10]

The second example is a literary one, and, while the 'stereotypes' of collective memory were uppermost in the newspaper headline, here the discourses which interact to produce meaning call upon not only a memory but a literary and critical skill. As readers, if we cannot recognize the exact history of the utterances, we may know where to look in order to unravel them; and if, this is impossible, discourse which has been elsewhere may signal itself as such even if its past incarnations cannot be determined precisely.[11] This example, in contrast to the first one, calls upon the third dialogic category, where the intersecting voices are those of author and hero within the text; and again intertextuality, the first category, provides the background for this intersection. This is an episode from Lowry's *Under the Volcano*, where Yvonne and Hugh are searching for the Consul in one bar after another: 'Yvonne felt with gratitude the hard road beneath her feet. The lights of the Hotel y Restaurant El Popo sprang up. Over a garage next door an electric sign was stabbing: *Euzkadi*.'[12] Although it is not a particularly marked instance of it, here we have the dialogic element missing from the newspaper headline. The voices, or intentions, of character and narrator are both present. In this case, it is the single word *Euzkadi* which has a pronounced dialogic role to play, as an instance of heteroglossia itself (it is a Basque word in an English text), in which various contexts (those of a brand name and a historical event), and two voices contend (it is the character who sees the tyre sign, but not necessarily with any awareness of its layers of meaning).

As the context of the garage suggests, Euzkadi is the name of a common brand of Mexican car tyre; it also carried associations from the Spanish Civil War, as the name of a short-lived secessionist Basque republic, which declared its independence in late 1936. Republican reluctance to help the separatist movement against Nationalist attack resulted in the bombing of Guernica in April 1937. (*Euzkadi* is still the Basques' word for their country.) These traces of past meaning, and the present meaning they contribute to, are hard to determine, although readers can agree that 'the sign makes an unspoken criticism of Hugh's dallying', as Ackerley and Clipper put it. Hugh delays in the search for the Consul, just as the Republicans, of whom he was one, delayed in helping Euzkadi, both with disastrous consequences. Interestingly, Lowry cut out clarifying utterances by the characters which appear in the drafts of

Under the Volcano. Typically of Lowry's rewriting practice, all that remains of the following scene is the word 'Euzkadi', as that was of most interest to him:

> They made a neat three-point landing in a field, coming to rest under an enormous advertisement for motor tires: *Euzkadi.*
>
> 'Isn't that the old name for the Basque country?' inquired Hugh, as he picked up the two little bags. 'It confuses me why it should be the name of a make of motor tires. Damn it, you can't get away from the thought of Spain at all.'[13]

Excising Hugh's rather unnatural speech from the published version of *Under the Volcano* has the effect, in the published version of the novel, of allowing dialogized heteroglossia to supersede exposition thinly disguised as a character's utterance. Meaning, in other words, arises more effectively from dialogic friction, not from explication. The reader's openness to the strands of past use in the word *'Euzkadi'* creates meaning; Lowry claimed that his novel called on the unconscious and memory of a European readership. In the draft version, the reader was distanced from the word by having its meaning spelled out. Dialogism is thus the 'characteristic epistemological mode' of our world,[14] in an especially concentrated form within a literary text and the reader's understanding of it.

Dialogized heteroglossia

In all these cases, double-voicedness, and the sensitivity of one language to those surrounding it, results not in peaceful relativity, or inert coexistence, but in a clash of discourses, as Bakhtin emphasizes:

> The authentic environment of an utterance, the environment in which it lives and takes shape, is dialogized heteroglossia, anonymous and social as language, but simultaneously concrete, filled with specific content and accented as an individual utterance. (DN 272)

'Dialogized heteroglossia' refers to the combative relations different languages enter into when they come into contact, most clearly perceptible in a text. The socially varying values and accents of novelistic languages result in unevenness, unstable positions, shifts up and down a hierarchy worked out in the novel itself, and dialogically related to external linguistic hierarchies. Textual meaning results from a specific context's discord. Bakhtin's phrase 'The word in language is half someone else's' (DN 293) conveys this sense of battle. If the word is half the 'private property' of another, pressure must be exerted to gain at least the remaining half of that word, or perhaps, temporarily, the whole of it: 'Expropriating [language], forcing it to submit to one's own intentions and accents, is a difficult and complicated process' (DN 294). Bakhtin emphasizes the fact that dialogism is 'a struggle among socio-linguistic points of view, not an intra-language struggle between individual wills or logical contradictions' (DN 273).

As we have seen, dialogism is the organizing principle of both polyphony and heteroglossia. In the latter, social registers of language interact in a friction-filled way to produce meaning. Polyphony is the name for one method by which heteroglossia can enter the novel, in the form of characters' discourse; these discourses are arranged in a way which allows them maximum freedom. They consist of dialogized heteroglossia in many of its variants: hidden polemic, the word with a loophole, microdialogue. Dialogism describes the way the languages of heteroglossia are arranged in a text. One of the results of this arrangement is the content of polyphonic characters' voices, as Bakhtin says: all the languages of heteroglossia, including narratorial and characters' discourse, permit 'a multiplicity of social voices and a wide variety of their links and their interrelationships (always more or less dialogized)' (DN 263) to enter the novel, which is thus a throughly 'social' phenomenon (DN 259):

> The living utterance, having taken meaning and shape at a particular historical moment in a socially specific environment, cannot fail to brush up against thousands of living dialogic threads, woven by socio-ideological consciousness around the given object of an utterance; it cannot fail to become an active participant in social dialogue. After all, the utterance arises out of this dialogue as a continuation of it and as a rejoinder to it – it does not approach the object from the sidelines. (DN 276)

It is often difficult to work out the precise relations between these concepts. Dialogism is a relational property, like carnival, while heteroglossia is a linguistic description, and polyphony and the chronotope are terms for literary forms. Where high and low registers of language dialogize each other in the historical context of folk humour, we can detect the presence of the carnivalesque. Bakhtin also links carnival laughter with polyglossia: 'the most ancient forms for representing language were organized by laughter – these were originally nothing more than the ridiculing of another's language and another's direct discourse' (PND 50). A novel's constituent chronotopes also interact dialogically.[15]

Some critics have suggested that dialogism is being made to do too much if it is enlisted both as a property of an aesthetic genre, the novel, and at the same time as an intrinsic property of language; and that the force of the distinction between 'dialogue' and 'dialogism' is precisely that the latter is a representational term, the former merely descriptive of an everyday activity. However, the premium placed on the overlap between dialogue and dialogism, which Hirschkop says is what makes Bakhtin's work interesting, is clear from a form Bakhtin often discusses in relation to dialogism, as we have seen: the newspaper. The supplements of daily and weekend newspapers have taken on the format of 'question and answer' columns with enthusiasm in the 1990s; for instance, the *Weekend* tabloid of the *Guardian* features, in the space of a few pages, one real and one fake questionnaire of this kind.[16] In an issue of American *Harper's* magazine appears an article on the March 1996 bombing of Tel Aviv which is not written as a straightforward eye-witness testimony or article but follows the format of 'Frequently Asked Questions' well-known to the computer-literate:

> FAQ files are typically used by Internet newsgroups to answer prospective participants' questions about how the group operates and which topics it covers; in his FAQ, [author] Hochstein summarized 'responses I have given to people who asked what happened to me' and also answered 'questions which no one asked me'.[17]

It is the fake questionnaires and the constructed nature of this FAQ file which are of most dialogic interest. The breakdown of a short article about holidays, and Hochstein's about the bombing, into two voices, one asking questions, and the other answering them, shares many elements with dialogic practice.

The example reproduced here, from the *Guardian*'s Pass Notes series, takes on a subject which might have appeared in a leading column, that archetypically monologic form, and breaks it down into two voices for both comic and ideological effect. There are two voices here where one would do. This is not akin to 'real-life' dialogue, which is conversation between two distinct subjects, but dialogism. Meaning, and humour, emerge from the interaction of the two voices; as Kristeva says of Socratic dialogue, such forms 'are characterized by opposition to any official monologism claiming to possess a ready-made truth'.[18] The format of Pass Notes is a stylized dialogue, with a straight voice and a funny voice, although they often swop roles. The first voice anticipates the response it will receive to such an extent that it is sometimes simply the pretext for the second voice. As Bakhtin says, 'every word is directed toward an *answer* and cannot escape the profound influence of the answering word that it anticipates [...] Responsive understanding is a fundamental force, one that participates in the formulation of discourse' (DN 280).[19] In 'The Problem of Speech Genres', he describes how each voice tries to act in accordance with the response it expects: 'I parry objections that I foresee, I make all kinds of provisos' (PSG 95). What we see here is not dialogue but a form of making meaning which looks like dialogue, and whose constituent voices are brought to the surface.[20]

The 'unevenness' discussed by Hirschkop as constitutive of dialogism, as different voices will invariably occupy different positions of power in relation to each other, is played around with here. The 'clear and irreversible distinction between speaker and listener' which Hirschkop uses as an example of such a power differential collapses into opacity and reversibility in the Pass Note. In this respect it is quite unlike the rhetorical magazine questions in Jenefer Shute's 1992 novel *Life-size*, where an 'irreversible' difference between speaker and reader, or consumer, is not only called upon but actually constructed: 'Only one thing matters for the rest of your life. Does what you are about to put in your mouth contain carbohydrates?'[21] This apparent dialogue is actually more akin to Bakhtin's definition of monologism as 'words that expect no answer' (PDP 63); it is a one-way 'addressivity'.[22] As Hirschkop argues, 'For true dialogue to take place one has to exchange not only statements or sentences but something else – ideas, positions – and one has to do so with a willingness to take on board those proferred by your interlocutor'.[23] Bakhtin emphasizes the fact that every speaker must also be a listener and respondent: 'He is not, after all, the first speaker, the one who disturbs the eternal silence of the universe' (PSG 69).

This Pass Note's dialogic relations extend beyond the two voices which are formally present.[24] Its format corresponds very closely, and so rather over-schematically, to Bakhtin's definition of dialogism. He points out that linguistics usually focuses only on dialogue 'as a compositional form in the structuring of speech', which is one level of what we see here, but ignores 'the internal dialogism of the word (which occurs in a monologic utterance as well as in a rejoinder), the dialogism that penetrates its entire

Pass Notes

No 839: The gay gene

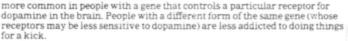

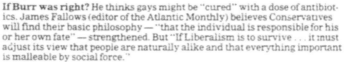

Hang on. Who says there is such a thing as a gay gene? Chandler Burr (right), author of A Separate Creation: How Biology Makes Us Gay.

He's rather cute! Your genes speak.

What's the evidence? Xq28. The 28th region of the q (long) arm of the X chromosome.

In plain English, please: The scientist Dean Hammer claims to have found a connection between Xq28 and homosexuality in a study of exclusively or mostly homosexual brothers.

Should we believe Chandler Burr? Maybe there's a gene which disposes us to believe such claims.

Oh come on! It's not so crazy. People's tendency to do things just for kicks, scientists have claimed, is more common in people with a gene that controls a particular receptor for dopamine in the brain. People with a different form of the same gene (whose receptors may be less sensitive to dopamine) are less addicted to doing things for a kick.

If Burr was right? He thinks gays might be "cured" with a dose of antibiotics. James Fallows (editor of the Atlantic Monthly) believes Conservatives will find their basic philosophy — "that the individual is responsible for his or her own fate" — strengthened. But "If Liberalism is to survive . . . it must adjust its view that people are naturally alike and that everything important is malleable by social force."

Science votes Republican? A good dose of antibiotics might cure Republicanism.

What would it mean if my genes made me gay? You might feel that "Nature" had sanctioned your behaviour; you might feel trapped, that "Nature" was determining your behaviour. If you weren't homosexual you might not be frightened of homosexuals and could spend less time (in the gym and the disco) trying to look hard; you might be determined to be homosexual and so prove that you were free (and spend more time in the gym and the disco).

So the knowledge of the existence of a gay gene might be a more powerful influence than the "gay gene" itself? Yes. And even Burr doesn't think the "gay gene" is the most important story.

Which is? Realising the extent to which biology determines our lives. Burr quotes Genesis: "And ye shall be as gods, knowing good and evil."

The serpent speaks: Where would we be if we had never listened?

You old optimist: It's epigenic (caused by genetic and environmental imputs).

Chandler Burr most likely to say: "Galileo was right, too."

Chandler Burr least likely to say: "Forget that guy's genes, it's how he *looks* in his jeans that interest me!"

structure' (DN 279). As we shall see, because the Pass Note does not really consist of two individual voices, its true dialogue is indeed present in its 'entire structure'.

Meaning here is constructed through question and answer; the questioner imitates the stance of a pupil, rather like the one in Plato's dialogues, where an acolyte's questions are answered by a master, in a parody of the notes sold to help students pass examinations. This particular Pass Note exhibits several of Bakhtin's concepts. The question which anticipates a certain kind of response and forms itself to get that response is so overt that the first speaker's questions end with a colon – 'In plain English, please:' – signalling that the voice (at this moment) exists only to elicit information. It recognizes the 'comic side of the truth that in social dialogue what I say to you somehow always already includes what you say to me, which in turn includes what I have said and may say to you', as Terry Eagleton puts it, adding that Bakhtin has built a whole theory of language around this irony.[25] The Pass Note also represents a carnivalesque debunking not only of monologically inclined politics – 'A good dose of antibiotics might cure Republicanism' – but of the possibility of any argument on such a subject as 'the gay gene': 'The serpent speaks: Where would we be if we had never listened?'

The Pass Note is characterized by a construction of meaning through roundabout means, arising from the dialogue itself and not from any authoritative commentary, either narratorial or authorial (the Note is unsigned). If the meaning of this Pass Note can be summarized as disagreement with Chandler Burr's theory, where does this become plain? The meaning is never uttered explicitly – the apparently naive questions get responses which seem, if you look only at their content, to be in agreement with Burr's thesis: 'What would it mean if my genes made me gay? ... If you weren't homosexual you might not be frightened of homosexuals and could spend less time (in the gym and the disco) trying to look hard ...' But, tongue in cheek, the second voice goes on 'naively' to emphasize the contradictions of the Burr position: 'you might be determined to be homosexual and so prove that you were free (and spend more time in the gym and the disco)'.

Only by looking at the utterance as a whole does its real, critical (or at least ridiculing) meaning become clear, *between* rather than *within* the voices.[26] As Bakhtin says, a grammatical analysis of the individual sentences of an utterance is not enough to reveal its dialogic construction, and its context and intonation as a whole must also be taken into account. Dialogism and carnival are used in this case to criticize an authoritarianism which wants to stifle dialogue.

'Dostoevsky could hear dialogic relationships everywhere'

Dostoevsky's work, according to Bakhtin, reveals the dialogic nature of the word with 'enormous force and an acute palpability' (PDP 265),[27] so much so that even critics find themselves drawn into a dialogic relation with his texts: 'One cannot talk about him; one can only address oneself to him' (251). *Problems of Dostoevsky's Poetics* is probably the most approachable of Bakhtin's works, especially for readers accustomed to literary critical texts. Bakhtin summarizes the work of other writers on Dostoevsky, how far short they fall or close they approach to recognizing the really distinctive feature of Dostoevsky's work, and then proceeds to analyse the latter to reveal its dialogic core. Bakhtin explains Dostoevsky's predisposition to dialogism:

> In every voice he could hear two contending voices, in every expression a crack, and the readiness to go over immediately to another contradictory expression; in every gesture he detected confidence and lack of confidence simultaneously; he perceived the profound ambiguity, even multiple ambiguity, of every phenomenon. (PDP 30)

Double-voiced discourse is not analysable, according to Bakhtin, using any kind of traditional linguistics. Bakhtin says that the object of his analysis is specifically Dostoevsky's *discourse*, by which he means 'language in its concrete living totality, and not language as the specific object of linguistics, something arrived at through a completely legitimate and necessary abstraction from various aspects of the concrete life of the word' (PDP 181). Conventional linguistics concentrates on small grammatical units, certainly not a whole utterance. Bakhtin discusses the artificiality of the sentence as a base-unit in 'The Problem of Speech Genres' (71–5), and says that instead the utterance is 'the *real unit* of speech communication', its boundaries marked by '*a change of speaking subjects*' (PSG 81).[28] Bakhtin terms his own approach to literary language 'metalinguistics', which aims to do those things unavailable to conventional linguistics: showing the difference between monologic and polyphonic language,[29] and 'treating the specific nature of dialogic relationships between rejoinders in a dialogue' (PDP 183). He observes that, while linguistics can give an account of an utterance's *'neutral signification'*, it cannot deal with its *'actual meaning'* (DN 281). The actual meaning is constituted by the dialogic interaction of heteroglot voices.

Bakhtin makes clear that dialogism operates formally, rather than by reliance on any particular content. Dostoevsky's 'struggle against a *reification* of man, of human relations [...] under the conditions of capitalism' takes place at the levels of both form and content (PDP 62). As is the case with the representation of the 'idea' in the polyphonic novel, Dostoevsky's greatest blows against this *'reifying devaluation'* take place not in his journalism so much as in the *'larger sense of his artistic form'*. Dialogism and polyphony develop together. An autonomous character is one which is able to reply to the 'author': 'By the very construction of the novel, the author speaks not *about* a character but *with* him' (PDP 63). The equality of voices in the polyphonic novel is realized dialogically, as being on the same plane means they can hear and respond to each other. The three elements dialogism, polyphony, and the chronotope work together, the latter facilitating the other two categories by placing the voices in the same space. Bakhtin's discussion of self-consciousness as the artistic dominant of Dostoevsky's dialogic novels shows both how chronotopically he views dialogism – the hero is 'actually present', although not on the 'territory' of a '"third person"' omniscient narrator – and how we might understand his use of the term 'author', as the following description of polyphony's role within dialogism suggests:

> Not a single element in [the novel's] atmosphere can be neutral: everything must touch the character to the quick, provoke him, interrogate him, even polemicize with him and taunt him; everything must be directed toward the hero himself, turned toward him, everything must make itself felt as discourse about someone actually present, as the word of a 'second' and not of a 'third' person. The semantic point of view of a 'third person', on whose territory a stable image of the hero is constructed, would destroy this atmosphere, and therefore such a point of view does not enter into Dosteovsky's creative world; and this is not because such a viewpoint is unavailable (due to the characters' autobiographical origins, or to Dostoevsky's extreme polemicism), but because it does not enter into Dostoevsky's creative design. (PDP 64)

The sense in which Bakhtin has used 'author', as the source of the voice which in another novel might be aloof and authoritative, is now taken over by 'atmosphere'; all the elements of the novel which the reader might expect to surround the hero inertly in the dialogic novel actually become involved with his fate.

In *Crime and Punishment* (1866), it is not the murder Raskolnikov commits, or the scandals and eccentricities that characterize Dostoevsky's other protagonists (PDP 64), which makes them into dialogized voices in a polyphonic novel but rather the other way round: 'the profound consciousness of [Raskolnikov, Sonya, Myshkin, Stavrogin, Ivan and Dmitry Karamazov's] own unfinalizability and indeterminacy is realized in very complex ways, by ideological thought, crime, or heroic deed' (PDP 59). Porfiry in *Crime and Punishment* knows that Raskolnikov is a murderer not through 'legal investigative psychology' but through 'a *special dialogic intuition* that allows him to penetrate the unfinalized and unresolved soul of Raskolnikov' (PDP 61).

As we will see in relation to polyphony and the chronotope, Bakhtin insists that Dostoevsky dramatizes in space rather than in time: 'One could say, in fact, that out of every contradiction within a single person Dostoevsky tries to create two persons, in order to dramatize the contradiction and develop it extensively' (PDP 28), as we saw happening in the format of the Pass Note. This observation shows how the different levels in Dostoevsky's work intersect. His dramatization is chronotopically spatial, rather than temporal; it is polyphonic, as the character reveals his or her own inner conflict, rather than being narrated from the outside; and it is dialogic, as what looks like a unitary voice turns out to be multiple and interactive. As an example, Bakhtin quotes from Raskolnikov's first interior monologue in *Crime and Punishment*, where he has just learnt of the engagement between his sister Dounia and Luzhin, made for his sake rather than Dounia's, from a letter from his mother: 'But my mother? It's all Rodya, precious Rodya, her firstborn! For such a son who would not sacrifice such a daughter! Oh, loving, over-partial hearts! Why, for his sake we would not shrink even from Sonya's fate' (quoted PDP 74). As Bakhtin describes, Raskolnikov in this section of his interior monologue 'recreates' the tones of his mother, and the reader can hear that

> in these words two voices are sounding simultaneously – [...] the mother's voice with her intonations of love and tenderness, and at the same time there is Raskolnikov's voice with its intonations of bitter irony, indignation (at the gesture of sacrifice), and sorrowful and reciprocal love. (PDP 75)

The voices of Dounia herself, Sonya and Marmeladov are also heard in the same monologue, showing that '[d]ialogue has penetrated inside every word, provoking in it a battle and the interruption of one voice by another', in a 'microdialogue'. These voices hear each other and call out to each other in small set pieces like this interior monologue; thus they are 'micro' versions of the dialogue of the novel as a whole.

Bakhtin points out that this interior monologue does not represent 'a psychological evolution of an idea within a single self-enclosed consciousness'. Rather, 'the consciousness of the solitary Raskolnikov becomes a field of battle for others' voices [...] and in this dialogue he tries to "get his thoughts straight"'. Any 'idea' which arises is the product of a 'live event', 'dialogic communion between consciousnesses'; it is at 'that point of contact between voice-consciousnesses the idea is born and lives' (PDP 88). As Bakhtin says, a particularly arresting example of this is the fact that Raskolnikov's letter to the newspaper, in which he puts forward his ideas, is never quoted in the text in its monologic form. It emerges only through dialogues, between Raskolnikov and Porfiry, Raskolnikov and Sonya, and Dounia and Svidrigailov; it is also implicitly questioned and tested by the events and various 'life-positions' within the novel. In this way, Bakhtin claims Raskolnikov's letter is '*an image of the idea*' (PDP 89), which is never represented in a formal, singular voice, but in this perspectival, multi-voiced manner.

A similar example is the letter Tess sends Angel Clare in Hardy's novel *Tess of the D'Urbervilles* (1891), in which she explains to him her past encounter with Alec D'Urberville, as a counter to his own confessions of past relationships. The letter is never quoted monologically, and in fact never read by Angel, but becomes known through the arguments Tess and Angel later have about her 'purity', and is again tested and questioned by the other 'ideas' and their exponents within the novel. Like Dostoevsky, Hardy has 'brought together ideas and world views, which in real life were absolutely estranged and deaf to one another, and forced them to quarrel' (PDP 91), in exemplary dialogic manner.

The fact that the 'idea' in question in *Crime and Punishment* is a letter to the newspaper gives it even greater force as an 'image' of the idea, and shows how 'genuine thought' can arise only 'when it enters into genuine dialogic relationships with other ideas, with the ideas of *others*' (PDP 88). The journalism of authors like Dostoevsky and Dickens has often been cited as evidence of their allegiance to ideas or causes which their novels then seem to contradict or throw into question. Dostoevsky's newspaper articles were monologic because they were journalistic, Bakhtin says; if the same idea were to appear in a novel, it would be an *image* of an idea, not the journalistic 'monologically confirmed' version. The novelist invariably triumphs over the journalist (PDP 92). Dostoevsky's artistic project was the representation of the permeation of the *'reifying devaluation of man'* into 'all the pores of contemporary life' (PDP 62), as expressed not through 'the journalistic side of his criticism, but rather the *larger sense of his artistic form*, which liberates and de-reifies the human being'.

In Dickens's case, it is equally true that, because he 'thought not in thoughts but in points of view, consciousnesses, voices' (93), his novels seem to contradict his stated, journalistic views. Again this is because the former operate dialogically, the latter monologically. Dickens's *Hard Times* (1864) is a case in point; in the novel, unions of workers and their leaders are presented sympathetically, but, at the same time, Dickens was also writing anti-union articles for the newspaper. What interests the analyst of dialogism is Dickens's 'idea-images', to quote the phrase Bakhtin uses of Dostoevsky, not the ideas themselves, and still less their monologically journalistic expression (PDP 91).

Dialogism and the novel

Bakhtin's approach to dialogism is central to his concept of the novel. The failure of traditional stylistics to deal with language is matched by its failure to deal with the novel; both have been seen as self-contained systems that cannot 'stand in a dialogic interrelationship with other languages' (DN 274). Bakhtin argues that most theories of the novel try to separate its style and its content, its 'formal' from its 'ideological' elements (DN 259). By contrast, he sees the novel as 'a social phenomenon', at the level of both form and content. They are both shaped by forces much larger than the '"private craftsmanship"' taking place in the 'artist's study', forces which include 'discourse in the open spaces of public squares, streets, cities and villages, of social groups, generation and epochs'. The novel is thus 'multiform in style and variform in speech and voice' (DN 261), and as a genre consists of a combination of distinct and interacting unities, which may include different languages. Bakhtin lists the 'basic types' of different elements out of which the novel is usually composed:

(1) Direct authorial literary-artistic narration (in all its diverse variants);
(2) Stylization of the various forms of oral everyday narration (*skaz*);
(3) Stylization of the various forms of semiliterary (written) everyday narration (the letter, the diary, etc.);
(4) Various forms of literary but extra-artistic authorial speech (moral, philosophical or scientific statements, oratory, ethnographic descriptions, memoranda and so forth);
(5) The stylistically individualized speech of characters. (DN 262)

Unravelling the layers of dialogic discourse in a novel, particularly one from a past era, may be hard work, as Bakhtin's description of the ideal dialogic critic suggests:[30] 'what is needed is a profound understanding of each language's socio-ideological meaning and an exact knowledge of the social distribution and ordering of all the other ideological voices of the era' (DN 417). It is, however, possible to identify the five categories of novelistic discourse in each of the novels cited in the present study as examples of Bakhtin's concepts.

Malcolm Lowry's *Under the Volcano* (1947) is the story of the last day in the life of Geoffrey Firmin, an alcoholic ex-consul living in Mexico, whose ex-wife Yvonne has come back to find him. Lowry's text is remarkable for its combination of polyphony, dialogized heteroglossia, and carnivalization of consciousness, and is therefore an example I will call upon frequently in this study. *Under the Volcano* features, first, a third-person narrator: 'Towards sunset on the Day of the Dead in November 1939, two men in white flannels sat on the main terrace of the Casino drinking *anís*'. Bakhtin's second category, *skaz*, is prominent in Lowry's novel, as the narrator frequently uses an 'everyday', oral-sounding discourse, particularly if it shades into free indirect discourse: 'It was too dark to see the bottom [of the ravine], but: here was finality indeed, and cleavage!'[31]

Third, there are many letters, newspaper articles, advertisements and notices in *Under the Volcano*, the 'everyday narration' of the third category, such as the Consul's letter to Yvonne, found by Laruelle after both are dead: '"So that when you left, Yvonne, I went to Oaxaca. There is no sadder word".' Bakhtin's fourth category, of literary but extra-artistic narration, is also widespread, as the novel's first sentence suggests, by sounding like a gazetteer: 'Two mountain chains traverse the republic roughly from north to south, forming between them a number of valleys and plateaux'.[32]

Finally, the speech of characters: this is Señor Bustamente recalling Geoffrey Firmin with his one-time friend Jacques Laruelle: '"But it was true, then, he was a Consul? For I remember him many time sitting here drinking: and often, the poor guy, he have no socks".' *Under the Volcano* also features languages other than English, for instance Italian and Spanish: '[Señor Bustamente] gave a little confused cough, an *appoggiatura*. "Your *amigo*, the *bicho* ... I did not mean bitch; I mean *bicho*, the one with the blue eyes"'; as well as stylized dialects of various kinds, including broken English: '"Why ah are you", shouted the fat policeman [...] "What ah are you for?"'.[33] All these different languages interact with one another; Bakhtin observes that traditional stylistics is 'deaf to dialogue' (DN 273), and unable to approach 'the distinctive social dialogue among languages that is present in the novel' (263).

Bakhtin distinguishes three kinds of dialogic relation between utterances in the novel: first, 'the primordial dialogism of discourse', between individuals' 'utterances inside a *single* language'; second, between '"social languages" within a single *national* language'; and third, between 'different national languages within the same *culture*' (DN 275). Examples of all three categories can be seen clearly in this exchange from *Under the Volcano*, between the Consul and an *abarrotes* owner, or grocer:

> 'You are – *diablo!*' There was a pause in which [Yvonne] heard the Consul saying something. '*Eggs!*' the good-humoured voice exploded again. 'You – *two diablos!* You *tree diablos.*' The voice crackled with glee. '*Eggs!*' Then: 'Who is the beautiful *layee?* – [...] *Eggs!*' ludicrously followed the Consul, who appeared at this moment, calmly smiling, on the pavement above Yvonne.
>
> 'In Tortu', he was saying [...] 'the ideal University ... where no application [...] is allowed to interfere with the business of – look out! - drinking'.[34]

Dialogic interaction occurs here within, first, a single national language (between the broken English of the *abarrotes*-owner and the conventional third-person narration, focalized through Yvonne); second, between different social languages within a national language (the Mexican's voice, although 'incredibly good-humoured', is lewd; the Consul's is learned but self-justifying); and, third, between different national languages, English and Spanish, within the single culture of Mexico (representing, among other things, the colonial Spanish past and the oppressive North American present).[35] As Bakhtin describes it, the languages of heteroglossia present together at any one moment in a text might include, for instance, 'the Ukrainian language, the language of the epic poem, of early Symbolism, of the student, of a particular generation of children, of the run-of-the-mill intellectual, of the Nietzschean and so on' (DN 291). All these languages acknowledge each other's existence in the text, speak to and relativize each other, and their interaction is thus dialogic. Both this list, and the list of different languages in *Under the Volcano* characterizing the encounter between the 'ruffianly' *abarrotes*-owner and the Consul, show that 'at any given moment of its historical existence, language is heteroglot from top to bottom'. Language represents all kinds of 'stratifying factors', including 'socio-ideological contradictions between the present and the past [and] [...] between different socio-ideological groups in the present' (DN 291). The interaction of English and Spanish in a Mexican context, or Ukrainian and Russian in a Soviet one, has exactly this kind of historical force. Again, this historicism is an effect which traditional stylistics cannot account for, as it imparts to a text a '"taste" of a profession, a genre, a tendency, a party, a particular work' (293), or a cultural conflict. Such apparently small-scale effects, 'the indices of heteroglossia', are excluded by conventional linguistics. Saussure, for instance, as Allon White puts it, 'consign[ed] them to the trash-can of "parole"'.[36]

STYLIZATION

Traditional stylistics is unable to account for the way various kinds of stylization work, Bakhtin points out, 'in *skaz*, in parodies and in various forms of verbal masquerade, "not talking straight"' (DN 275). The fact that Bakhtin's own stylistics *can* analyse this dialogue is what makes it not only innovative but revolutionary. Only by paying attention to the context of the utterance can such features as 'not talking straight' be recognized and analysed. By 'stylization', Bakhtin means the borrowing by one voice of the recognizable style and timbre of another; it is 'an artistic image of another's language' (DN 362). Stylization is one example of 'hybridity', which means any 'mixture of two social languages within the limits of a single utterance', languages which are 'separated from one another by an epoch, by social differentiation or by some other factor'. The spectrum of hybridity ranges from stylization to parody with many sub-varieties of 'mutually illuminated' languages in between (DN 364).[37] Obliteration of the second voice is not the point; nor is imitation, as this would also result in just one voice.[38] Parody also consists of two voices, but the relation between them is more likely to be one of disagreement, the first holding the second up to ridicule. The following are brief examples of each variety of stylization:

(1) *skaz*: we have already seen an example of this from *Under the Volcano*, and from *Notes from Underground* in the chapter on heteroglossia; here, the narrator of Helen Zahavi's *Dirty Weekend* reports that Bella liked to sit on a bench in Brunswick Square, and then adds, 'Something wrong with that? Something abnormal? Is she taking too much? Is she too grasping? Is she gobbling up altogether too much?'[39] As *skaz*, this utterance is both everyday and a stylized – and therefore double-voiced – version of oral discourse, as the insistent rhetorical questions suggest.

(2) parody: Bakhtin rather disconcertingly observes that in world literature 'there are probably many works whose parodic nature has not even been suspected' (DN 374). A recent example of unsuspected (non-literary) parody, although those involved did know 'the alien discourse' of its 'second context', is Alan Sokal's 1996 article, 'Transgressing the Boundaries: Toward a Trans-formative Hermeneutics of Quantum Gravity', published in the journal *Social Text* as a straightforward attempt to link contemporary science with postmodern theory. Professor Sokal's admission that his article was a parody of postmodern discourse, and surprise that the 'fundamental silliness' of what he said was not noticed by the journal editors, has unleashed a wide-ranging debate.[40] Sokal's hoax depended on his article sounding single-voiced to those who would not hear its double-voiced attack. The central 'silliness' of his parodic article, according to Sokal, was his taking for granted the questionability of physical reality. This is a representative quotation from Sokal's article:

> the truth claims of science are inherently theory-laden and self-referential; and consequently [...] the discourse of the scientific community, for all its undeniable value, cannot assert a privileged epistemological status with respect to counterhegemonic narratives emanating from dissident or marginalized communities.

It is worth dwelling on Sokal's parody, as it is a stylization of a genre – postmodern literary theory – where, in his view, '[i]ncomprehensibility becomes a virtue; allusions, metaphors, and puns substitute for evidence and logic'. Sokal satirizes this aspect of postmodernism, and its tendency towards 'subjectivist thinking' and a denial of 'the existence of objective realities'. From a Bakhtinian point of view, what is most interesting about Sokal's 'spoof' is that he argues that his 'utterly serious' criticism of this way of thinking could be made only parodically. His target is, he says, an 'academic subculture that typically ignores (or disdains) reasoned criticism from the outside', and in order to 'show that the emperor has no clothes', the 'best weapon' is satire.

(3) 'not talking straight': Leo Rosten quotes an apocryphal example of this double-voicedness. After the death of Lenin, with Trotsky exiled, Stalin receives this cablegram at a mass rally in Red Square:

> Joseph Stalin
> Kremlin
> Moscow
> You were right and I was wrong. You are the true heir of Lenin. I should apologize.
>
> Trotsky

A simple tailor in the crowd tells the triumphant Stalin he has not read the cablegram with the right feeling, and renders it himself:

> You were right and I was *wrong*? *You* are the true heir of Lenin? *I* should apologize???!
>
> Trotsky![41]

Post-colonial studies has developed the term 'hybridity', a concept analogous to hybridization. Although the fact that the two terms sound so alike is coincidental, the definition of 'hybridity' in post-colonial discourse is a striking example of antagonistic double-voicedness. The notion of 'hybridization' refers to combinations of European and indigenous discourse within post-colonial texts. It includes the idea of Europeanization, the imposition of an authoritative and foreign language, but also testifies to the continuing life of local culture during and after colonial rule.[42] Hybridization in this sense means a textual form of mimicry, in which '"the words of the master"' are not simply copied or ventriloquized but rewritten: 'misreadings and incongruities expose the uncertainties and ambivalences of the colonial text and deny it an authorizing presence'.[43] The hybrid writer 'is already open to two worlds', as Kumkum Sangari points out in a discussion of Gabriel García Marquez's novels.[44]

THE BATTLE OF LANGUAGES

As these examples remind us, the discourse of every novel is very varied, composed of all kinds of different discourse; as Bakhtin puts it, 'the style of a novel is to be found in the combination of its styles; the language of a novel is the system of its "languages"' (DN 262). The definition of the novel is, according to Bakhtin, 'a diversity of social speech types (sometimes even diversity of languages) and a diversity of individual voices, artistically organized'. When these languages within the novel take account of each other, answer each other back, include alien fragments within themselves, then that novel is dialogic.

Bakhtin's distinction between 'individual voices' and 'artistic organization' underlies a point Ken Hirschkop makes, as we will see below. The novel's relation to heteroglossia – 'social speech types' – is of course one of citation and aesthetic organization, not mere reproduction. Bakhtin describes the function of all the five features listed above as 'those fundamental compositional unities *with whose help* heteroglossia can enter the novel' (DN 263, my italics).

It is very important to note which way round this relationship operates; the diversity of the novel has developed in order to allow any novelistic theme to move through as many 'different languages and speech types' as possible, rather than the theme itself giving rise to diverse languages. For this reason, novelistic language, and the fragmentary novelistic subject, is contrasted by Bakhtin to poetic genres, where, he argues, unity of style and 'the unity of an individual person realizing himself in this language' are prerequisite. In the novel, '[t]he plot itself is subordinated to the task of coordinating and exposing languages to each other', as 'the primary stylistic project of the novel as a genre is to create images of languages'. The skill it calls upon and fosters in its readers is 'a sharpening in our perception of socio-linguistic differentiations', and a sensitivity to the '"internal form" ... of an alien language, and to the "internal form" of one's own language as an alien form' (DN 365–7). Hirschkop detects in Bakhtin's comments here on plot a preference for simultaneity over the evolution of narrative, which aims 'to disconnect completely the narrative structure of such novels from the dialogue of ideologically charged languages within them'. Bakhtin's own examples actually run counter to his own argument, as the nineteenth-century novels he cites are far from suspending 'all social description and explanation'. What is distinctive about Dostoevsky's nineteenth-century novels, and Helen Zahavi's late twentieth-century novel *Dirty Weekend*, discussed below, is that, rather than attempting any kind of 'explanation' of a discourse, they represent its 'testing'.[45]

Although Bakhtin does not necessarily mean different national languages when he describes them as 'alien', in *Lost in Translation: Life in a New Language* (1989) Eva Hoffman describes the disconcerting effect of being confronted with the 'brute materiality' (DN 367) of her native and her adopted languages when her family leave Poland for North America in 1968:

> But mostly, the problem is that the signifier has become severed from the signified. The words I learn now don't stand for things in the same unquestioned way they did in my native tongue. 'River' in Polish was a vital sound, energized with the essence of riverhood, of my rivers, or my being immersed in rivers. 'River' in English is cold – a word without an aura.[46]

The act of describing such a process naturally gets mixed up with the process itself. Instead of using the Polish word for 'river', Hoffman repeats the English word twice, despite its 'coldness', signalling that regret for the Polish word is in the past, and the present consists of this text's perfect and controlled English. Polish words rarely feature at all in Hoffman's text; revealingly the one quoted most often is the Polish for 'nostalgia', 'tęsknota'. As Bakhtin says, '[a] deeply involved participation in alien cultures and languages [...] inevitably leads to an awareness of the disassociation between language and intentions, language and thought, language and expression' (DN 369), a perception echoed by Hoffman, whose participation in an alien culture was as an immigrant. Her description of an encounter with a Canadian family suggests just this 'disassociation':

> Now my mind gropes for some description of them, but nothing fits. They're a different species from anyone I've ever met in Poland, and Polish words slip off of them without sticking. English words don't hook on to anything. I try, deliberately, to come up with a few. Are these people pleasant or dull? Kindly or silly? The words flow in an uncertain space.[47]

Eva's single consciousness 'participates equally in several languages' (DN 368), although the reader is again saved from such participation directly, gaining access to it only as a non-literal artistic image. This is a method of representing heteroglossia which, like Roth's *Call It Sleep*, avoids offering first-hand experience of different dialects or national languages in the way that *Under the Volcano*, for instance, does. The confused perceptions of a transplanted, bilingual adolescent are rendered in flawless prose in a single national language. In the case of *Lost in Translation*, the book's title itself suggests that the Polish subject, named Ewa Wydra, has been entirely replaced by the American one, Eva Hoffman, as the apparent ambiguity of 'Now my mind gropes' suggests. That 'now' is long past, and its momentary resemblance to a comment on the text's composition in the present simply emphasizes the distance between Ewa then and Eva now.

UNRELIABLE NARRATORS

Bakhtin goes further than his argument that plot is subordinated to the exposure of languages to each other, and suggests that the presence of a 'direct and unmediated' word in the novel is so 'impermissably naive' that it is at once dialogized by taking on the nature of 'an internal polemic' (DN 278). That is, an apparently univocal word exists as a *representation* of such a word, and must interact dialogically with the other words around it. The same is true even if heteroglossia remains outside the novel and the 'novelist comes forward with his own unitary and fully affirming language'. The very fact that a unitary language is 'uttered in a heteroglot environment' and that such a language must be 'championed, purified, defended', forces it to interact dialogically with heteroglossia (DN 332).

An example of this process is the device of an unreliable narrator, whose word is the only one we read, but whose 'unitary language' is dialogized by the unspoken surrounding of other languages, including the reader's. John Dowell in Ford Madox Ford's *The Good Soldier* (1915) is one such example. Dowell is a sophisticated version of the 'the image of the fool – either of an actual simpleton or the image of the mask of a rogue'. It is impossible to know whether Dowell is a simpleton or a rogue, so Bakhtin's description of the ancient figure of the fool fits Dowell, a modern instance, very aptly. As an organizing function in *The Good Soldier*, Dowell acts as a means of '*not grasping* the conventions of society [...] not understanding lofty pathos-charged labels, things and events – such incomprehension remains almost everywhere an essential ingredient of prose style' (DN 402). For example, Dowell appears not to 'know' of his wife Florence's promiscuous past, or that she spent the night before their wedding with a lover; he does not 'understand' that she feigns a heart condition in order to avoid sexual relations with him, and he does not read correctly the signs of her adultery, even when it involves the 'good soldier' of the title, his friend Edward Ashburnham. The text purports to be the revelation by this simple narrator of what Dowell has since found out and been told by Edward's widow Leonora. Some critics have taken his 'fool' persona as a smokescreen, and suggest that it is an elaborate cover-up by a clever but impecunious 'rogue' who has murdered his wife and her lover, among others, for monetary gain; his alibi is his 'simpleness'. Either way, the reader is presented with incomprehension and failure to grasp conventions.[48]

Another example of this kind of 'deliberate stupidity', which polemicizes and dialogically interacts with 'a lofty pseudo intelligence' in the novel, is the device of the child's-eye view. Bakhtin mentions 'the cult of the child in Romantic literature', which was the 'image of the fool' chosen by that particular 'artistic trend' (DN 403-4). In the case of Henry James's novel *What Maisie Knew* (1897), for instance, the innocence of the young girl Maisie in the face of adult sexual arrangements may be a truer 'knowledge' than the adults' apparent sophistication. The contrast between Maisie's childlike perceptions and the Jamesian narrator emphasizes this gulf: 'Her researches had hitherto indicated that to incur a second parent of the same sex you usually had to lose the first'.[49] There exists here a dialogic friction around several words, in general surrounding the gap between the Jamesian diction and the childish world it renders: 'researches' is too formal a term for Maisie's unhappy experiences; 'incur' neatly suggests that parents and stepparents may be liabilities. Maisie differs as an image of innocence from John Dowell because his narration was in the first person, while James points out in his Preface that, although all the action is seen through Maisie's eyes, it is not expressed in her own terms.

James appears to have had a Bakhtinian motive for choosing this subject and the means to represent it. The fictional situation arises out of artistic or abstract impulses, for instance James's technical interest in having 'Everything take place before Maisie'.[50] James is aware that the dialogical interaction between ignorance and knowledge can result in a reversal of the two terms, and that one voice of knowledge may never appear within the text:

> I recall that my first view of this neat possibility was as the attaching problem of the picture restricted (while yet achieving, as I say, completeness and coherency) to what the child might be conceived to have *understood* – to have been able to to interpret and appreciate.[51]

The picture may be restricted to Maisie's view, but that view's dialogic interaction with other, absent, discourses produces 'coherency', if not polyphony.

Following Bakhtin's observation above, in this case it is clearly the form which determines the content, and thus the particular intersection of languages within a text, rather than the other way round. While Ford's novel was an example of representation 'through the words of a *narrator* who does not understand this world', in the case of James's novel it is the '*character* who does not understand' (DN 402).[52]

Bakhtin argues that the various novelistic images of incomprehension and deception – the rogue, the clown, the fool – are 'the three dialogic categories that had organized heteroglossia in the novel at the dawn of its history', and persist in altered form, as we have seen, in the present (DN 405). Although categorizing them like this shows the ambivalence of the roles, one could call John Dowell the 'symbolic image' of the rogue, Maisie of the fool, and a contemporary example of a clown, who maliciously distorts high languages and turns them 'inside out', might be, again, the Consul in *Under the Volcano*. For instance, the sight of a golf course inspires him to distort the high languages of Donne's poetry and the jargon of golf, partly in drunken (if unuttered) word-play, and partly, as he is a tragic clown, as an ironized comment on his own destiny and uncertain salvation:

> I should become a sort of Donne of the fairways at least. Poet of the unreplaced turf.– Who holds the flag while I hole out in three? Who hunts my Zodiac Zone along the shore? And who, upon that last and final green, though I hole out in four, accepts my ten and three score ... Though I have more.[53]

In all three cases, the 'stylistic functions' of these figures in the novel are 'determined by [their] relationship to heteroglossia', which each one helps to introduce. The rogue parodies high languages; the fool is 'naively incomprehending' of the high languages s/he comes into contact with; the clown 'unmasks' high languages and has licence to utter the otherwise unacceptable. Heteroglossia is dialogized by these human figures, as it becomes double-voiced through being parodied, and relativized by different viewpoints.

Although in the examples we have examined the rogue, fool, and clown are central characters, Bakhtin also describes how the lineaments of novelistic heroes have not always been psychologically motivated but depend on contemporary habits of representing human images. Novels of the hero's trial, picaresque novels, the *Bildungsroman*, the confessional novel,[54] all include particular kinds of hero, determined by the text's historical position, precursors and successors, and 'extraliterary rhetorical genres'. Such a list of novelistic elements reveals the difficulties of analysing fully the dialogic layers in older texts; as Bakhtin argues, 'historico-linguistic research into the language systems and styles available to a given era (social, professional, generic, tendentious)' can help such an approach, along with more orthodox linguistic analysis (DN 417).

Bakhtin points out that heroes in early novels of trial are represented as 'static', without any element of 'becoming' or internal change. This is the result of certain kinds of contemporary discourse about human subjects: 'The unity of a man and the coherence of his acts (his deeds) are of a rhetorical and legal character and therefore, viewed from a later psychological concept of the human personality, they appear external and merely formal' (DN 407). Bakhtin suggests that the kind of novel which succeeded the trial novel, the picaresque, drove a wedge between the image of a man and of his deeds, because of the ambivalence of the picaresque hero. As an example, Bakhtin mentions the character Gil Blas, from Lesage's eighteenth-century French novel of that name; other examples include Henry Fielding's Tom Jones, or, more recently, Fevvers in Angela Carter's picaresque novel *Nights at the Circus*, (1984) who is a symbol of ambivalence. Her identity and commercial success depend upon being poised between a freak of nature who really has wings, and a confidence trickster pretending to have them. Thus '[a]ll the old links between a man and his act, between an event and those who participate in it, fall apart' (DN 408): almost literally in Fevvers's case, as her 'act' is that of a trapeze artist, and she is thought by some to be covering up the fact that she is really a man.

The novel and rhetoric

Bakhtin suggests that describing the novel as a rhetorical, rather than an artistic, genre, can be helpful, and points out that the novel is as close to 'living rhetorical genres (journalistic, moral, philosophical and others)' as to the artistic genres, 'epic, dramatic, lyric' (269). Rhetoric aims to impress or persuade; it thus has a quality of *address*, to the listener, and of formal construction, which the novel shares. Allon White points out that the word's internal dialogism consists partly in its expectation of an answer,[55] which means it takes up a certain orientation towards the addressee, as the speaker – the word – 'strives to get a reading on his own word', as Bakhtin puts it:

> The listener and his response are regularly taken into account when it comes to everyday dialogue and rhetoric, but every other sort of discourse as well is oriented towards an understanding that is 'responsive' although this orientation is not particularized in an independent act and is not compositionally marked. (DN 280)

White argues that this orientation by the novelistic word towards 'the imagined resistance of its addressee' extends to the form of the novel as a whole, and includes an area of study Bakhtin notoriously omits, the dialogic relation between reader and text: 'A kind of reader-oriented self-consciousness, [this line of dialogism] can be compared to the effect created in discourse by the "implicit reader" spoken of by Wolfgang Iser'.[56]

Bakhtin contrasts the novel's gravitation towards 'the realities of heteroglossia', which produces a network of dialogic, interactive relations in the text, with what he calls 'unitary language' (DN 270). This aims to *unify and centralize the verbal-ideological world*. An example of such a unifying force is any system of linguistic norms, Bakhtin says, meaning not just abstract grammatical rules but a verbal-ideological force which aims to keep a national language free from foreign or heteroglot influences. Contemporary instances of the activity of such a unitary force include the 'English Only constitutional amendment proposed in the United States and [...] the political use of received standard pronunciation in the United Kingdom';[57] and the Académie française's disapproval of English words imported into French. Bakhtin calls this impetus 'centripetal', meaning that it aims to draw all language back to a central focus; it is contrasted with 'centrifugal' heteroglot forces, which tend to move away from such a centre. Bakhtin emphasizes differential social relations here, as a central passage on unitary language suggests:

> The victory of one reigning language (dialect) over the others, the supplanting of languages, their enslavement, the process of illuminating them with the True Word, the incorporation of barbarians and lower social strata into a unitary language of culture and truth, the canonization of ideological systems, philology with its methods of studying and teaching dead languages [...] all this determined the content and power of the category of 'unitary language'. (DN 271)

This is very persuasive rhetoric itself. An instance in *Under the Volcano* illustrates a centrifugal, heteroglot overcoming of such centripetal forces. The Consul finds abandoned a child's exercise book, in which he reads:

> Escruch is an old man [...] His is a miser. No one loves Scrooge and Scrooge loves no one. He has no friends. He is alone in the world. The man (*el hombre*): the house (*la casa*): the poor (*los pobres*): he lives (*él vive*) [...] Is Scrooge rich or poor? Has he friends? How does he live? Alone. World. On.[58]

On the face of it, a child's English grammar lesson should show exemplary centripetal qualities: it is about correct usage and learning a unitary, fixed 'langue'. Bakhtin argues that

> To speak of discourse as one might speak of any other subject, that is, thematically, without any dialogized transmission of it, is possible only when such discourse is utterly reified, a thing; it is possible, for example, to talk about the word in such a way in grammar, where it is precisely the dead, thing-like shell of the word that interests us. (DN 355)

However, the instance of this kind of centripetality from *Under the Volcano* is undermined by the incursions of heteroglossia, in the form of incorrect English ('Escruch is an old man ... His is a miser'). The grammar lesson is already a representation of correctness, rather than the thing itself, because it is what the child has copied down; and being included within the dialogic whole of a novel makes it a representation on that level as well. Grammatical correctness is also undermined by the Consul's drunken reading: it is not clear if the final list of words is isolated by the Consul himself, who sees his own story in Scrooge's, or a list of new vocabulary for the student to memorize: 'Alone. World. On'. As Bakhtin puts it, 'alongside verbal-ideological centralization and unification, the uninterrupted processes of decentralization and disunification go forward' (DN 272).

Equally, this episode represents a typical novelistic 'testing [the hero's] discourse', which distinguishes the novel from epic, according to Bakhtin (DN 388). The tension in this extract between the various different languages – broken and standard English, Spanish, the nod towards Dickens, the well-known format of the grammar lesson with its comprehension exercises, and the Consul's final comment, 'bloody old Scrooge; how queer to meet him here!'[59] – makes this a miniature example of Bakhtin's comment on the 'authentic environment of an utterance' as 'dialogized heteroglossia, anonymous and social as language, but simultaneously concrete, filled with specific content and accented as an individual utterance' (DN 272). The representation of heteroglossia here has rescued the word from its reifying context, and forced the grammar-book into a dialogic relation with its surrounding languages.

Dialogue and dialogism

It is worth noting here the emphasis Bakhtin places on the idea of dialogue itself, although, as Kristeva points out, 'For Bakhtin, dialogue can be monological, and what is called monologue can be dialogical'.[60] Ken Hirschkop suggests that Bakhtin declares dialogue in general to be constitutive of language, when in fact he has in mind various specific kinds of literal dialogue, both the kind that characterizes Western liberal political debate and the kind which underpins the philosophy of ethics. Hirschkop detects in *Problems of Dostoevsky's Poetics* Bakhtin's allegiance to the philosophies of Immanuel Kant and Martin Buber, 'smuggled' into what purports to be an objective description of language. Kant's and Buber's are 'projects with an interesting and chequered political history, not realizations of ontological attributes of language'.[61] It looks as if Bakhtin is prey to his own theory: rather than presenting a successfully monologic account of dialogism as a property of both the novel and language itself, another, submerged voice speaks differently, of the specific philosophical heritage of dialogism. Hirschkop describes Bakhtin's apparent slide from dialogue to dialogism as 'the not so surreptitious introduction of a central political concept, that of equal rights, into a description of linguistic style'. Hirschkop's point is that stylistically it is impossible to distinguish a voice with 'equal rights' from one without, although Bakhtin's account of polyphony, and his approach to dealing with the utterance as a whole, suggests that he thinks this is untrue.[62]

Hirschkop suggests that the novel, as an aesthetic form 'orchestrated' by an author, cannot reproduce the features of dialogue: 'whatever the values made flesh in the novel, the openness and spontaneity we deem essential to dialogue aren't found there'. Instead, the novel is one of the 'modernist' genres which cites and represents rather than enacting. Bakhtin appears to be over-valuing dialogue, but, dialogically, a different voice emerges in his writing on this subject: 'it is Bakhtin's point, even though he does not seem to know it', according to Hirschkop, that 'there is something wrong with the assumption that dialogue represents all we should hope for in the political and social life of language'. Hirschkop adds that the novel makes the public square, valued by Bakhtin for a rather different kind of dialogue, intelligible. The raw data of heteroglossia can make little sense aesthetically until they are 'orchestrated' into novelistic form: if dialogue is an 'impoverished ideal' in the modern world, '[b]etter to admit that there might be something to those genres which cite and represent, something they have that the public square lacks. Perhaps dialogism, to coin a phrase, reaches those parts dialogue cannot reach.'[63]

Hirschkop's argument is extremely persuasive in distinguishing the various voices in Bakhtin's discussion of multi-voicedness (again, he emphasizes that Bakhtin 'does not seem to know' the dialogism of his own discourse), but some of what he presents as being a submerged voice seems to be much nearer the surface of Bakhtin's work (see for instance his insistence on the 'neutrality' of speech structures, and his comments on the novel as a 'secondary speech genre': 'primary genres lose their immediate relation to actual reality and to the real utterances of others' in the novel, PSG 62). Hirschkop's case against dialogue seems by its very strength to over-value the claims made for dialogue either by Bakhtin or by Western democracies. However, Hirschkop concludes with a modified version of dialogism: his is 'a vision of language as unevenly structured, full of forms which don't respond, as in a dialogue, but represent'.[64] This is a very useful definition and working model for dialogism; and it fits with the representational emphases of heteroglossia, with its 'images' of language, and polyphony, with its freedom within representational boundaries.

'Poetic in the narrow sense'

Bakhtin is notorious for arguing that poetry cannot be dialogic, and that poetic language runs the risk of becoming 'authoritarian, dogmatic and conservative, cutting itself off from the influence of extraliterary social dialects' (DN 287). According to Hirschkop, Bakhtin sees poetry as 'a style which imposes [...] the Saussurean model of language on the actual practice of discourse.' Many critics have argued that, on the contrary, Bakhtin's theories can be very helpful when read with poetry in mind.[65] Lodge suggests that Browning, who uses double-voiced discourse in his poetic mono- logues, and T. S. Eliot, whose The Waste Land (1922) is constructed particularly polyglottically, seem to be counter-examples to Bakhtin's distinction of the novel's polyglossia and poetry's monoglossia. Robert Crawford finds Bakhtin's categories 'exciting' and fruitful when considering Scottish poetry, as 'one may consider writing in Scots as having the effect of what Bakhtin calls "dialogized heteroglossia", that is, utterance or writing in which there is clear friction of "argument" between different discourses'. Crawford also uses a passage from 'Author and Hero in Aesthetic Activity' to illuminate T. S. Eliot's J. Alfred Prufrock.[66] Donald Wesling, in his essay 'Bakhtin and the Social Poetics of Dialect', contrasts two dialect poems – Tom Leonard's 'Unrelated Incident (3)' and Linton Kwesi Johnson's 'It dread inna Inglan' – and concludes that Leonard's refutes Bakhtin's slurs against the poetic, while Johnson's supports them. Leonard's poem, according to Wesling, offers internal dialogization in the clash between the voices of a 'Glasgow scruff' and a BBC news announcer: 'This is proof that double-voicing exists in poetry as a mode', Wesling concludes. Johnson's poem, on the other hand, does not feature the Volosinovian 'struggle within the sign', and the same claims cannot be made for his work: 'We found a fissure down the middle of each word in Leonard, but nothing of the sort in Kwesi Johnson'.[67]

Bakhtin agrees that dialogized *images* may appear in all genres of poetry, even the lyric (DN 278), which he considers the least dialogic literary form as it purports to be the univocal utterance of a single subject. In his identification of the poet's language with the unified poetic self, Bakhtin seems to be making the common error of reading a poet's lyric persona biographically, assuming that, as Todorov puts it, 'the poem is an uttering act, while the novel represents one'.[68] A classic example of this is the many critics who erroneously believed, having read her poem 'For Johnny Pole on the Forgotten Beach' (1958), about the death of the speaker's brother during the Second World War, that Anne Sexton herself had lost a brother.[69] Bakhtin argues,

> The language of the poet is his language, he is utterly immersed in it, inseparable from it, he makes use of each form, each word, each expression according to its unmediated power to assign meaning (as it were, 'without quotation marks'), that is, as a pure and direct expression of his own intention. (DN 285)

Bakhtin's apparent refusal to credit the poetic persona with qualities similar to that of the prose narrator is akin to critics' inability to read Sexton's poem as a form of artistry. Acknowledging that there may be two voices in a poem, the represented and the representing, as there are in a work of fiction, would allow poetry to be dialogic, and Sexton to be constructing a voice with such verisimilitude that it appears to be confessional. The construction of her persona or 'mask' fits with the carnival activities that accompanied poetry's accomplishment of 'cultural, national and political centralization' (DN 273).[70] On the stages of 'local fairs and buffoon spectacles', language was simultaneously being decentred and ridiculed: 'where there was no language-center at all, where there was to be found a lively play with the 'languages' of poets, scholars, monks, knights and others, where all 'languages' were masks and where no language could claim to be an authentic, incontestable face' (DN 273). However, Bakhtin's argument obviously does not only rest on a simple confusion between the 'unified' language of the lyric poem with its author's language. It is almost as if the definition makes better sense in reverse: the term for any literary utterance which is not self-reflexive, and in which 'the representation of discourse [...] isn't aesthetically valorized as it is in prose', is 'poetry'. The reader's and writer's awareness of the surrounding heteroglossia is suspended 'by convention' (DN 285).[71]

As Galin Tihanov puts it, in Bakhtin's writing, the 'concept of poetry vacillates between the strict meaning of a given genre, whose essence is captured in the lyric [...], and the broader meaning of all direct, canonical genres'.[72] Bakhtin is contrasting 'two form-shaping ideologies', novelness and and lyricness, rather than 'empirical generalizations' about specific novels and poems.[73] As with his broader theory of dialogism, the historical and the normative are easily confused when considering Bakhtin's comments on poetry, despite his own *caveat*: 'It goes without saying that we continually advance as typical the extreme to which poetic genres aspire; in concrete examples of poetic works it is possible to find features fundamental to prose, and numerous hybrids of various generic types' (DN 287). It is thus no contradiction that Bakhtin analyses lyric poetry himself; Pushkin's 'Parting' is discussed in both *Art and Answerability* (211–21) and *Towards a Philosophy of the Act* (65–73; though it is fair to note that the context alters more than the discussion of the poem in these two locations). Morson and Emerson's description of Bakhtin's 'hostility' to lyric poetry[74] seems not quite right. As Carol McGuirk points out, it is not poetry itself which is the villain, but the 'superior status' granted to poetry within the hierarchies of classical stylistics.[75] When he is not contrasting lyricness with novelness, poetry can yield concisely expressed examples for other parts of Bakhtin's theory of discourse.

As well as 'dialogized images', Bakhtin discusses local dialogic effects which may appear in poetry, like the obvious presence of several voices in a single word or utterance. He suggests that, although elements of heteroglossia may enter poetic discourse, they are not on the same level as the 'real language of the work'; they are simply depicted things (DN 287). These dialogized images cannot alter the tone of the poetry: 'even discourse about doubts must be cast in a discourse that cannot be doubted'. As Morson and Emerson put it, the novelist's language, by contrast, 'is one of doubt, not because he uses language to express doubts, but because he doubts his own language'.[76] Poetic tropes themselves never unfold into 'two meanings parceled out between two separate voices' (DN 328). They can possess only a 'single-voiced double or multiple meaning' (DN 330). This seems to be true even of Crawford's analysis: what he says of Scots as 'dialogized heteroglossia' imparting a dialogic element to the work of Scottish poets is equally true of prose writers, and his comment on Prufrock is simply on an image, not the poem's language. Wesling argues that poetic language can be dialogized by heteroglossia, and claims that both his examples show that 'the social, whether it be [Tom Leonard's Scottish] border culture or [Linton Kwesi Johnson's British West Indian] diaspora culture, penetrates in poetry down to the level of form'.[77]

Poetry, Bakhtin argues, is immune to the 'internal dialogism of the word', that is, the presence of two voices within an utterance, without compositional markings (DN 283). In poetry, style 'permeates the object directly and without any mediation' (DN 378). Even a parodic poem, which would automatically be double-voiced, is not part of the genre it parodies, and therefore not a poem at all (PND 59).[78] In the novel, as we have seen, internal dialogization is very important; in poetry, 'the internal dialogization of discourse is not put to artistic use', but is 'artificially extinguished' (DN 284). Bakhtin claims that anything that enters the poetic work '*must immerse itself in Lethe, and forget its previous life in any other contexts*'. Rhythm itself helps in this amnesiac process, as it 'destroys in embryo those social worlds of speech and of persons that are potentially embedded in the word' (DN 298). Even in eras of 'language crises', when poetry too is forced to change, it quickly re-canonizes the new language and behaves 'as if no other language existed' (DN 399).

Morson and Emerson conclude that this makes poetry a

utopian form, as the 'contingencies of history and the messiness of daily life are thought away', and replaced by a language which 'sees into the essence of things'. The novel is again quite opposite to this, an anti-utopian form – although it may represent utopian worlds – because it 'presuppose[s] the impossibility of a single language of truth and imagine[s] social discourse as an unfinalizable discovery of new and unforeseeable truths'.[79] However, as Morson observes of Tolstoy's 'absolute' novelistic language, even apparent monologism must become dialogized when it is represented. Poetic practice is defined by its relation to other discourses, just like the novelistic; it does not so much repress social relations within discourse, as produce particular hierarchical ones.[80]

Epic

Epic is another literary genre which Bakhtin contrasts negatively with the novel. Although he does not discuss any specific examples in detail, he cites Homer's *Iliad*, the epic of the Trojan war, and Dante's *Divine Comedy*. Neither of these facts – epic as less than the novel, and Bakhtin's failure to supply instances of it – is as simple as it seems.

In the first place, as Rachel Falconer has pointed out, when 'Epic and Novel' is read alongside Bakhtin's theory of the chronotope, it seems that he is being particularly polemical about the temporal arrangement of epic. Like all other genres, epic possesses its own chronotopes, although Bakhtin does not use this word in relation to it.[81] Epic, Bakhtin argues, has been supplanted by the novel, with its superior temporal structure, but his addition of value judgements to such an observation (he describes epic using such adjectives as 'stilted', pre-packaged', 'narrow and unlifelike', EN 10) is due to the fact that, as he suggests elsewhere, epic and novel are not so very different. As Falconer puts it, 'the central importance of the chronotope in Bakhtin's definition of genre necessitates a close, indeed a contingent relation between epic, novel and romance'.[82] Todorov also points out that in other writings, Bakhtin defines the novel in such a way that it shares features of epic (and drama, for good measure).[83] To maintain the difference between epic and novel which his 'valorization' of the latter calls for, Bakhtin must insist on a qualitative distinction between the genres.

In the second place, Bakhtin is strategic in not discussing particular examples of epic, for the same reason that he does not discuss examples in his comparisons of poetry with the novel. His concern is with genre; with '"epicness"', not particular epics, and this makes it difficult to argue against his position, if one feels his points are best dealt with at the level of specific counter-examples.[84]

In 'Epic and the Novel', Bakhtin describes epic's three constitutive features. First, its subject is 'a national epic past' (EN 13). This kind of past is 'valorized', taken to be better by definition than the present; epic's relative terms, such as 'beginning', 'earlier', 'ancestor', are not 'merely temporal categories, but *valorized* temporal categories' (15). They appear to be descriptive, but are value judgements, in this realm of '"firsts" and "bests"'. They contrast with comic temporal and spatial categories, which are closer to the era depicted, and take up more varied perspectives on it: 'above, below, in front of, behind [...] past, present, brief (momentary)' (24). Epic time is 'walled off' from anything after it, particularly from the time in which the 'singer and his listeners' are located (16). As Bakhtin revealingly puts it, epic time knows no 'loopholes' through which to glimpse the future, and epic has uttered the final word, in a manner quite different from the novel's allegiance to loopholes, and its inability to produce a final word.

Second, the source of epic is 'national tradition', rather than 'personal experience'. Epic's reliance on an exclusively 'impersonal and sacrosanct tradition' is a formal quality, which has nothing to do with the accuracy of its factual sources, none of which is accessible to the listener in any case.

Third, 'an absolute epic distance separates the epic world from contemporary reality'. The orientation of epic is towards the past, and it works formally by the transfer 'of a represented world into the past' (EN 13). Bakhtin emphasizes that the epic's interest in the past does not just mean that its content is about past events, as the first category pointed out, but that formal elements go to make epic's represented world inaccessible, unquestionable, sanctified. It is in this sense that epic is about the past. This distinguishes it from the novel, which faces towards the future (EN 15), and is based on 'experience, knowledge and practice'.

The difference between the two genres is summed up by Bakhtin's observation that '[p]rophecy is characteristic for the epic, prediction for the novel' (EN 31). The grandiloquent, Biblical associations of prophecy, and the implication that its relation to the future is already set, as prophecies are supposed to come true, is quite different from the more mundane and risky future-orientation of prediction. Bakhtin also discusses the epic's reliance on 'memory' (EN 15), which is distinct from the '"de-heroizing"' personal memory of autobiography and memoir, and novelistic 'memory' which will span only a single life: 'there are no fathers or generations' (EN 24 n. 2) in such treatment of memory.

As we have seen, the content-related element of distance in epic has formal implications. The distance between the present audience and the heroes of epic is such that, in Bakhtin's image, they cannot be seen or touched, experienced or evaluated, but must be accepted with reverence. Thus 'point of view and evaluation are fused with the subject into one inseparable whole' (EN 17). It is impossible to become interested in the plot of epic, Bakhtin argues, in the sense that 'the condition of not knowing' does not apply to the audience of epic (EN 32). Homer's *Iliad*, for instance, is not a mystery story; no one, according to Bakhtin, would ever ask about it, '"How does the war end? Who wins? What will happen to Achilles?".'[85] The whole event is already known to the audience.[86]

The epic feature of 'always knowing' is particularly clear in Milton's epic, *Paradise Lost* (1667), where the story of the poem's plot is the Bible. When reading, for instance, of Satan's approach to Eve in Book 10, there is a spatial clash: the distance of the images, as Bakhtin puts it, means that there should be no suspense here, and no questions of the kind, Will Eve really eat the fruit? What will happen to her next? should arise. However, Satan's characterization introduces the zone of familiar contact into this epic, and with it does come a kind of meta-epic suspense. It is as if the reader sees Satan struggling with the 'adamantine chains' of the precursor text as much as with the chains of now having a hellish nature. The Biblical precursor text acts for Satan like a kind of predestination, meaning he *must* tempt Eve and cause humankind to fall. This seems to be one way out of the radical dichotomy between epic and novel which Bakhtin describes. *Paradise Lost* conforms in many central ways to Bakhtin's discussion of epic, but does not fall into the trap Gogol's *Dead Souls* (1842) landed in, by attempting a novelistic version of Dante's *Divine Comedy*; *Paradise Lost*'s self-consciousness as an epic becomes a novelistic element. During the temptation scene at least, Satan does not act like the epic hero who 'coincides with himself', and there is, momentarily, a gap between his 'authentic essence and its external manifestation' (EN 34). It is as if, like the hero of a novel, Satan's clothes are for a while 'too tight' on him (EN 37), although they become a perfect fit after this episode.[87]

These three features make epic the opposite to the folk

humour, eventually transposed into literary form, which Bakhtin discusses in *Rabelais and His World*. The literature of folk humour is characterized by a contemporaneity which is 'flowing and transitory, "low", present – [a] life without beginning or end' (EN 20). Humour is absent from epic, in which the absolute past, its events and characters, cannot be looked at from any but the determined point of view: 'it is impossible to experience it, analyse it, take it apart, penetrate into its core' (EN 16). Humour, as we have seen, is central to the 'low', serio-comic genres out of which the novel was born, and as a principle it offers an exactly opposite perspective to that of epic:

> Laughter has the remarkable power of making an object come up close, of drawing it into a zone of crude contact where one can finger it familiarly on all sides, turn it upside down, inside out, peer at it from above and below, break open its external shell, look into its centre, doubt it, take it apart, dismember it, lay it bare and expose it, examine it freely and experiment with it. (EN 23)

In the comic genres, temporality and spatiality are altered. Memory and tradition are informal at best, more often than not entirely absent, as '[o]ne ridicules in order to forget'. Distance no longer exists, as 'one can disrespectfully walk around whole objects' and see that object's 'back and rear portion [...] (and also its innards, not normally accessible for viewing)'.

Bakhtin's example of Gogol's *Dead Souls*, which was supposed to be a contemporary epic modelled on Dante's *Divine Comedy*, is an interesting one.[88] Gogol's attempt to combine epic and novelistic genres failed, because the 'distanced images of the epic and images of familiar contact can never meet on the same field of representation', and Gogol 'got muddled somewhere between memory and familiar contact' (EN 28). Instead of a Russian epic, Gogol accidentally wrote a Menippean satire, in which ideas are put to the test in a multi-styled whole, rather than being epically affirmed within a monologic whole. Menippean satire, a genre dear to Bakhtin's heart, is named after the freed slave Menippus, who lived in the third century BCE. Menippus wrote satires of any learned form, and so the term 'Menippean satire' refers to parodies of serious, 'high' kinds of writing, satires which feature exaggeration, mimicry, and mixtures of genre (in Menippus' case, of prose and verse). In the menippea, epic cosmogonies are turned into 'zone[s] of crude contact'; characters move with extreme freedom between the realms of heaven and earth, and encounters between heroes of the absolute past and living contemporaries often occur. In complete opposition to epic, 'this confrontation of times from the point of view of the present is extremely characteristic' (EN 26). In 'From the Prehistory of Novelistic Discourse', Bakhtin cites the figure of a 'comic Odysseus', popular in satyr plays, and Aeschylus' parody of Homer's epic of the Trojan War, 'particularly the episode involving Odysseus' quarrel with Achilles and Diomedes, where a stinking chamber pot is thrown at Odysseus' head' (FPND 54).

Joyce's *Ulysses* (1922) has a framework which could be seen in the same light as Gogol's novel. In the former, the 'confrontation of times' is so near at hand that fusion has occurred between the characters of the absolute epic past and the uncongealed novelistic present. The high myth of Homer's Ulysses is brought down to earth if Leopold Bloom, advertising salesman and consumer of kidneys for breakfast, is seen as the new representative of this classical figure. The same is true of the names of the episodes in Joyce's *Ulysses*; and each mythic figure has an everyday, mock-heroic version, so that Penelope becomes Molly, Cyclops the one-eyed Citizen, and so on. Joyce has made Homer's epic the *Odyssey* more obviously carnivalesque and dialogic, by placing Greek heroes in human form in twentieth-century Dublin and doing away with an omniscient narrator. Joyce is not just satirizing the pretensions of the old style of epic but giving his own characters something of the glamour of the classical heroes. As Anthony Burgess puts this, 'The invocation of the Odyssey may reduce Ulysses to Bloom, but it also exalts Bloom to Ulysses',[89] or even vice versa. Joyce did not suffer from an inability to 'find the proper focus on his binoculars', as Bakhtin says Gogol did, as this is a clear example of the 'novelization' of epic (EN 39).

As with poetry, critics have contested Bakhtin's dismissal of epic, and have reserved the right to use his categories to discuss epic.[90] Bakhtin has an epic view of epic; he sees it as consigned to the distant past, untouchable, the product of an era which did not know novelization. Polyglot Roman texts started the process of epic's disintegration (EN 21–2), and the Renaissance dealt the final blow to epic, as it had a different temporal view: the present 'began to sense itself not only as an incomplete continuation of the past, but as something like a new and heroic beginning' (EN 40). Todorov detects in Bakhtin's lack of specificity on epic (the lack of examples, use of phrases like 'epic time' as a means of tautologously defining epic) a failure to describe a genre at all, as Tihanov does for poetry;

Todorov sees Bakhtin's argument rather as a description of 'categories of discourse in general [...] whose occurrence is not confined to a single historical moment'.[91]

Two case studies

Each of the following two textual examples gains from a dialogically aware analysis, in ways which show its extremely varied potential as a method of critical practice. Helen Zahavi's 1991 novel *Dirty Weekend* benefits from attention to its deployment of socio-ideological languages (DN 272). The dialogic effects in this novel are close to the surface, as its discourse consists of 'tendentious', parodically hybridized languages with a particularly direct address to the reader. The novel's dialogism depends upon gender imbalances, but its self-consciousness makes it equally concerned with linguistic issues. James Kelman's 1994 novel *How Late It Was, How Late* is characterized not by the parodic hybrids of Zahavi's novel but by the double-voiced discourse of reported speech, and represented dialect. These features interact in a way which is greatly clarified by Volosinov's discussion of reported speech in *Marxism and the Philosophy of Language*.[92]

DIALOGISM AND GENDER: POLEMIC IN HELEN ZAHAVI, *DIRTY WEEKEND*

Helen Zahavi's novel *Dirty Weekend* caused a minor furore when it was published, because of its content: it is a version of the rape-revenge narrative, usually more common in films than in novels. Like Ridley Scott's film *Thelma and Louise*, it was both praised for defamiliarizing male violence against women and criticized for appearing simply to reverse the terms of that violence. As Bakhtin says, an exclusive interest in the subject of a novel implies that the novel's discourse is 'an artistically neutral means of communication', and allows the critic to perform 'purely thematic analyses' of the novel instead of stylistic ones (DN 261). On the other hand, Bakhtin also criticizes those whose exclusive interest in stylistics and the utterance's '*neutral signification*' blinds them to its '*actual meaning*'. Clearly the most fruitful way to approach a text, particularly one like *Dirty Weekend* where both style and theme are by turns parodic and defamiliarizing, is to see each element as an inextricable aspect of the other.

In Zahavi's novel, Bella, the central character, decides that the only way to rid herself of a nuisance phone-caller is to kill him; she then acquires a gun, and spends the rest of the weekend in Brighton 'cleaning up', vigilante-style. Bella may seem like an extreme version of the 'testing [...] of the emancipated woman' and her discourse (DN 390); Bakhtin describes the testing of a character's discourse as a fundamental property of the novel and one which 'radically distinguishes it from the epic' (DN 388). What Hirschkop says of Dostoevsky's novels could also be said of Zahavi's: the latter is not only constructed out of an ideological argument but 'argument punctuated with events which test the ideas, by submitting them to a kind of fictional experiment'.[93]

However, once the central role of the novel's style is taken into account, as well as its plot, the issue becomes more complex; a more style-based approach to *Dirty Weekend* confirms Bakhtin's observation that 'the study of verbal art can and must overcome the divorce between an abstract "formal" apprach and an equally abstract "ideological" approach' (DN 259), as '[f]orm and content in discourse are one'. *Dirty Weekend* works as one of the 'externally most marked' examples of dialogic construction which Bakhtin discusses (DN 274); its narration is characterized by irony, satire, linguistic playfulness and a consciousness of its own literariness. All these features can be ascribed to the narrator, who is well aware throughout that she has an unusual story to tell, as the following description of Bella's first killing, of the obscene phone-caller, suggests:

> Timothy's life ended with both a bang and a whimper. With her final blow, she terminated that particular cycle of deprivation forever.
>
> There are certain laws of nature, she reflected, certain iron laws, that you flout at your peril. People in glass houses shouldn't throw stones. Men with thin skulls shouldn't try to involve randomly selected women in their fantasies.[94]

The narratorial voice frequently exhibits these features: first, recognizable quotations from such sources as Shakespeare and the Bible – here, T. S. Eliot – are used in a literalized way (the bang on the head causes Timothy to whimper); second, clichés are also used literally, and given a gender-conscious slant ('People' is transformed into 'men'); third, hybrid construction is prominent, in which the voices of narrator and character coexist within one utterance, as the absence of inverted commas in even Bella's directly reported reflection about the laws of nature suggests. The latter feature is taken to extremes on occasions of particular significance for both character and narrator, for instance when Bella in the gun-shop realizes the gun she is being offered does not shoot bullets:

> 'A hundred and twenty for cash. And I'll pump up the shells for you.'
>> Pump up the shells?
> 'Pump up the *shells*?'[95]

In this case, Bella's disappointment is conveyed by the emergence of direct speech out of hybridity; the direct utterance repeats aloud, with an increased outrage signalled by the italics, the original hybrid perception of the gun's non-deadliness. This feature brings the idea of hybridity so close to the novel's surface that it suggests a closeness or even identity between the narrator, whose voice is so personally polemical an example of *skaz* that she almost attains the status of a subject, and Bella, the character, who is narrated in the third person. As well as representing languages, however, the discourse of this narrator is of course itself represented (DN 336).

The text's self-consciousness arises from features like these: the foregrounding of its own units of composition, such as hybridity and intertextuality, and the intermittent awareness of the character that she is someone within a narrative. This self-consciousness is linked also to the novel's close intertwining of the formal and the ideological: the way in which it is metafictional – that is, conscious of its own status as a fiction – is also a reminder that this kind of narrative is not usually one told about women. Bella does not commit suicide in despair at her victimized state because of the thought 'of having been, and gone, and left no mark. The thought that if she finished it, she would have had no story. The thought that no-one even knew her name'.[96] The ways in which she does 'make a mark', 'have a story' and get her name known are equally by serial killing and by the writing of a book about it. The hyperbolic link between the acts of murder and of writing is recognized by Andrea Dworkin's review of the book – 'Poor Martin Amis, poor D. M. Thomas. The game's over, boys – literary terrorism and the fun on the streets'[97] – and by the arch author's biography, which duplicates the train journey Bella makes at the end of the novel to continue her endeavours: 'Helen Zahavi has recently moved from Brighton to London. *Dirty Weekend* is her first novel.'[98] The 'terrorism' in the novel is as much formal as ideological.

Bakhtin defines the novel as 'a diversity of social speech types (sometimes even diversity of languages) and a diversity of individual voices, artistically organized'. He observes that the novel depends on the 'internal stratification' of its national language, and lists what such a stratification might consist of:

> social dialects, characteristic group behavior, professional jargons, generic languages, languages of generations and age-groups, tendentious languages, languages of the authorities, of various circles and of passing fashions, languages [...] of the hour (each day has its own slogan, its own vocabulary, even its own emphases). (DN 262)

As in the case of the chronotope, gender is conspicuously absent from this list of the social components of language. Zahavi's novel dialogically redresses this balance by enlisting what are usually the epic utterances of reassurance and authority to disquieting and even murderous effect, by making them speak twice. Her recycling of cliché and quotation makes them very stark examples of the utterance as 'a contradiction-ridden, tension-filled unity of two embattled tendencies in the life of language' (DN 272). For instance, the Apollo moon-landing soundbite is made not only to reveal its concealment of women within 'mankind', but to comment upon Bella unprecedentedly daring to leave her house in the middle of the night, in order to kill Timothy: 'One small step for Bella, but a huge leap for womankind'.[99] Again, a standard feature of the novel as described by Bakhtin is brought to the surface in a particularly stark way, in this case the presence of 'pronouncements and maxims' which frequently have 'an ironic or directly parodic character', thus casting a 'a mantle of materiality' over the text as a whole, forcing the reader to suspect the presence of 'parodic stylization' (DN 374). This mantle of materiality is very clear in *Dirty Weekend*, and its parodic stylization scarcely needs to be 'suspected'; but its precise nature is not as easy to discern.

In a reverse movement to the Apollo maxim, the discourse of misogyny in the novel is made to express its own violent origins by being taken literally, and by being repeated out of context without any significant alteration to the discourse itself. As she sallies forth on her streetcleaning mission, Bella's state of mind is described in the following way: 'You know how it is when you need to have a man? When you get the sudden urge to put your arms around a man? When the heat gets too hot, and you're burning for a man?'[100] The words 'have', 'put your arms around' and 'burning for' are all double-voiced here; they remember their origins in the language of misogynist projections but also speak here of the urge to exact bloody (and feminist) revenge. Bakhtin's description of the 'dialogic orientation' of prose, which we have seen before, is especially appropriate to this kind of language-use:

> The living utterance, having taken meaning and shape at a particular historical moment in a socially specific environment, cannot fail to brush up against thousands of living dialogic threads woven by socio-ideological consciousness around the given object of an utterance; it cannot fail to become an active participant in social dialogue. (DN 276)

This is exactly what happens linguistically in *Dirty Weekend*; neutral-seeming 'living utterances' do indeed 'brush up against' the concealed power relations of 'murderers, victims and spectators', into which the clairvoyant Bella visits claims the world is divided.[101] These utterances take their meaning from a rather violent 'brushing' in the novel, just as Bella is forced 'to become an active participant', as Bakhtin puts it, because the luxury of being a bystander is denied her. This bystanding position of non-involvement is reserved for the reader of the text, as is suggested by the constant narratorial address to 'you'. 'You just try making with the dignity when you're being violated', the narrator challengingly observes of Bella's first personal encounter with Timothy, and advises, 'Don't judge her unless you've been there' after the first phone-call,[102] drawing attention to the difference between the victim's and the voyeur's role.

As Bakhtin says, rhetoric, like the satire of *Dirty Weekend*, is blatantly oriented towards 'the listener and his answer', and, as the second-person address shows very clearly in the novel, the relationship with the listener 'enters into the very internal construction of rhetorical discourse'. Bakhtin argues that this kind of 'responsive understanding' is not usually 'compositionally marked' (DN 280), although in this case it has been brought to the text's surface, and that it is an active understanding which 'discourse senses as resistance or support enriching the discourse'. Again, this is literally true in *Dirty Weekend*; the listener implied by the second-person address alternates in both subject position and gender, although the address itself remains the same. In the instance discussed above – 'You know how it is when you need to have a man?' – the identification implied is between women; in other instances, it seems to be between men: 'Do you wonder what she's doing, out alone so late? Do you [...] wonder why she couldn't find anyone to hurriedly take her home, and take her hurriedly when he's got her home?'.[103]

However, it is the foregrounding of the construct of rhetorical discourse itself which is of interest in the text, rather than its specific orientation; Bakhtin contrasts this kind of 'internal dialogism of the word' with that 'determined by an encounter with an alien word', because it is the 'subjective belief system' of the listener which is the site for double-voicedness, not just the object of the discourse.

This kind of dialogism 'bears a more subjective, psychological and (frequently) random character, sometimes crassly accommodating, sometimes provocatively polemical' (DN 282). This is exactly how the narrator of *Dirty Weekend* appears; 'subjective dialogism' is clearly what constitutes this narrator's discourse, and what appear to be her character traits. As Bakhtin says, 'The internal politics of style (how the elements are put together) is determined by its external politics (its relationship to alien discourse)' (DN 284). In a sense, this is the subject of *Dirty Weekend*. It is not only about a woman's murderous relationship to men but also about the relationship of the politics of style to external discourse; the murderous subject simply makes this relationship much more pointed.

The central example of 'socio-ideological consciousness' against which the discourse of *Dirty Weekend* brushes is romantic fiction. This is a tidier, more orthodox way for the sexes to relate than the one Bella chooses, and one more usually found in fiction, as the novel's title (and its packaging: it resembles a holiday romance) suggests. The metaphorical 'dirt' of Bella's seaside weekend is not sexual, but deathly. A dialogic analysis of this satirical joke can reveal the disgust on which the original metaphor is based,[104] and the potential this disgust gives for turning the phrase into a battleground for meaning. In Bella's mouth, the marriage service ('"Speak now, or forever hold your piece"', she says to Timothy during one of his phone-calls) and anxieties about marriageability ('Is he just after her money? Are his intentions therefore honourable?', she wonders of the gun-dealer) are jokingly parodied, and made to refer double-voicedly to the threat of sexual violence, rather than monologically to romantic propriety.[105] As Bakhtin puts it,

> By manipulating the effects of context, it is very easy to emphasize the brute materiality of another's words, and to stimulate dialogic reactions associated with such 'brute materiality'; thus it is, for instance, very easy to make even the most serious utterance comical. (DN 340)

The 'brute materiality' of the phrases Bella and her narrator quote out of context is made very plain by transforming their meanings into brutal ones.

The meanings gathered by words such as 'pay', 'have' and 'give' in the discourse of *Dirty Weekend* similarly become dialogic battlegrounds; these words are already unpleasantly double-voiced in misogynist discourse. Women must 'pay' in kind if they let men 'pay' the bill, or, if they refuse, must 'pay' the penalty. These meanings are implicit in, for example, 'to make them pay is woman's way', as the narrator comments when Bella lets the gun-dealer buy her a drink and looks forward to other ways in which she will make 'them' pay when the deal is done. Equally, if women are not 'giving' enough spontaneously, someone will 'give' it to them forcibly; or they may be too giving, as Bella's red dress suggests ('Any one of us could have taken what you're giving'). Again, the already fraught nature of these terms allows them to speak opposite meanings, while continuing to look like the most crassly sexist utterance. The narrator points out that Norman, Bella's second victim, was not singled out: 'She would have given any one of them all she had to give. But he'd been the one. He'd seen her and he'd wanted her. And he was going to have her.'[106] The knowingly double-voiced ambiguity of the last phrase is enabled by exploiting the potential of hybrid construction, of which Bakhtin says it is an utterance that 'belongs, by its grammatical (syntactic) and compositional markers, to a single speaker, but that actually contains mixed within it two utterances, two speech manners, two styles, two "languages", two semantic and axiological belief systems' (DN 304). Even a single word, as we have seen of 'pay' and 'give', can belong 'simultaneously to two languages, two belief systems that intersect in a hybrid construction'. In the above example, it is not Norman's voice we hear mixed with the narrator's, pronouncing his intention ('going to have her'), but Bella's voice, using words which might indeed have been more suited to him, expressing her own rather different sense of inevitability (Norman will have her wrath wreaked upon him). As Bakhtin puts it, 'The linguistic significance of a given utterance is understood [...] against the background of other concrete utterances on the same theme, a background made up of contradictory opinions, points of view and value judgments' (DN 281).

In *Dirty Weekend* as a whole, this exposure of the 'contradiction-ridden, tension-filled unity of two embattled tendencies' in language works best with the reversed metaphor of romance, and romance becomes a metaphor for this process itself. The 'two embattled tendencies' (DN 272) in this novel are the irresolvable ones of masculinity and femininity. As Bakhtin points out, in all cases social discourse precedes individuals, particularly in the novel, where characters are the means of increasing the number of languages represented, but perhaps particularly in this case: 'Oppositions between individuals are only surface upheavals of the untamed elements in social heteroglossia, surface manifestations of those elements that play on such individual oppositions, make them contradictory' (DN 326). Thus the novelistic hybrid is not just double-voiced and double-accented but also double-languaged, because it contains not just 'two individual consciousnesses, two voices, two accents', but also 'two socio-linguistic consciousnesses, two epochs [...] that come together and consciously fight it out on the territory of the utterance' (DN 360). In *Dirty Weekend* the discourse of romance is frequently enlisted to describe something quite different. Bella's recollection of waking up Timothy in order to bludgeon him is described as the moment when she 'said her goodbyes' to him; realizing Mr Brown has a gun to sell her prompts Bella to tell him, '"We're made for each other"'; and this potential is more materially realized in Bella's encounter with the Geordie serial killer, as she thinks, 'To stab him [...] was to know him'.[107]

The distance between the positions of masculine and feminine in this novel is signalled in Norman's hotel room, when the narrator explains the respective fears men and women entertain of the most 'devastating' thing they can do to each other: 'He fears her ridicule. She fears his rage. She might laugh at him. He might kill her.' The lack of 'balance' in these fears requires Bella, the narrator declares, to put the balance straight, as if she were indeed some dialogic principle required to set free the several voices, or power roles, implicit in both everyday behaviour and in the language which characterizes it. As Bella tells Norman just before she kills him, '"You're unlucky because the rules have changed, and nobody let you know".'[108] She is simply conforming to Bakhtin's observation that recognizing the several-voiced nature of the utterance means there is potential for further reversals and rejoinders:

> Forming itself in an atmosphere of the already spoken, the word is at the same time determined by that which has not yet been said but which is needed and in fact anticipated by the answering word. Such is the situation in any living dialogue. (DN 280)

What Bella has done is unleash a dialogic process, by revealing the concealed voices and implicit power relations in a particular kind of discourse, but of course hers is not the final word either: 'Fewer and fewer neutral, hard elements ("rock bottom truths") remain that are not drawn into dialogue' (DN 300).[109]

The debate over its political morality ignored the fact that *Dirty Weekend* is not a realist text, and it is rather that the intractable and monologic appearance of the discourse of gender relations, and of 'literary terrorism', makes it a particularly interesting case to try and throw into crisis, and into dialogue. Its particular parodic effect is most economically described using dialogic categories. Although Bakhtin is less explicitly interested in the subversive or liberatory effects of dialogic analysis than he is in relation to carnival, this potential is registered in *Dirty Weekend*, as the narrator suggests moments before the death of Timothy: 'She's grinning like the peasant grins, before he forks the landlord'.[110]

DIALOGISM AND REPORTED SPEECH IN JAMES KELMAN, *HOW LATE IT WAS, HOW LATE*

In James Kelman's novel *How Late It Was, How Late*, a dialogic analysis reveals not the parodic impulse of *Dirty Weekend*, but a subtle use of hybrid construction, a use linked to the presence of Glaswegian dialect, which is both represented and representing in the text. This is Kelman's first full-length excursion into 'the consistent use of marked dialect lexis, grammar and phonology (the last through orthography) in the narrative prose as well as the dialogue'.[111] As James Robertson points out in the introduction to a collection of contemporary short stories written in Scots, traces still remain of the eighteenth- and nineteenth-century literary division between a representing language, English, and a represented one, Scots: 'English was for seriousness, for moral and intellectual discourse, high culture, narrative in fiction; Scots was for humour, sentimentality, nostalgia, slavishly Burnsian verse, dialogue in fiction.[112] The decision to reject English forms in favour of Scots ones is political as much as phonetic, Robertson observes, in a Bakhtinian reminder that the reality of linguistics does not have the final word. The novelist Duncan McLean says he chooses not to write phonetically, '"believing that Standard English spelling stands equally for all dialects – I'm not willing to let Standard English become any more firmly associated with a single accent/dialect than it is already"'.[113] This is a similar political point, with a different linguistic result, to Kelman's statement in an interview:

[neither] of them [Graham Greene and Evelyn Waugh] seems to have bothered working out that this 'third party voice' they use to tell their stories is totally biased and elitist, economically secure, eats good food and plenty of it, is upper middle-class paternalist.[114]

In *How Late It Was*, neither Sammy nor the narrator, who sounds so like him that the reader infers he is from the same social background, possesses any of these features. As Robert Crawford puts it in the introduction to his *Identifying Poets: Self and Territory in Twentieth-Century Poetry*, 'if discourse is always a blend of discourses (scientific, demotic, jargons, dialects) – then, like Caribbean or Australian writing, Scottish writing, in which this blending is frequently explicit, becomes typical rather than eccentric'.[115]

Kelman's text is dialogic almost by definition; Sammy Samuels, the central character, goes blind on page 10 of the novel, and is therefore reduced to apprehension through voice alone, in a literalization of Bakhtin's words on Dostoevsky's relation to dialogism: he hears voices everywhere. Sammy is also in some unspecified trouble with the police, and interrogation becomes the site for stylized and forced dialogue and confession, as do Sammy's encounters with medical and social security officials. As he says during one of the police interrogations, 'I just hear voices, yez're coming at me from all directions'. Of course, dialogism arises from the reader's point of view. Sammy may well rely on hearing voices, as he can no longer see, but for the reader spoken utterance is not the point, as the double-voiced effect of what Sammy says and hears would be lost 'if read aloud' (DN 136).[116] As we will see, this text does not, despite, or because of, appearances, aim for a realistic portrayal of spoken dialect.

Because he is blind, Sammy cannot describe the people he encounters bodily, so instead their voices are both rendered and commented upon: 'It was funny how people had their own voices, everybody in the world, everybody who had ever been'. The receptionist at the Medical Centre 'had one of these mental ding dong middle-class accents ye get in Glasgow that go up and down all the time and have these big long sounds'; the doctor's receptionist is similarly identified by a voice which consists solely of class-based accent, and Sammy thinks of her as 'Missis La di da'. Sammy listens to the 'fucking raspberry fucking trifle' voices on the radio, as the television is no longer a means of communication for him; silences or responses become much more charged and important, and he addresses people who are not there.[117]

Sammy's blindness is linked to the narratorial form of the novel; as well as producing Sammy's reliance on the utterance, it produces his reliance on bodily proximity and attempted independence from the gaze of others.[118] Sammy cannot see himself, but can imagine how he must look to the sighted world; this is a particularly clear example of what Bakhtin calls 'transgredience', or 'outsideness.' Discussing the latter in 'Author and Hero', Bakhtin observes that the self will always see more of the other than the latter can of himself, such as 'parts of his body that are inaccessible to his own gaze, [...] the world behind his back' (AH 23). This 'excess of seeing' is literally what almost anyone Sammy meets enjoys, at his expense. The 'outsideness' which characterizes Sammy's representation is most effectively rendered in free indirect discourse, with its substitution of past tenses for present, and third person for first: 'Okay. All these cunts watching him; there he goes, yer blind-as-a-bat Sammy, the bold yin, heading for a piss'.[119] As Sammy imagines being watched, the narrative in the quotation above is clearly divided between narrator and character; at other times, when he is alone, or forgets even to consider whether or not people are looking at him, the narrative becomes more blurred, and character and narrator blend together: 'Ye had to look the part [...] Yer man, he had a reputation; Sammy, he was a style-conscious guy, know what I'm talking about, sweating auld fucking trainers; ye kidding!'[120] At this moment, it is as if Sammy is thinking about himself as someone else would discuss him ('Yer man ... Sammy'), so much so that two voices emerge out of one (is it Sammy or another who calls him(self) 'I'?). This is made possible by the fact that the quotation is, technically speaking, a mixture of free indirect and free direct discourse in a hybrid construction, which allows for the first, second, and third person to appear in one sentence.

Shlomith Rimmon-Kenan defines free indirect discourse as being '[g]rammatically and mimetically intermediate between indirect and direct discourse', the former of which is 'mimetic to some degree' while being mostly concerned with reporting the content of an utterance, the latter a '"quotation" of a monologue or dialogue' creating the 'illusion of "pure" mimesis'. Rimmon-Kenan defines free direct discourse as '[d]irect discourse shorn of its conventional orthographical cues. This is the typical form of first-person interior monologue', well known for instance from James Joyce's *Ulysses*.[121]

It is the mixture of both of these kinds of discourse in a single utterance in *How Late It Was* which produces its particular version of double-voiced discourse. In the extract above about the trainers, the way free indirect discourse works in '[d]eletion of reporting verb + conjunction "that"' is clearly present; 'he was a style-conscious guy' follows this pattern. In direct discourse it would rather have appeared as something like 'Sammy thought, "I'm a style-conscious guy"'; in indirect discourse, it would have been, 'Sammy thought that he was a style-conscious guy', the presence of his own word 'guy' attesting to the fact that indirect discourse is still 'mimetic to some degree'. This is all obvious enough.

However, confusion arises since this indirection is mixed with free direct discourse, that is, 'direct discourse shorn of its conventional orthographic cues': 'know what I'm talking about'. This is a representation of Sammy's own word about himself, his own 'style' in both senses, but its place within the context of the verbal tense-scheme and subject construction of free indirect discourse has the effect of making it seem like the word of another person, perhaps a personalized narrator who shares Sammy's dialect, or the 'guardian angel' he thinks about at one point.[122] Whereas free indirect discourse uses the past tense and the third person, free direct discourse, as we see here, uses the present and the first person. Volosinov discusses cases like this where the 'narrator's speech is just as individualized, colorful, and nonauthoritative as is the speech of the characters' (MPL 121).[123] He places this in his second category of reported speech, the 'pictorial' style, in which mixtures and modifications of methods are common, and which combines an obliteration of the boundaries of reported speech with a high degree of individualization: exactly the case in *How Late It Was*.

As critics have noted,[124] Sammy's inner discourse alternates between a material and precise realism (details of his struggles to walk home and use the lift when he is newly blind; the encounters with officialdom, such as DSS employees and the doctor) and a Beckettian existentialism (he ponders on the hardships of life, the reasons for carrying on, lessons to be learned from prison, and so on). The two merge, of course, becoming together an example of speech which 'loses almost all its referential meaning and becomes decor instead, on a par with clothing, appearance, furnishings, etc.' (MPL 121).

Volosinov quotes an example from Gogol of direct and indirect discourse becoming mixed together, although in this case attributes it to the absence in Russian of those distinctive features of indirect discourse we have been concerned with, the 'special usage of tenses, moods, conjunctions, personal forms'. Volosinov quotes

Osip from *The Inspector General* (1836): 'The innkeeper said *that I* won't give *you* anything to eat until you pay for what you've had'. Volosinov attributes the undeveloped nature of syntactic patterns for reporting speech in Russian to the fact that

> the history of the Russian language knows no Cartesian, rational-
> istic period, during which an objective 'authorial context',
> self-confident in its power of reason, had analyzed and dissected
> the referential structure of the speech to be reported and created
> complex and remarkble devices for the indirect transmission of
> speech. (127)

This is akin to Bakhtin's suggestion that the history of capitalism's rapid introduction into Russia has allowed the flourishing of the carnivalesque. Although the pictorial style of reportage predomi-nates in Russian, according to Volosinov, it is without that sense of 'boundaries forced and resistance overcome' which is exactly how the movement within one sentence from third to first person in Sammy's discourse may strike the reader. As Makiko Minow-Pinkney puts it of Virginia Woolf's similar mixing of the direct and indirect in *Mrs Dalloway*:

> The text presents itself as a homogeneous unity in the conventional
> narrative guise of third-person past tense, but is in fact radically
> heterogeneous. Subjects of sentences are continually shifting [...]
> Whenever we try to pinpoint the locus of the subject, we get lost
> in a discursive mist.[125]

The dialogic interaction of these two modes of speech repre-sentation frequently produces a defamiliarizing and double-voiced effect in Kelman's text. Volosinov points out that the analysis of novelistic reported speech gives the critic insight into the reception of another's utterance into the 'inner-speech consciousness of the recipient' (MPL 117). He goes further, and suggests that the history of speech representation in the novel registers the history of 'socioideological communication' as a whole (MPL 123). Technical analysis of the construction of reported speech in Kelman's novel reveals Sammy's self-address, how he sees himself as he imagines others see him, and how not only the words but the mode of address of others affect his 'inner-speech consciousness': hence the alternation between first, second, and third person, all addressed to and by just one character. The unsettling mixture of person can be explained in narratological terms, but again its *effect* can best be described using Bakhtin's notion of dialogism. As Volosinov puts it in *Marxism and the Philosophy of Language*, 'what is expressed in the forms employed for reporting speech is an active relation of one message to another, and it is expressed, moreover, not on the level of the theme but in the stabilized constructional patterns of the language itself' (116). On the first page of *How Late It Was*, there is a mildly disconcerting shift from second to third person: 'Edging back into awareness, of where ye are: here, slumped in this corner, with these thoughts filling ye. And oh christ his back was sore; stiff, and the head pounding'.[126] Either second or third person narration, used consistently, would present few problems;[127] it is their combination and the dialogue between them that is striking here. The 'constructional' conventions of free indirect discourse allow the use of either 'you' or 'he', but the movement from one to another produces a complex 'thematic' effect: of Sammy's waking up after an alcoholic black-out, his return to his body, his gradual realization of where he is: in a novel, apart from anything else. The imprecation 'oh christ', although it can easily be reconciled here with the past tense of free indirect discourse, actually belongs to the mode of direct discourse, which also features; the imprecation takes place in the present moment, otherwise it would have been rendered in the past tense: 'oh christ, he thought, his back was sore'. The ostensible reason for this shift to the present and to free direct discourse is that it is impossible to convert some kinds of utterance 'mechanically' into reported speech without producing a farcical – 'grammatically correct and stylistically inadmissible' – effect, as Volosinov's example of a fable treated in this way suggests:

> The Ass, bowing his head to the ground, says to the Nightingale *that not bad, that no kidding, it's nice listening to him sing, but that what a shame he doesn't know their Rooster, that he could sharpen up his singing quite a bit, if he'd take some lessons from him.* (MPL 127)[128]

This example, according to Volosinov, is 'bogus and highly objectionable' because it fails to take into account the fact that indirect discourse is concerned with the 'analytic transmission of someone's speech', and that 'the compositional and inflectional peculiarities of interrogative, exclamatory, and imperative sentences are relinquished in indirect discourse'. The mixture of direct with indirect in *How Late It Was*, however, does succeed in retaining Sammy's inflections. It gets around the problem Volosinov notes, that 'the lexical tint of expressions such as "not bad" and "sharpen up" does not fully harmonize with the analytical spirit of indirect discourse' because these expressions 'are too colorful: they not only convey the exact meaning of what was said but they also suggest the manner of speech [...] of the Ass as protagonist' (MPL 129). Colour and manner of speech are indeed preserved in the indirect discourse of Kelman's novel, as the following examples show:

1   Helen had never been to England. Hard to believe somebody that was an adult had never been to England, no even on a visit. But there ye are man that's fucking Helen for ye.[129]

This passage starts out as if it is an omniscient narratorial description of Helen, but the second sentence makes it clear that the past tense of the description – she 'had never been' – is attributable to the tense schemes of indirect discourse, rather than direct narratorial address. In the second sentence, however, the same tense – 'had never been' – has a different function, as part of free direct discourse; it is what Sammy is thinking in the present, a 'direct quotation' of his thought but without orthographical pointers such as quotation marks.

2   He wasnay exactly Dracula's fucking uncle. She maybe fancied him. Who knows.[130]

In this example, the first sentence refutes Volosinov's comment that inflection cannot be preserved in indirect discourse. It is an indirect version of, 'I'm not exactly Dracula's fucking uncle', expressed in the past tense of indirection – 'wasnay' – but keeping the exclamatory tone of present, direct discourse – again, 'wasnay', and 'fucking'. This is an example of how the presence of dialect in this text intersects with its complex layers of reported speech. Both are to do with representing speech, and the 'wasnay' in the first sentence of this extract already disrupts its indirect appearance by remaining colourful and distinctive, rather than analytical. In fact, the word 'wasnay' does not even appear in the direct utterance this is supposedly replacing, as that utterance would be in the present tense and first person, perhaps: 'I'm no exactly Dracula's fucking uncle'. Even the orthodox tense shifts of indirection, when they appear in *How Late It Was*, are coloured by the voice (and, literally, 'accent') of the character.[131]

The use of indirection throughout the novel, rather than first-person narrative, undermines attempts to describe the effect as 'realism'. As Leech and Short point out, 'because the correspondence between graphological and phonological features is far from precise, it cannot be said that a writer has actually represented the speech style of a character. Graphological conventions are exploited impressionistically.[132] Representing accent and dialect is of course a matter of literary convention rather than verisimilitude.[133] This is also true of Sammy's frequent use of expletive, *pace* James Wood.[134] Volosinov's discussion of a passage from Dostoevsky's *A Writer's Diary* (1876) is helpful here (MPL 103–5). In this passage, a group of six artisans have a conversation in Dostoevsky's hearing which consists solely of one unprintable noun, used with varying intonations to convey emotion, expression and reasoning. Volosinov uses the passage to support his theory of '*expressive intonation*', of which he says, 'In living speech, intonation often does have a meaning quite independent of the semantic intonation of speech'. It is certainly true that all of the four thousand or so instances of the word 'fuck' in Kelman's text are expressive only, and, to quote Bakhtin, 'universal and far removed from pornography' (RW 146). The word is not once used literally, and instead becomes an intensifier, meaning 'extremely' or 'very', its obscene sense quite defamiliarized after a few pages. We lose the idea that, as Bakhtin says of Rabelais, it was at first 'hard to weave these coarse [billingsgate] words into the artistic texture of the novel'. The resistance of some critics and readers to this facet of Kelman's novel can be ascribed to Bakhtin's analysis of modern views of abuse and cursing: 'almost nothing has remained of the ambivalent meaning whereby [oaths and other unprintable expressions] would also be revived' from their graveyard depths; 'only the bare cynicism and insult have survived'. Equally, the 'attraction' such language can still exert is due to a 'vague memory of past carnival liberties and carnival truth' which 'still slumbers in these modern forms of abuse' (RW 28). While Bakhtin sees misunderstandings of Rabelais arising out of historical distance, one might say that similar misunderstandings of *How Late It Was* arise out of distances 'of class, education, profession or location'.[135]

Quotation (2) is an extreme version of what Volosinov calls '*texture-analyzing* modification' (MPL 130), which incorporates into indirect discourse expressions typical of the 'subjective and stylistic physiognomy of the message', although usually this takes place on a more submerged level, as Volosinov's own examples from Dostoevsky suggest, and smacks more of 'making strange' and irony at the expense of the character. The absence of irony in the presentation of Sammy's discourse may mean that he is constructed polyphonically, but not dialogically. The low level of narratorial intervention, and the precedence of character over narrator, suggests polyphony, but not the presence of two voices equal enough for dialogic interaction. However, the presence of 'texture-analyzing modification' is again why two voices seem to emerge from a single one. The easiest explanation for the odd 'wasnay' is that the narrator speaks in the same way as Sammy – like Ally, the narrator is his 'rep', someone with a similar history (Ally too has 'supped the porridge') and background. The following is perhaps the clearest example in the text of an apparent separation of not just two voices but two different *subjects*, character and narrator, from one voice: 'He got to sleep eventually so that was fine, though how long he was out for I don't know'.[136] However, even this narrator-like utterance could be ascribed to the free indirect discourse of a character. It is retrospective, reported when Sammy has woken up (he evaluates the experience: 'so that was fine'), and the obtrusive 'I don't know' is his own utterance, again reported in free direct discourse. In this view, 'I don't know' appears in the present and the first person because it is a cliché, like 'know what I'm talking about' above. It is not a comment by the narrator on his shaky omniscience (an utterance nearer to the zone of 'referent-analyzing modification', as Volosinov would say), as it may sound, but a texture-aware representation of an exclamation. 'I don't know' would make no sense if it were transposed into the other persons and tenses of indirection, as 'that was fine' seems to be. This is an example of the 'puzzle' Volosinov mentions in relation to certain kinds of reported speech, in which the reader must guess who is speaking: 'from the standpoint of abstract grammar, it is the author who speaks; from the standpoint of the actual sense of the whole context, it is a character who speaks' (MPL 144). Where Volosinov says 'author', we would substitute 'narrator'; and the example from *How Late It Was* is even more ambiguous than this description suggests, as from the standpoint of sense, as we have seen, 'I don't know' could indeed be the utterance of either narrator or character.

The question remains, why is this obtrusive effect, moving so abruptly between persons within one subjectivity, sought? One answer is that it defamiliarizes the processes of reported speech, and continues the 'subversive' pattern of showing the narrator to be from the same social realm as the character.[137] Their technical indistinguishability is one way of showing their social and, more importantly, their dialectal indistinguishability.[138] Volosinov sees the process moving from narrator to character – 'authorial [*sic*] intonations freely stream into the reported speech' (MPL 146). Cairns Craig puts it the other way round of Kelman's texts: the 'linguistic equality between speech and narration [...] allows the narrator to adopt the speech idiom of his characters';[139] however, in this case, it is impossible to tell whose intonation is streaming into whose.

A second answer to the same question – why is this obtrusive effect, moving abruptly between persons within one subjectivity, sought? – might be that it undermines the apparently neutral judgements of linguistics on the use of dialect by a central character and/or narrator. Leech and Short claim that it has a 'distancing and stigmatizing effect' in a novel to use 'non-standard forms of language, including deviant spellings', and the 'very fact of using such forms implies that the character deviates from the norm of the author's own standard language'.[140] Quite apart from the fact that this is not true of Kelman, who shares at least an accent with his character (he 'was born in Glasgow and will probably die there', according to the blurb for *Some Recent Attacks: Essays Cultural and Political*[141]), this rather tendentious 'linguistic' analysis moves into the territory of author biography. A more Bakhtinian point would be that the *effect* of movement between persons may be created by having the narrator and character speak in different dialects, particularly if the former's language is more 'standard' than the latter. Confusion arises in Kelman's novel because narrator and character sound so alike, *and* so non-standardly, that they may be one entity. Indeed, *How Late It Was* is a rare example of a novel in which some characters speak more 'standardly' than the narrator, as the case of doctor and receptionist show.

Leech and Short go on to argue that '"dialect suppression"' is common in nineteenth-century novels where the main character speaks in standard English despite his or her origins; this is true of George Eliot's Adam Bede and Hardy's Tess.[142] They suggest that a 'linguistic' reason for this is just as compelling as ascribing it to 'Victorian delicacy or snobbery', which is 'that non-standard language often implies remoteness from the author's own language, and hence from the central standards of judgement in a novel'.[143] Bakhtin's and Volosinov's metalinguistics allow the reader to avoid such approaches as these in relation to *How Late It Was*.

Volosinov observes that the materiality of language, which precedes 'inner personality', 'determines differentiation in a society, its sociopolitical order; it organizes society hierarchically and deploys persons interacting within it' (MPL 153). Kelman uses a particular combination of ways of reporting speech and defamiliarizes their properties through the device of shared dialect and social status, offering a threat to the order and hierarchy of the society represented in his novel, because 'the vicissitudes of utterance and speaking personality in language reflect the social vicissitudes of verbal interaction, of verbal-ideological communication, in their most vital tendencies' (MPL 157). The representation of Sammy almost amounts to a case of 'acting out' a character, discussed by Volosinov as a rare and extreme case of the quasi-direct.

Volosinov concludes *Marxism and the Philosophy of Language* with a chapter on what he calls 'quasi-direct discourse', that is, free indirect discourse,[144] which he describes as the most 'double-faced' (MPL 144) and 'dialogized' of forms of reporting speech. As we have seen, *How Late It Was* represents a mixture of free direct and free indirect discourse, and in this way it conforms to some extent to Volosinov's description of the quasi-direct, which 'derives its tone and word order from direct discourse and its verbal tenses and persons from indirect discourse' (MPL 142). According to Volosinov, the development of indirect discourse in European languages is part of a more general process of reliance on 'opinion' rather than direct truth, and interest in an utterance's construction rather than its content, a de-essentializing trend which appears also in novels such as Kelman's. The signifier has taken precedence over the signified, at the expense of 'the word with its theme intact, the word permeated with confident and categorical social value judgment, the word that really means and takes responsibility for what it says' (MPL 159).[145] As Renfrew says, the distinction between English and Scots is only one of a range of possible dialectal interactions,[146] but it serves in the case of *How Late It Was* to throw into relief the ideologically charged nature of novelistic processes like the reporting of speech. Kelman, in interview, says that he is not aiming to do away with the narrator as such, 'just the standard third party one, the one that most people don't think of as a "voice" at all – except maybe the voice of God – and they take for granted that it is unbiased and objective. But it's no such thing.'[147] Craig discusses Kelman's 'very specific means of overcoming the distinction between English (as the medium of narration) and Scots (as the medium of dialogue)',[148] and it seems most helpful to see *How Late It Was* in this light: as a kind of test case for upsetting the usual hierarchy of narrator and character, using dialect to highlight this process of upsetting. However, describing it like this makes clear that the process may have more relevance to polyphony than to dialogism.

It has been argued that Kelman's novel is not dialogic for two reasons: first, standard English, the implied dialogic adversary, is hardly represented at all, and the novel is 'characterized by the antithesis of diversity of speech'. Indeed, Renfrew argues, 'Sammy's (authoritarian, oppressive) tormentors speak the same language as he does'. The dialogic interaction is implied rather than seen.[149] One kind of monologue has simply been replaced by another. Second, there is little chance of the development in *How Late It Was* of 'an arena in which *two* intonations, *two* points of view, *two* speech acts converge and clash' (MPL 135), when character and narrator are so closely, so polyphonically, identified. No one is ironic at Sammy's expense: he is politically correct in his internal and external utterances on the subjects of women, gay men, and racial difference. The 'acting out' of reported speech mentioned above is a problem here; without the usual 'embracing context' of narratorial utterance, the text may begin to resemble a play (MPL 157). However, the use of dialect by both narrator and character makes the hybrid constructions so marked that the impression gained by the reader is, again, most similar to that of the slipping subject in Modernist fiction by Woolf or Mansfield. This markedness of hybrid constructions suggests that *How Late It Was* is dialogic, even if its particular, dialectal form of dialogism does not include other unevenly structured differences, such as gender.

Notes

1 It can also mean 'double-wordedness'; see Michael Holquist's discussion of the Russian word '*slovo*', 'Glossary', DN 427.
2 Ken Hirschkop, 'Introduction', Hirschkop and David Shepherd, in eds, *Bakhtin and Cultural Theory*, Manchester University Press, Manchester 1989, p. 6; and the same author's 'Bakhtin, Discourse and Democracy', *New Left Review* 160, November/December 1986: dialogism 'is both an essential feature of all discourse and a specific oppositional practice within in it', p. 103. In Bakhtin's terms, the novel's 'lack of success in subversion is inexplicable', *ibid.*, p. 106, because Bakhtin omits a satisfactory discussion of 'the institutional forms which bring [the novel] into being'.
3 Hirschkop goes on to discuss the ambiguity's genesis, 'Introduction', pp. 9, 20.
4 *Ibid.*, pp. 11, 16.
5 Julia Kristeva, 'Word, Dialogue, and Novel', *Desire in Language: A Semiotic Approach to Literature and Art*, Basil Blackwell, Oxford 1980, pp. 68, 70.
6 *Ibid.*, p. 66.
7 Carol Adlam, 'In the Name of Bakhtin: Russian and Anglo-American Readings of the Literary Writings 1990-1996', in A. Renfrew and Graham Roberts, eds, *Exploiting Bakhtin*, Strathclyde Modern Language Studies, new series, 2, 1997, p. 88.
8 *Guardian*, Saturday 10 August 1996. (In Irvine Welsh's 'A Smart Cunt', the

protagonist's father says of junkies on his housing estate, '"Well, we will fight them on the beaches, as they say"', at which his son thinks, 'The pompous auld fuck' (*The Acid House*, Jonathan Cape, London 1994, pp. 189–90).)

9 Anthony Wall and Clive Thomson say that context 'is an intrinsically chronotopic notion [which] necessarily implies both space and time', 'Cleaning Up Bakhtin's Carnival Act', *Diacritics* 23 (2), summer 1993, pp. 47–70, p. 59.

10 Tzvetan Todorov, *Mikhail Bakhtin: The Dialogical Principle*, University of Minnesota Press, Minneapolis, Minnesota 1984, p. 10.

11 Raymond Williams's *Keywords*, for instance, helps trace some of these trails of changing meaning for certain words with an especially significant literary involvement, like 'country', 'racial', 'ideology'. All kinds of multiple voices intersect in these words, in 'an elastic environment of other alien words about the same object, the same theme' (DN 276). Utterances structure themselves in anticipation of a response, particularly in the mouths of characters in literary texts, but also in the case of any of the multiple languages of heteroglossia.

12 Malcolm Lowry, *Under the Volcano*, Picador, London 1990, p. 324.

13 Chris Ackerley and Lawrence J. Clipper, *A Companion to 'Under the Volcano'*, University of British Columbia Press, Vancouver 1984, p. 404.

14 Holquist, 'Glossary', DN 426.

15 See FTC 255, *pace* Hirschkop, 'Introduction', p. 30.

16 Ice-T discussed his beliefs in 'The Questionnaire'; in the Travel Section, facts about New York weekends were treated in a question-and-answer format (*Guardian* Weekend Supplement, 15 June 1996).

17 Joseph Hochstein, 'An Afternoon in Tel Aviv', *Harper's*, July 1996, pp. 15–17.

18 Kristeva, 'Word, Dialogue, and Novel', p. 81. Ken Hirschkop points out the radical difference between the 'folky stylization of recent journalism' and Bakhtin's philosophical project of 'depicting the human being at a moment of crisis, as open-ended, etc.'. This is quite right, but I think the Pass Note format of modern, 'degraded' dialogism is none the less revealing.

19 See also PSG 69.

20 This is also a fruitful way to approach the 'Ithaca' episode in Joyce's *Ulysses*, when Stephen Dedalus and Leopold Bloom are in Bloom's kitchen late at night, particularly the part which is structured as a dialogue between two unnamed parties, and which has foxed critics trying to describe what is going in conventional narratological terms. See Bernard Benstock, *Narrative Con/Texts in 'Ulysses'*, University of Illinois Press, Urbana Chicago, Illinois 1991, pp. 92–105.

21 Jenefer Shute, *Life-size*, Secker and Warburg 1992, p. 113.

22 See 'The Problem of Speech Genres', 95; addressivity is defined as 'the quality of turning to someone', without which the utterance cannot exist, p. 99.

23 Hirschkop, 'Bakhtin, Discourse and Democracy', p. 103.

24 See Bakhin's discussion of speaker and listener in 'The Problem of Speech

Genres', pp. 67 ff.

25 Kristeva, 'Word, Dialogue, and Novel', p. 66.

26 Terry Eagleton, *Walter Benjamin, or Towards a Revolutionary Criticism*, New Left Books, London 1981, p. 149; interestingly his reference credits Volosinov.

27 The heading is from PDP 40.

28 See Allon White, 'Bakhtin, Sociolinguistics, Deconstruction', in *Carnival, Hysteria and Writing: Collected Essays and an Autobiography*, Oxford University Press, Oxford 1994, p. 130, on the problem with Saussure.

29 Elsewhere 'homophony' is used as the opposite of polyphony, PDP 220.

30 These categories are discussed in more detail by Bakhtin in 'Discourse in the Novel', pp. 312–24; the speaking subect, pp. 332–55. The difficulties of the dialogic critic are compounded by having to detect tiny shifts of 'canonization' and 're-accentuation', pp. 417–22.

31 Lowry, *Under the Volcano*, pp. 4, 15.

32 *Ibid.*, p. 35; Ackerley and Clipper, *A Companion*, pp. 3, 9.

33 Lowry, *Under the Volcano*, pp. 28, 357.

34 *Ibid.*, p. 56.

35 See Ackerley and Clipper's discussion of the *abarrotes*-owner's lewdness: the Spanish for eggs, *huevos*, also means 'testicles', so the 'ruffianly male laughter hence implies that those in the shop think the Consul is trying to buy virility, to cope with "the beautiful *layee*". In fact, he is probably having a hair-of-the dog prairie oyster or a similar egg-based drink to steady himself' (*A Companion*, p. 91). They go on to discuss exactly why the Consul mentions Tortu (or rather Tartu, in Estonia), *ibid.*

36 White, 'Bakhtin', p. 152.

37 Bakhtin writes that in parody, 'two languages are crossed with each other, as well as two styles, two linguistic points of view, and in the final analysis two speaking subjects', PND 76. Within stylization, even if the first voice is in agreement with the second voice, two voices will sound out, because, according to Gary Saul Morson and Caryl Emerson, this is what the first voice aims for (*Mikhail Bakhtin: The Creation of a Prosaics*, Stanford University Press, Stanford, California 1990, p. 151); see also Todorov, *Mikhail Bakhtin*, pp. 71–3.

38 See Lynne Pearce, *Reading Dialogics*, Edward Arnold 1994, p. 51; David Lodge, *After Bakhtin*, Routledge, London 1990, p. 59.

39 Helen Zahavi, *Dirty Weekend*, Flamingo, London 1991, p. 15. (Thanks to John Slaytor, Millie Slaytor and Pip Vice for providing the atmosphere in which I wrote this section.)

40 *Social Text* (spring/summer 1996); and A. Sokal, 'A Physicist Experiments with Cultural Studies', *Lingua Franca*, May/June 1996, p. 63; and letter from *Social Text* editor Andrew Ross in *The Nation*, 8 July 1996. I am grateful to Catherine Ciepiela for drawing the Sokal saga to my attention; and Paul Tyrer for pointing out the gleeful reception of Sokal's parody by, for instance, shock jock Rush Limbaugh, who sees it as a move against those who make claims such as that Cleopatra was black.

41 Leo Rosten, *The Joys of Yiddish*, W. H. Allen, London 1970, p. xxv. Rosten comments on the difficulty of writing rather than reciting such

jokes, which depend on intonation for their double-voiced effect; Wall and Thomson note the lack of attention paid to writing in Bakhtin's work, which would help approach the issue of his use of the 'voice' metaphor, and 'allow for a fuller understanding of how everyday language is supposed to enter the novel' ('Cleaning Up Bakhtin's Carnival Act', p. 59).

42 Bill Ashcroft, Gareth Griffiths and Helen Tiffin, eds, *The Post-Colonial Studies Reader*, Routledge, London 1995, p. 10.

43 Quoted from Homi Bhabha, in Benita Parry, 'Problems in Current Theories of Colonial Discourse', in Ashcroft *et al.*, *Post-Colonial Studies Reader*, p. 42.

44 Mae Gwendolyn Henderson (in Henry Louis Gates, Jr, ed., *Reading Black, Reading Feminist*, Meridian Books, New York 1990, pp. 116–44), discusses a 'dialogic of difference': 'What distinguishes black women's writing, then, is the privileging [...] of "the other in ourselves"', and dialogic interaction between this other's various voices (p. 119); see also Peter Hitchcock's *Dialogics of the Oppressed*, University of Minnesota Press, Minneapolis 1993. Gates, in his *Figures in Black: Words, Signs, and the 'Racial' Self* (Oxford University Press, New York and London 1987) uses Bakhtinian double-voiced discourse in conjunction with the practice of 'signifying', 'the black rhetorical strategy' (p. 48), 'the trope of revision, of repetition and difference' (p. xxxi).

45 Hirschkop, 'Introduction', pp. 24–6.

46 Eva Hoffman, *Lost in Translation: Life in a New Language*, Minerva, London 1991, p. 106.

47 *Ibid.*, p. 108.

48 Kim Newman says the following in a review of a remake of Clouzot's 1955 *Les Diaboliques*, a film 'that has coined clichés: whenever a wealthy character married to a poor one complains of a weak heart, it's a sure tip-off that they are about to fall victim to an "it's-all-a-plot" plot' (*Diabolique*, *Sight and Sound*, September 1996, p. 39). On Ford and the 'it's all a plot' theme, see Roger Poole, 'The Real Plot Line of Ford Madox Ford's *The Good Soldier*: An Essay in Applied Deconstruction', *Textual Practice* 4, 1990 (I am grateful to Tim Armstrong for this reference).

49 Henry James, *What Maisie Knew*, Penguin, Harmondsworth 1966 [1897], p. 78.

50 *The Notebooks of Henry James*, eds F. O. Matthiessen and K. B. Murdock, Oxford University Press, Oxford 1963, p. 238.

51 Henry James, 'Preface to "What Maisie Knew"' *The Art of the Novel*, Charles Scribner's Sons, New York 1934, pp. 140–58, p. 145.

52 Bakhtin adds, 'or, finally, the direct style of the author himself involves a deliberate (polemical) failure to understand the habitual way of conceiving the world (this happens, for example, in Tolstoy)'.

53 Lowry, *Under the Volcano*, p. 203; Jonathan Arac calls this simply 'fun', 'The Form of Carnival in *Under the Volcano*', *PMLA* 92, 1977, p. 483.

54 Bakhtin discusses this further DN 406–14, and in 'The *Bildungsroman*', SG. See also Ed Cohen's discussion of the trial of Oscar Wilde in Bakhtinian terms: 'the narratives of Wilde's legal proceeding can be suitated within a historical pattern of interpretation that privileged the trial as a site for the

production of meaning' (*Talk on the Wilde Side*, Routledge, London 1993, p. 129).

55 White, 'Bakhtin', p. 140.

56 *Ibid.*, p. 141.

57 Donald Wesling, 'Mikhail Bakhtin and the Social Poetics of Dialect', *Papers in Language and Literature* 29 (3), 1993, pp. 303–22, p. 303.

58 Lowry, *Under the Volcano*, p. 223.

59 *Ibid.*, p. 224.

60 Kristeva, 'Word, Dialogue, and Novel', p. 67.

61 Hirschkop, 'Is Dialogism for Real?', *Social Text* 30, 1987, p. 106; he also claims that for Bakhtin 'an ethical plea for the recognition of the social nature of our existence finds its expression in a theory of language' (p. 103).

62 *Ibid.*, p. 105.

63 *Ibid.*, pp. 107, 109, 111, 108, 111 respectively.

64 *Ibid.*, p. 112.

65 The heading is from DN 284; among critics who have discussed this issue, David Lodge distinguishes between poetry and verse, claiming that Bakhtin nowhere states that the latter is necessarily monologic' (*After Bakhtin*, p. 96), which is, as we will see, not the case, though Lodge is right that Bakhtin does frequently use Pushkin's poem *Eugene Onegin* as an example. Bakhtin discusses his own use of *Onegin* at PND 43 ff., especially 47, and as Todorov points out, Bakhtin treats Pushkin's text as novelistic, not poetic (*Mikhail Bakhtin*, p. 64). Other critics on this subject include Donald Wesling, who has categorized current Bakhtinian work on poetics in his paper '"The Buds of Future Form and Content": Mikhail Bakhtin on Poetry and Poetics', on the 'double-voiced lyric' of Marina Tsvetaeva, delivered at the Seventh International Biennial Bakhtin conference, Moscow, June 1995, into 'Utterance Study' (Robert Crawford, Don Bialostosky's work on Wordsworth), 'Intonation Study', and 'History and Society: Poetics of Discourse in Politics' (Roland Barthes, Yurii Streidter, Graham Pechey, Dana Polan); see also Karen Simroth James, '*On veult responce avoir*: Pernett du Guillet's Dialogic Poetics', in Karen Hohne and Helen Wussow, eds, *A Dialogue of Voices: Feminist Literary Theory and Bakhtin*, University of Minnesota Press, Minneapolis, Minnesota 1994, pp. 171–98; Tatiana Bubnova, 'In Defence of Authoritarianism, or Poetry as an Ethical Act', paper given at Moscow, June 1995, again on Eliot, p. 99; the debate on Robert Burns and heteroglossia (David Morris, 'Burns and Heteroglossia', *The Eighteenth Century: Theory and Interpretation* 28 (1), 1987, pp. 3–27, and Carol McGuirk 'Burns, Bakhtin, and the Opposition of Poetic and Novelistic Discourse: A Response to David Morris', *The Eighteenth Century: Theory and Interpretation* 32 (1), 1991, pp. 58–71).

66 Robert Crawford, *Identifying Poets: Self and Territory in Twentieth-Century Poetry*, Edinburgh University Press, Edinburgh 1994, p. 7; Crawford mentions two poets whose practice has been influenced by Bakhtin: American 'Language' poet Michael Palmer and British Ian Gregson (p. 10).

67 Wesling, 'Mikhail Bakhtin and the Social Poetics of Dialect', pp. 316, 320.

68 Torodov, *Mikhail Bakhtin*, p. 65.

69 Anne Sexton, *No Evil Star: Selected Essays, Interviews, and Prose*, ed. Steven E. Colburn, University of Michigan Press, Ann Arbor, Michigan 1985, p. 136.

70 Sexton uses the same term, 'mask', in an interview, *No Evil Star*, p. 137, and so does her biographer Diane Middlebrook, *Anne Sexton: A Biography*, Virago, London 1992, p. 114.

71 Todorov, *Mikhail Bakhtin*, p. 64; of course counter-examples at once spring to mind, again despite Bakhtin's caveat: Philip Larkin's 'they fuck you up, your Mum and Dad', in 'This Be the Verse' (see Neil Roberts's forthcoming *Narrative and Voice in Post-War Poetry*, Longman, Harlow 1998, on the mixture of registers in Larkin's poetry).

72 Galin Tihanov, 'Bakhtin, Lukács and German Romanticism: The Case of Epic and Irony', in C. Adlam, R. Falconer, V. Maklin and A. Renfrew, eds, *Face to Face: Bakhtin in Russia and the West*, Sheffield Academic Press, Sheffield 1997.

73 Morson and Emerson, *Mikhail Bakhtin*, p. 319.

74 Gary Saul Morson and Caryl Emerson, eds, *Rethinking Bakhtin: Extensions and Challenges*, Northwestern University Press, Evanston, Illinois 1989, p. 6, in a discussion of TPA before it was translated. Nor is he 'hostile' to drama, as his discussions of Shakespeare suggest: e.g. RQ 4–5.

75 McGuirk, 'Burns, Bakhtin, and the Opposition of Poetic and Novelistic Discourse', p. 67.

76 Morson and Emerson, *Mikhail Bakhtin*, p. 322.

77 Wesling, 'Mikhail Bakhtin and the Social Poetics of Dialect', p. 309.

78 Gary Saul Morson, in 'Who Speaks for Bakhtin?', points out that while 'mock-epic is quite a different thing from epic, the history of the novel includes parodies of the novel [... which] are for Bakhtin the quintessence [...] of "novelness"' (in Morson, ed., *Bakhtin: Essays and Dialogues on His Work*, University of Chicago Press, Chicago 1986, p. 13).

79 Morson and Emerson, *Mikhail Bakhtin*, p. 323; see Paul de Man, 'Dialogue and Dialogism', in Morson and Emerson, eds, *Rethinking Bakhtin*, and Mathew Roberts, 'Poetics Hermeneutics Dialogics: Bakhtin and Paul de Man', *ibid.*

80 Hirschkop, 'Bakhtin, Discourse and Democracy', p. 108.

81 Morson and Emerson, *Mikhail Bakhtin*, p. 419; and see Rachel Falconer, 'Bakhtin and the Epic Chronotope', in Adlam *et al.*, eds, *Face to Face*, p. 255; FTC 85.

82 Falconer, 'Bakhtin and the Epic Chronotope', p. 255 ff; cf. FTC 155, 241.

83 Todorov, *Mikhail Bakhtin*, p. 90; see also Tihanov, who points out that the source for Bakhtin's 'high evaluation' of the novel is Friedrich Schlegel and German Romanticism in general, which valued both novel and epic equally highly ('Bakhtin, Lukács and German Romanticism', 11 ms).

84 Morson and Emerson, *Mikhail Bakhtin*, p. 421; Falconer, 'Bakhtin and the Epic Chronotope', p. 257, cites particular epics in refutation of Bakhtin, although she also argues in general for the 'polychronicity' of epic, pp. 6–7.

85 A contemporary twist to this syndrome, in which 'not knowing' is not what provides the text with narrative impetus, is the case of 'epic' block-

buster films, such as the Arnold Schwarzenegger vehicle *Eraser*. Film reviewer Jonathan Romney argues that in this film we are 'asked to take an interest in events that have no consequences, as if nothing that happened could possibly matter in the long run [...] As Steven Spielberg recently put it, "we've moved from the 'What if?' cinema of the 1970s and 1980s to a 'What the heck?' cinema", in which anything might as well happen, simply because the technology is available' (*Guardian*, Friday 30 August 1996). This 'What the heck?' film-narrative is a 'debased' contemporary counterpart to the reverential lack of interest in plot development in epic which Bakhtin discusses.

86 Yet the *Iliad* can be seen as a '"subversive epic"', according to Joan Malory Webber, quoted in Falconer, 'Bakhtin and the Epic Chronontope', p. 261, in which '"only unremitting destruction, and dissension"' are made clear.

87 Falconer (*ibid.*) says that Bakhtin's argument that the absence of loopholes in epic deprivileges the reader is 'a fascinating point with regard to *Paradise Lost* since the subject of Milton's epic is precisely how people lose their capacity for free choice, and not only in Arcadia, but here and now'; 'Looking back, *Paradise Lost* also offers its reader the possibility for a radical freedom of choice that history once offered, and if re-visited, might offer again. This is, very precisely, a loop-holing of time', pp. 266, 269. The same 'loopholing' may be perceived in other texts which return to the past, and give a forward glance to a future which looks undetermined from this vantage point. An example is Steven Spielberg's film *Schindler's List* (1993), in which such loopholing takes the form of disrupted linear time, movements between past and present, and a return to a time before knowledge of gas-chambers was commonplace. (I am grateful to John Watkins for planting the idea of Satan bound by the Bible in my mind.)

88 Other texts which take Dante as a model and intertext include two Holocaust works: Primo Levi's *If This is a Man* (1959), and Louis Begley's *Wartime Lies* (1991).

89 Anthony Burgess, 'Introduction', James Joyce, *Ulysses*, Minerva, London 1992, p. xii.

90 Neil Roberts argues in 'Epic and Novel in George Eliot' (in Adlam *et al.*, *Face to Face*) that the struggle between novel and epic is part of the plot of *Middlemarch*, as 'generic conflict' extends itself to the characters, particularly Dorothea; in *Daniel Deronda*, in a reverse movement, the novelistic is subdued by the epic.

91 Todorov, *Mikhail Bakhtin*, pp. 88, 90–1.

92 See Gary Saul Morson and Caryl Emerson, *Mikhail Bakhtin: The Creation of a Prosaics*, Stanford University Press, Stanford, California 1990, on the Russian for these terms, pp. 160, 163, 167.

93 Ken Hirschkop, 'Introduction', in Hirschkop and David Shepherd, eds, *Bakhtin and Cultural Theory*, Manchester University Press, Manchester 1989, p. 27.

94 Helen Zahavi, *Dirty Weekend*, Flamingo, London 1992, p. 60.

95 *Ibid.*, p. 74.

96 *Ibid.*, p. 2.

97 Andrea Dworkin's review is quoted on the back cover of *Dirty Weekend*.

98 Zahavi, *Dirty Weekend*, p. i; Irvine Welsh's *Trainspotting* (1993) similarly ends with the central character, Mark Renton, fleeing to Amsterdam, the city in which Welsh wrote the novel.

99 Zahavi, *Dirty Weekend*, p. 49.

100 *Ibid.*, p. 92.

101 *Ibid.*, p. 39.

102 *Ibid.*, pp. 17, 11.

103 *Ibid.*, pp. 92, 130.

104 See the discussion of sexualized dirt in Peter Stallybrass and Allon White, *The Politics and Poetics of Transgression*, Methuen, London 1987.

105 Zahavi, *Dirty Weekend*, pp. 47, 77.

106 *Ibid.*, pp. 114, 83, 101, 98.

107 *Ibid.*, pp. 65, 80, 183.

108 *Ibid.*, pp. 108, 114.

109 The symmetry between Bella and the Geordie serial killer at the end may seem too close for comfort.

110 Zahavi, *Dirty Weekend*, p. 56.

111 Liam Rodger, 'Tense, Aspect and *The Busconductor Hines* – the Literary Function of Non-Standard Language in the Fiction of James Kelman', Edinburgh Working Papers on Applied Linguistics, 3, 1992; Rodger, who wrote this article before *How Late It Was* was published, says 'Novel-length texts of this type are rare', p. 117. (I am grateful to University of Sheffield Information Studies MA students Hazel Lee, Helen Maskell, and Ruth Soper, who located this and other articles for me.)

112 James Robertson, 'Introduction', in Robertson, ed., *A Tongue in Yer Heid*, B&W Publishing, Edinburgh 1994, p. x.

113 Quoted *ibid.*, p. xii.

114 Quoted in Rodger, 'Tense, Aspect and *The Busconductor Hines*', p. 118.

115 Crawford, *Identifying Poets*, p. 7; see Bakhtin on Walter Scott, B 53; and Norman Blake, *Non-standard Language in English Literature*, André Deutsch, London 1981, p. 11, says non-standard language may act as a sign of past-ness.

116 James Kelman, *How Late It Was, How Late*, Minerva, London 1995, pp. 163, 136. See also Renfrew's discussion of attempts to reproduce 'authentically' spoken utterance in written form as the ultimate referential illusion ('Them and Us? Representation of Speech in Contemporary Scottish Fiction', in Renfrew, Alastair, and Graham Roberts, eds, *Exploiting Bakhtin*, Strathclyde Modern Language Studies, new series, 2, 1997, p. 16).

117 *Ibid.*, pp. 207, 123, 212, 113.

118 *Ibid.*, pp. 116, 127; according to Alastair Renfrew, Sammy's blindness is also linked to the concentration on inner speech, which is the way to merge the character's and the 'authorial [*sic*] voice' ('Them and Us?', ms 4).

119 Kelman, *How Late It Was*, p. 284. Bakhtin's discussion of 'outsideness' acknowledges its metafictional potential, as well as its philosophical and ethical importance; the subject 'authors' the object through his (*sic*) gaze. We will see how this works in Chapter 4 in the section on Jenefer Shute's novel *Life-size*, where, as in the present case, such authoring is symbolically

represented in the text: in Shute's case by an anorexic woman, in Kelman's by a blind man. See AH, 27, 50–1.

120 Kelman, *How Late It Was*, p. 76.

121 Shlomith Rimmon-Kenan, *Narrative Fiction: Contemporary Poetics*, Methuen, London 1983, pp. 109–10.

122 Kelman, *How Late It Was*, p. 260; Leech and Short just say it is 'imaginary speech' (Geoffrey Leech and Michael Short, *Style in Fiction*, Longman, London 1982, p. 171), in an instance of linguistics' failure to get to grips with subtle shifts within utterances.

123 However, Volosinov still takes the author's role for granted.

124 James Wood, 'In Defence of Kelman', *Guardian*, 2 October 1994, p. 9.

125 Makiko Minow-Pinkney, *Virginia Woolf and the Problem of the Subject*, Harvester, Brighton 1987, pp. 56, 58.

126 Kelman, *How Late It Was*, p. 1.

127 Novels written in the second person include Jay McInerney's *Bright Lights, Bright City* (1984), and Ron Butlin's *The Sound of My Voice* (1991) (see 'Notes and Queries', *Guardian*, 6 December 1995 for a fuller discussion).

128 Volosinov reproduces grammarian A. M. Peskovkij's italics.

129 Kelman, *How Late It Was*, p. 254.

130 *Ibid.*, p. 287.

131 Volosinov discusses linguistician Tobler's observations on the origin of quasi-direct discourse: 'A speaker, relating past events, cites another person's utterance in an autonomous form just as it sounded in the past. In the process, the speaker changes the present tense of the original utterance to the imperfect in order to show the utterance is contemporaneous with the past event being related. He then make some additional changes (persons of the verbs and pronouns) so that the utterance not be mistaken for the relator's own' (MPL 142). Volosinov argues that Tobler mistakes an '*entirely new*' form of reporting speech for a mixture of two old ones here (143).

132 Leech and Short, *Style in Fiction*, p. 132; see also pp. 167–73.

133 See also Blake, *Non-standard Language*, p. 17.

134 Wood, 'In Defence of Kelman': 'reading [*How*] *Late It Was, How Late* is like being grabbed by an elaborately angry Glaswegian man. Kelman's authenticity seems to me to be intense', although he does recognize its 'stylized' qualities as well.

135 Robertson, 'Introduction', p. ix.

136 Kelman, *How Late It Was*, p. 333. I am grateful to Stephen Owen for his observation that Ally, the rep, is a candidate for narrator.

137 Cairns Craig, 'Resisting Arrest: James Kelman', in Gavin Wallace and Randall Stevenson, eds, *The Scottish Novel since the Seventies*, Edinburgh University Press, Edinburgh 1993, p. 103.

138 Blake, *Non-standard Language*, pp. 12, 20. He does not include dialect in his study because, in works where dialect is omnipresent, it is not 'non-standard', a term he uses as contrast between forms of language, p. 12.

139 Craig, 'Resisting Arrest', p. 103.

140 Leech and Short, *Style in Fiction*, p. 170; cf. Blake, *Non-standard Language*, p. 15, who uses the phrase 'deviant pronunciation'.

141 James Kelman, *Some Recent Attacks: Essays Cultural and Political*, AK Press, Stirling 1992.

142 Robertson points out that 'English as spoken by the upper classes of England is so far from being "standard" these days that increasingly it is – and should be – seen as just one of the many forms of English', 'Introduction', p. x.

143 Leech and Short, *Style in Fiction*, p. 170.

144 Volosinov uses French (MPL 144) and German terms (147).

145 Tihanov argues illuminatingly that Bakhtin endorses, while Volosinov regrets, such irony, 'Bakhtin, Lukács and German Romanticism'.

146 This is *pace* Crawford, who says of the fact that his book concentrates on male poets, 'I suggest [...] that the prime identifying gestures of female poets, especially as the century ends, may relate to gender rather than to territory', as if gender were only a quality of writing by women (*Identifying Poets*, p. 14). Dorothy McMillan, in an article on Scottish fiction, draws attention to the fact that 'gender' is not simply a synonym for 'femininity': 'All the versions of Scottishness I have discussed so far are by men; they are also clearly gendered versions' ('Constructed out of Bewilderment: Stories of Scotland', in Ian A. Bell, ed., *Peripheral Visions: Images of Nationhood in Contemporary British Fiction*, University of Wales Press, Cardiff 1995, p. 93).

147 Quoted in Rodger, 'Tense, Aspect and *The Busconductor Hines*', p. 118.

148 Craig, 'Resisting Arrest', p. 103.

149 Alastair Renfrew, 'Them and Us?', p. 24; Robertson, 'Introduction', p. xv.

3

Polyphony: voices with equal rights

Introduction

Although polyphony has often been taken to be synoymous with either dialogism or heteroglossia,[1] it refers precisely to the construction of the voices of characters and narrator in the novel, as its etymology – the Greek for 'many voices' – suggests. As Roger Fowler points out, the term's 'simple' (PDP 22) musical metaphor 'refers to the co-presence of independent but interconnected voices'.[2] Bakhtin argues that characters and narrators are known by their voices, rather than by any other features, within a text, and it is the way in which these voices are arranged that determines whether or not a work is polyphonic. Bakhtin takes the novels of Dostoevsky as his central example of the polyphonic text, as he argues that here character and narrator exist on the same plane, the latter does not take precedence over the former but has equal right to speak. The polyphonic novel is a democratic one, in which equality of utterance is central.

Polyphony is dialogic in form, and the dialogic nature of Dostoevsky's work is in part due to its presence (PDP 18), but it is not reducible to dialogism. Polyphony refers to the autonomy of the characters' voices. The voices which make up the polyphonic novel are dialogic: they interact dialogically, and the language of which they are composed is dialogic. Not only did Dostoevsky hear conflicting voices everywhere, which he transposed into the novel, but the voices he heard were dialogic, internally riven into conflicting opinions (PDP 90): the 'polyphonic novel is dialogic through and through [...] dialogue penetrates within, into every word of the novel, making it double-voiced, into every gesture, every mimic movement on the hero's face, making it convulsive and anguished' (PDP 40). The dialogic content of the voices which are constructed polyphonically is made clear in Bakhtin's discussion of Raskolnikov's dialogized interior monologue from *Crime and Punishment*:

'all the words in it are double-voiced, and in each of them a conflict of voices takes place' (PDP 74). At the same time, '[t]he author retains for himself no essential "surplus" of meaning and enters on an equal footing with Raskolnikov into the great dialogue of the novel as a whole'. In the polyphonic novel, the constituent voices are dialogic ones. Without polyphony, dialogism is impossible, because, as in the 'monologic' writings of Tolstoy, according to Bakhtin, only *one cognitive subject is present*, everything else being 'merely *objects* of its cognition'. In the Dostoevskian polyphonic novel, by contrast, Bakhtin says that the author (or, rather, narrator) acts as a 'participant in the dialogue without retaining for himself the final word' (PDP 72).

Equally, polyphony is a way of realizing heteroglossia in the novel, without being identical to heteroglossia. 'Polyphony' means 'multi-voicedness', while 'heteroglossia' means 'multi-languagedness', and this apparently small difference in meaning is very significant. Polyphony refers to the arrangement of heteroglot variety into an aesthetic pattern. One of the principal ways of ensuring the presence of the different voices of heteroglossia in the novel is the creation of fictional characters. These characters may contribute in a number of ways to the heteroglot whole of the novel, both by using a particular kind of language and by having a particular viewpoint on the world around them. Characters may use a distinctive dialect, jargon, or personal idiosyncrasy of utterance, as most of Dickens's characters do, adding to the variety of styles which make up the novel's style as a whole.

In *Little Dorrit* (1857), for instance, the chapter 'Fellow Travellers', half-way through the book, at first allows the characters to speak without naming them for fifteen pages: they are heard and not seen in a very obvious way. However, so sharply differentiated have their voices been until this point that the reader has no trouble in recognizing who each one is, even though they are eventually named, without the help of the narrator, when the 'insinuating traveller' reads their names in the hotel's visitors' book. Pam Morris describes this Dickensian process:

> Each character's sharply particularized 'voice' or 'discourse' articulates a recognizable social viewpoint – of class, or profession, or religion and so on. Orchestrated together, these voices offer us a verbal image of the contentious social dialogue taking place in mid-Victorian England.[3]

This variety is a contribution to novelistic heteroglossia, which is the *raison d'être* of having such constructions as characters in the novel. The way in which characters are represented, their relation to the narrator, the autonomy which their voices and viewpoints have within the text, determines whether or not their construction is truly polyphonic.

The polyphonic character

In a polyphonic novel, characters are represented not as objects, who are manipulated and commented upon by an omniscient narrator, but as subjects, on an equal footing with the narrator (their voices are constructed in exactly the same way as this figure's voice), whose own word about themselves and each other is all that we know about them. Bakhtin sees proof of this fact in the response of critics to Dostoevsky's characters: so autonomous do the voices of Raskolnikov, Myshkin and Ivan Karamazov sound that they are responded to as if they were authors in their own right:

> In the consciousness of the critics, the direct and fully weighted signifying power of the characters' word destroys the monologic word of the novel and calls forth an unmediated response – as if the character were not an object of authorial discourse, but rather a fully valid, autonomous carrier of his own individual word. (PDP 5)

Polyphony, in this case, thus creates the conditions for dialogism: so independent do these characters' voices seem, that readers feel it appropriate to enter directly into debate with them.

Other examples of this process spring readily to mind: feeling that, for instance, Leopold Bloom in *Ulysses* seems like a 'real person' is testimony to the same effect of dialogized polyphony. It means that his voice is constructed polyphonically, he seems capable of offering his own replies, that he speaks as a subject and not as an object who is manipulated and commented upon. Bakhtin describes the Dostoevskian character in terms which could equally be used of Bloom: 'he is perceived as the author of a fully weighted ideological conception of his own, and not as the object of Dostoevsky's finalizing artistic vision' (PDP 5). Polyphony, or the 'freedom' of the character's voice from the narrator's, is a central question in any study of character construction, a version of which is implicit in D. H. Lawrence's insistence that one must trust the tale, not the teller; John Bayley's that some novelists respect their characters' privacy more than others; and in Wayne Booth's relief that 'impartiality' of authors towards characters is impossible: 'Is

Ulysses fair to the bourgeois Irish characters that throng about Bloom and Stephen and Molly? We can thank our stars that it is not.'[4] Booth seems to suggest that some characters can be more polyphonic than others.

However, even if there is such a thing as a novelist's respect for her or his characters, it is only further testimony to the author's complete control over the text and its occupants, which he or she may choose whether or not to express artistically. As Bakhtin puts it,

> It might seem that the independence of a character contradicts the fact that he exists, entirely and solely, as an aspect of a work of art, and consequently is wholly created from beginning to end by the author. In fact there is no such contradiction. The characters' freedom we speak of here exists within the limits of the artistic design, and in that sense is just as much a created thing as is the unfreedom of the objectivized hero. (PDP 64)

The formal choice to represent character in a certain way itself pushes the author in a particular direction; he or she may create, but not invent, as '[h]aving set a specific task for himself, the creator must subordinate himself to this order'. In his discussion of carnival laughter, Bakhtin sees no conflict between the concept of polyphony and ascribing ultimate power to the author, who may even use that power for unauthorizing, dialogic purposes: 'the author causes [the heroes' world-views] all to collide in the "great dialogue" of the novel, leaves that dialogue open and puts no finalizing period at the end' (PDP 165). The character's discourse is indeed created by the author, but 'created in such a way that it can develop to the full its inner logic and independence as *someone else's discourse*, the word of the *character himself*' (PDP 65). This effect is reached by formal means.[5]

The irony of this is clearly that the freer such a character appears, the more it is likely to be testimony to a definite 'artistic vision' on the part of the author, even if that vision is open-ended rather than finalizing. It is interesting that it is almost as if a particularly strict pattern of textual construction results in what seems like freedom; as we will see in the case of the Consul in Malcolm Lowry's *Under the Volcano*, traits of construction which appear as character traits, as if these traits were not evidence of fictionality but of subjectivity, work especially effectively to create this illusion of the character having an autonomous word, and to call forth a reader's 'unmediated response'. Like the Underground Man, the

Consul's 'real-life characterological definition [...] and the artistic dominant of his image are fused into one' (PDP 51).

The character in the polyphonic novel is allowed to speak for him- or herself, without the intrusion of overbearing narratorial comment. The corollary of this is that, instead of taking for granted the narrator's explanatory word about heroes, the reader has to rely on the word of the characters about themselves. The hero *is* a 'particular point of view on the world and on oneself'; fixed images of the hero and his/her world from the outside are not what appear in the polyphonic novel, which concentrates instead on 'how the world appears' to the hero, and 'how the hero appears to himself' (PDP 47). Although 'we do not see him, we hear him' (PDP 53), a triangulated picture of the character may be built up by the reader, from the words of other characters, as well as obliquely from the character's own words; but no external picture will be provided, in the manner of, for instance, George Eliot. In *The Mill on the Floss* (1860), to summarize rather crudely, the central character Maggie Tulliver grows up from an awkward tomboy into a beautiful young woman. Both stages are described in a mixture of monologism and polyphony, as the following two extracts suggest. First, we meet Maggie as a child:

> Maggie, as she threw off her bonnet, painfully confirmed her mother's accusation: Mrs Tulliver, desiring her daughter to have a curled crop, 'like other folks's children', had cut it too short in front to be pushed behind the ears; and as it was usually straight an hour after it had been taken out of paper, Maggie was incessantly tossing her head to keep the dark heavy locks out of her gleaming black eyes – an action which gave her very much the air of a small Shetland pony.

Although 'painfully confirmed' is a phrase with a glance at Mrs Tulliver's words, which are also quoted verbatim, and held at a slight distance, to signal their ungrammatical nature ('"like other folks's children"'), the rest of the description of Maggie is just that: a report by the narrator. Even here the narrator seems to try, monologically, to convey the attractiveness of the young girl ('dark heavy locks', 'gleaming black eyes'), of which her father has already been, in more polyphonic fashion, the advocate: '"Pooh, nonsense!" said Mr Tulliver, "she's as straight a black-eyed wench as anyone need wish to see"'.[6] When Maggie has fulfilled this potential, and emerged as a handsome young woman, this is again conveyed by a combination of the narrator's monologic utterance, and by the more polyphonic means of other characters' words. The narrator speaks of Maggie's 'dark eyes' and 'fine throat'; and in the scene where Maggie meets Stephen Guest, fiancé of her cousin Lucy, who is 'pretty, but not to a maddening extent', her attractiveness is conveyed for the most part unpolyphonically:

> For one instant Stephen could not conceal his astonishment at the sight of this tall dark-eyed nymph with her jet-black coronet of hair; the next, Maggie felt herself, for the first time in her life, receiving the tribute of a very deep blush and a very deep bow from a person towards whom she herself was conscious of timidity. This new experience was very agreeable to her – so agreeable, that it almost effaced her previous emotion about Philip. There was a new brightness in her eyes, and a very becoming flush on her cheek, as she seated herself.[7]

It is true that at least some of this description of Maggie is subjective, and not the omniscient word of a narrator; it is through Stephen's eyes that we see her as a 'nymph' wearing a 'coronet', although whether these particular words are likely to be his own is rather more doubtful. However, we are told about Maggie's own response to this attention, and how she herself looks, in no uncertain terms: she now has 'a very becoming flush on her cheek', which prompts the narrator to speak over Maggie's head, using a vocative phrase often on its lips: 'Poor Maggie! She was so unused to society that she could take nothing as a matter of course ...'[8] This is perhaps the grown-up equivalent of the narrator's earlier observation about the Shetland pony, which suggests a condescending fondness not really in keeping with polyphonic objectivity.

By contrast, we find out about the appearance of Yvonne in *Under the Volcano* in a different way, which suggests that it is not her appearance which is important, but, first, the texture of the language itself, and, second, the consciousness of the characters involved.[9] There are all kinds of lines of interference involved in any 'description', or, more accurately, the reader's awareness of the physical appearance of any of the characters, as it often only conveyed as the way one character imagines how the other sees them, or as they may be seen by others. The Consul's first sight of Yvonne in the novel is narrated from her point of view: 'Then he looked up abruptly and saw her [...] standing there as she knew he must see her, half jaunty, a little diffident' (51).[10] From Hugh's point of view,

> Yvonne stood below smiling up at him, hands in the pockets of her

slacks, feet wide apart like a boy. Her breasts stood up under her blouse embroidered with birds and flowers and pyramids she had probably bought or brought for Geoff's benefit, and once more Hugh felt the pain in his heart and looked away.[11]

The presence of polyphony here offers a kind of structural jealousy: rather than a fixed portrait of Yvonne, we get instead Hugh's perception of Yvonne appealing to Geoffrey, as Geoffrey thinks in turn: 'She was no longer his: someone had doubtless approved her smart slate-blue travelling suit: it had not been he'.[12] Again, we learn what Yvonne is wearing, but only with a view to establishing what this means to someone else.

The following development from a draft version of *Under the Volcano* shows the transfer of external narration, to the polyphonic construction of pure self-consciousness. In the draft, Yvonne is the Consul's daughter, not his wife, and speaks up with rather soap-operatic directness in the scene where she comes upon her father in a cantina early in the morning, the early version of the scene quoted above: '"Oh, for the love of Pete … Cockeyed, in your dress clothes, at seven o'clock in the morning, howling about a corpse —"'[13] The wifely Yvonne, however, in the same scene but this time from the published version, is rendered polyphonically: 'Geoffrey, she went on, wondering if she seemed pathetic sitting there, all her carefully thought-out speeches, her plans and tact so obviously vanishing in the gloom, or merely repellent – she felt slightly repellent – because she wouldn't have a drink'.[14] Instead of a presentation of daughter-Yvonne's impatience, which is followed by tears and more exhortation, we hear wife-Yvonne's unuttered self-consciousness. This is consonant with the considerable reduction in direct utterance in the published version of the novel; instead of the long speeches and addresses of the draft, the characters in *Under the Volcano* indulge in only 'minimalist and bizarre' utterance, the majority of the text's images of language consisting of free indirect discourse[15] and silent utterance.

In the Consul's chapter, Yvonne herself tries for a direct response: '"How do I look?" She seemed to have said'; the Consul is not sure whether or not he actually answers her, but recalls her record of the words of others about her: 'she had been at fifteen, she'd told him […] a girl of whom people said, "She is not pretty but she is going to be beautiful"'.[16] Finally, Yvonne herself recalls a magazine interview from her Hollywood days, in which the presence of stylized language coexists with the repetition of certain themes;[17] as a subsidiary effect, the word of the interviewer about her physical appearance is also heard:

> *I found her the other day at her beach home, a honey-tanned Venus just emerging from the surf. As we talked she gazed out over the water with her slumbrous dark eyes and the Pacific breezes played with her thick dark hair ... the torso's still terrific, and the energy is still absolutely unparalleled!*[18]

We are far removed here from any direct assertion of Yvonne's appearance on the part of the narrator, even though thematically Yvonne is treated like an object: she is 'the torso'. When the narrator does this, as in the case of Maggie in *The Mill on the Floss*, whose subjective experience and objective appearance were both available for monologic comment, the effect is quite different.

Even in his earliest works, such as *The Double* (1846), Bakhtin's arch-exemplar Dostoevsky depicts 'not the "poor government clerk" but the *self-consciousness* of the poor clerk' (PDP 48), who is for instance seen looking into the mirror.[19] How the character appears to her- or himself is all that is shown, as Bakhtin describes in a central paragraph:

> All the stable and objective qualities of a hero – his social position, the degree to which he is sociologically or characterologically typical, his habitus, his spiritual profile and even his very physical appearance – that is, everything that usually serves an author in creating a fixed and stable image of the hero, 'who he is', becomes in Dostoevsky the object of the hero's own introspection, the subject of his self-consciousness; and the subject of the author's visualization and representation turns out to be in fact a function of this self-consciousness. (PDP 48)

This description gives a very clear way of seeing polyphony in action. It is not so much that real 'freedom' has been granted to the character in the polyphonic novel, but rather that the way s/he is represented always follows a certain form. Instead of expending energy on a narrator and an authoritative voice, the polyphonic novelist expends it on representing the self-consciousness of the characters. As Bakhtin emphasizes, this is a formal and aesthetic choice, which may have radical origins in a struggle against a '*reifying devaluation*' of the person (PDP 62), but otherwise is still the result of artistic activity on the part of the author. 'The issue here is not an absence of, but a *radical change in, the author's position*' (PDP 67).

One might ask why, for instance, Lowry went to such lengths

to represent the Consul without breaking the consistency of the characters' own viewpoints; it was presumably less because he imagined he was really respecting the rights of the characters, or even 'loving' them and their autonomy, but because of his own interest in the conflicting voices of the day, in the ludic possibilities of language when left to its own devices, and because of the increased pathos of a person's death if not externally narrated. As Bakhtin argues, this kind of polyphonic construction replaces the official, omniscient narrator with a different effect: '[n]ot only the reality of the hero himself, but even the external world and the everyday life surrounding him are drawn into the process of self-awareness, are transferred from the author's to the hero's field of vision' (PDP 49). Any information we gain is *from* the character, not *about* him or her; and, as the only way this can easily be managed is to have the characters tell about themselves and each other, the effect may be, for instance, one of great self-preoccupation, as is the case with the Underground Man, and with the Consul in *Under the Volcano*. Stephen Spender speaks of the latter's 'desperate isolation of consciousness' and 'failure to love',[20] both of which are rendered in the novel by means of a self-sufficient and self-defining voice. The isolation of the alcoholic becomes rather like a figure for polyphony; such a character is of necessity solipsistic, sees things others do not see (an old woman in a bar, for instance), will not tell the truth, is not sure when s/he has spoken aloud or silently thought: all are character traits of (a textual portrait of) an alcoholic, and also of a polyphonically constructed character. This is true of many features of the Consul's 'personality', including his habit of identification with other people or even objects (such as the tomb-like toilet: '"It is what I deserve ... It is what I am", thought the Consul').[21] The Consul hears voices all around him – 'Why am I here, says the silence, what have I done, echoes the emptiness, why have I ruined myself in this wilful manner, chuckles the money in the till, why have I been brought so low, wheedles the thoroughfare, to which the only answer was – The square gave him no answer'[22] - both because he is drunkenly hearing voices from all around and because he is in a polyphonic novel.

GENDER AND THE POLYPHONIC CHARACTER

Being an alcoholic character is an ideal accounting device for all of the novelistic features Bakhtin discusses: for polyphony, if the alcoholic's aural hallucinations seem independent and real; for dialogism, as the voices interact, either by actually taking issue with each other or simply through the 'friction' of coexistence; and for heteroglossia, owing to the variety of voices which assail such a character, who cannot sort out those which are worth listening to from those which are not – from the items on a mistranslated menu and advertising slogans to quotations from Dante and the Bible.

An intriguing problem which arises here is the possibility of a novel having as a character an entity without self-consciousness; can such a being be represented polyphonically? Of the tree in Tolstoy's story 'Three Deaths', Bakhtin notes that it is 'by its very nature incapable of understanding the wisdom and beauty of its death – the author does that for it' (PDP 70). Efforts have been made, however, to represent the consciousness of a variety of beings, for instance by James Joyce of the infant Stephen Dedalus's consciousness in *A Portrait of the Artist as a Young Man* (1915), by William Golding of Neanderthals in *The Inheritors* (1955), by Anna Sewell of a horse.

An example of the transfer from the author to the character's field of vision is the matching up of a certain inability to interpret on the part of the character with a similar blankness on the part of the narrator in particular novels: Margaret Atwood's *The Edible Woman* (1969) and Sylvia Plath's *The Bell Jar* (1963) both feature first-personal (intermittently, in the case of the former), female characters. Bakhtin says that the device of a first-person narrator is not in itself enough to ensure polyphony in its elimination of authorial discourse, but in both these texts a character trait does also become a narratorial trait. The central character in each – Marian in *The Edible Woman*, Esther in *The Bell Jar* – is at a particular turning point in her life, the former about to get married, the latter about to go to university. Each reacts strongly to her predicament, but in a way which is left opaque to the reader, a narratorial refusal to explain which represents a lack of vocabulary for rendering certain kinds of experience. Betty Friedan describes this in *The Feminine Mystique*, published in 1963, the year Plath's novel was published, and six years before Atwood's, in a chapter entitled 'The Problem with No Name':

> The problem lay buried, unspoken, for many years in the minds of American women. Each suburban housewife struggled with it alone. As she made the beds, shopped for groceries, matched slip-cover material, ate peanut butter sandwiches with her children, chauffeured Cub Scouts and Brownies, lay beside her husband at night, she was afraid to ask even of herself the silent question: 'Is this all?'[23]

Esther, like the Consul, as we will see, acts in a way she cannot understand and does not interpret, and reports her own behaviour with bemusement. During the summer, Esther feels suicidal but spends a day at the beach with friends:

> We browned hot dogs on the public grills on the beach, and by watching Jody and Mark and Cal very carefully I managed to cook my hotdog just the right amount of time and didn't burn it or drop it into the fire, the way I was afraid of doing. Then, when nobody was looking, I buried it in the sand.[24]

As with her other rebellions, Esther here conforms in scrupulous detail and is outwardly successful: she wins prizes and awards, and then at the last minute does something inexplicable and self-destructive, like throwing all her expensive new clothes off the roof of her New York hotel at the end of her editorial job at *Ladies Day*. The technical disorientation that results from a striking absence of explanation for this kind of behaviour acts as a figure for Esther's disruptive and contradictory existence. She cannot admit her real thoughts to herself, her urge both to rebel and conform as a woman.[25] In this first-person narrative, the technical reasons for not providing explanations for apparently aberrant behaviour are the same as the psychological ones.

In *The Edible Woman*, the division between femininity as Marian experiences it, and femininity as a construct or representation which she finds herself fitting into, is more explicit, although it is again expressed both psychologically and technically by Marian's inability to account, even to herself, for why she starts doing things like sliding under beds and running away from parties. This kind of behaviour follows the development of a clear split within Marian, and the conventions of portraying character are exploited to emphasize this. After Peter proposes to her, an alien persona takes Marian over and speaks through her; he asks when they should get married, and instead of her usual facetious evasion, 'instead I heard a soft flannelly voice I barely recognized, saying, "I'd rather have you decide that. I'd rather leave the big decisions up to you".'[26]

This internal split results, infamously, in Marian presenting Peter with a cake shaped like a female body. The process of making the cake is not made clear to the reader until it is brought out of the oven; this is a polyphonic absence of external comment, and at the same time a demonstration that Marian herself does not know exactly what she is doing or why. As further confirmation of her divided self, the chapter is narrated in the third person: 'Marian had a swift vision of her own monumental silliness, of how infantile and undignified she would seem in the eyes of any rational observer',[27] the narrator comments as she brings the cake out to Peter, but not in the manner of an omniscient, authoritative narrator, as all we learn here is about Marian's self-consciousness, not about the 'truth' of her motives and actions.

This particular version of polyphonic construction unites the features Bakhtin sees in Dostoevsky: social upheaval, in this case the brink of first-wave feminism in both texts, and the McCarthy-era electrocution of the Rosenbergs in *The Bell Jar*, is represented by heroines who do not coincide with themselves (PDP 59), whose self-consciousness rather than outer form is shown, and about whose appearance, world, and actions no finalizing narratorial pronouncement is made.

The polyphonic narrator

In *Problems of Dostoevsky's Poetics*, Bakhtin describes the polyphonic novel in varying ways, emphasizing slightly different aspects of it each time he mentions it. It consists of a '*plurality of independent and unmerged voices and consciousnesses* [...] a *plurality of consciousnesses, with equal rights and each with its own world*' (PDP 6); like each of Dostoevsky's novels, the polyphonic is one which 'is *multi-accented* and contradictory in its values' (PDP 15); '[n]ot a single element of the work is structured from the point of view of a nonparticipating "third person"', and it unites a 'plurality of equally authoritative ideological positions and an extreme heterogeneity of material' (PDP 18); it 'affirms the independence, internal freedom, unfinalizability, and indeterminacy of the hero [who] is not "he" and not "I" but a fully valid "thou"': that is, '*someone actually present*', another 'autonomous "I"' who can hear and answer the author (PDP 63). A possible image for Dostoevskian polyphony would be a church, Bakhtin suggests, 'a communion of unmerged souls, where sinners and righteous men come together' (PDP 26).

Bakhtin emphasizes that polyphony is a formal property of the text, and that asserting the freedom of characters as part of the novel's content is not enough to make it polyphonic: 'As the ethico-religious postulate of an author or as an important theme in a work, the affirmation of someone else's consciousness does not in itself create a new form or a new type of novelistic construction' (10). Polyphony is a practical, formal matter: 'The uniqueness of Dostoevsky [...] lies in the fact that that he was able, in an objective and artistic way, to visualize and portray personality as another, as someone else's personality, without making it lyrical or merging it with his own voice' (PDP 12). It is not just the high value placed on personality which distinguishes Dostoevsky from other, monologic writers, but the 'artistic image' of it in his work. The aesthetic and ideological dimensions of the novel are indistinguishable, as Bakhtin implies: 'Dostoevsky, like Goethe's Prometheus, creates not voiceless slaves (as does Zeus), but free people, capable of standing alongside their creator, capable of not agreeing with him and even of rebelling against him' (PDP 6). As we will see in relation to the chronotope, the accusation of even textual slavery is a serious one for Bakhtin. By contrast, he ascribes the polyphony of Dostoevsky's works to the author's conception of the world as 'personalized': he 'perceives and represents every thought as the position of a personality' (PDP 9), a subject with equal rights and not an object or slave.

Polyphony helps to generate the distinctive chronotope of Dostoevsky's novels. The first level of chronotopic construction, in which the effects of public events make themselves felt, represents the 'epoch itself [...] the multi-leveledness of [Dostoevsky's] own time' (PDP 27), with its pre-revolutionary, post-emancipation ethos; the second, more local level of the text itself enables Dostoevsky to show these contradictions 'as forces coexisting simultaneously'. There is thus a chronotopic and polyphonic impetus for the array of different voices in Dostoevsky's texts, and a dramatization of issues in space rather than time, especially internal debates. A character may be made to 'converse with his own double, with the devil, with his alter ego, with his own caricature' (PDP 28). An image for this extensive representation of events might be the newspaper, rather than the church; a newspaper is 'a living reflection of the contradictions of contemporary society in the cross-section of a single day, where the most diverse and contradictory material is laid out' (PDP 30). The representation of a newspaper is a common device for just such a multiplication of voices in a text, 'extensively', and for their enforced interaction and relativization. The voices in a newspaper are already both polyphonic and dialogic: they are autonomous, unorchestrated utterances in which extremely heterogenous material rubs shoulders, ranging from world news to cartoons, *faits divers* to advertisements. In *Under the Volcano*, drunken misreadings and incorrect renderings of English multiply even further both polyphonic and dialogic aspects of the English page of the Mexican *El*

Universal which the Consul reads while his half-brother Hugh gives him a shave:

> 'Kink unhappy in exile.' I don't believe it myself. 'Town counts dog's noses'. I don't believe that either, do you Hugh? [...]
>   'Or a Cadillac for 500 pesos. Original price 200 ... And what would this mean, do you suppose? "And a white horse also." Apply at box seven ... Strange ... Anti-alcoholic fish. Don't like the sound of that. But here's something for you. "A centricle apartment suitable for love nest.' Or alternately, a serious, *discrete* –"
>   '–ha–'
>   '"apartment" ...'[28]

The newspaper's voices address the Consul directly and demand a response, offering not just the (personal) news of the day before – his suspicions about Hugh's relations with his wife – but a prediction of the future – the horse which will loom so large in the rest of the day's events appears here, in one of its incarnations even accompanied by a Cadillac.[29] There is further word-play here – the Consul and the reader enjoy the misspelling of 'discreet', while Hugh, not seeing the spelling, scoffs at the idea of discretion. Later on, when the Consul is drunker, newspaper headlines offer an even more direct commentary on his fate, and the fate of the world embroiled in the Spanish Civil War, a directness signalled by the seamless passage, free of quotation marks, between the words and the Consul's response:

> A boy dashed up to them selling papers. Sangriento Combate en Mora de Ebro. Los Aviones de los Rebeldes Bombardean Barcelona. Es inevitable la muerte del Papa. The Consul started; this time, an instant, he had thought the headlines referred to himself. But of course it was only the poor Pope whose death was inevitable. As if everyone else's death were not inevitable too![30]

Polyphony therefore has temporal implications as well as spatial ones. Bakhtin argues that in Dostoevsky's novels 'the author's discourse about a character is organized as discourse about *someone actually present*, someone who hears him (the author) and is *capable of answering him*' (PDP 63). The double meaning of 'present' suggests this: 'author', or narrator, and hero exist in the same time-frame, as well as the same location.

The evocation of slavery may be one of the analogies of which Bakhtin says that they are only partly metaphor, as is also the case in his invocation of Einsteinian relativity in 'Forms of Time and

Chronotope in the Novel'. Bakhtin mentions Dostoevsky's political investment in the compositional forms he chooses, and the dangers of isolationist thinking, exemplified by the Underground Man's spiralling, spiteful utterances (PDP 287). On the part of the author her/himself, paradoxically, the only way in which an individual will expresses itself is through the urge to lose itself among others: 'the artistic will of polyphony is a will to combine many wills, a will to the event'.[31] One of the reasons why it is very unlikely that there could be 'a confident and calmly meditative consciousness' mono-logically narrating in Dostoevsky's works is due, Bakhtin argues, to their roots in the recent history of Russia, 'where capitalism set in almost catastrophically, and where it came upon an untouched multitude of diverse worlds and social groups which had not been weakened in their individual isolation'. Thus 'the objective precon-ditions were created for the multi-leveledness and multi-voicedness of the polyphonic novel' (PDP 20); isolated social groups were forced into massively dialogic contact even to the point of conflict, their world-views relativized, with no transcendent overseer to mediate the process. In the real world, this process resulted in 'that coexistence of distinct languages which seems to define heteroglos-sia', as Ken Hirschkop puts it.[32] In Bakhtin's materialist view, all this has its analogy in the formal properties of Dostoevsky's novels, which will 'outlive capitalism' (PDP 35): the artistic significance of polyphony will remain even when the era which gave rise to it is over. This is an important point; although capitalism is still not yet over, polyphony has indeed already been transplanted to quite different epochs from Dostoevsky's, and in different languages, most recently the English-speaking, postmodern, ecofeminist, film-going world of the late twentieth century.

THE PROBLEM OF THE AUTHOR

It is worth noting again here that, despite his insistence on the 'structural' constitution of the characters in a novel, Bakhtin adheres to the idea of an author as the centre of intention and achievement behind even the freeing up of characters' voices. Where Bakhtin, therefore, says 'author', it is often clearer to replace this with 'narrator'. He does distinguish between the two – discussing the different kind of orientation of the monologic novel, he observes that this applies to 'narration by the author, by a narra-tor, or by one of the characters' (PDP 7) – but it is hard to see how this distinction could be realized in practice, except perhaps by invoking Wayne Booth's distinction between actual and implied author. The former is not perceptible in the text, but the latter may be, as 'a construct inferred and assembled by the reader from all the components of the text'.[33] As Booth puts it, 'It is only by distinguishing between the author and his implied image that we can avoid pointless and unverifiable talk about such qualities as "sincerity" or "seriousness" in the author'[34] - or indeed such qualities as loving freedom and respecting the privacy of others. Bakhtin's slide between author and narrator is clear in his discussion of Dostoevsky's *The Double*, of which he observes that, 'the narrator is literally fettered to his hero', and, a paragraph later, 'Dostoevsky had no "distance perspective" on the hero and the event' (PDP 225). Even if Bakhtin is aware here of a distinction between narrator and author, he assumes that the construction of the former can be explained in terms of the latter's personal foibles.[35]

Bakhtin's omission of a helpful distinction between author and narrator is an important clue to the genesis of his notions of polyphony and dialogism. His assumption that it is the *author's* voice we frequently hear in the novel, more in the monologic kind than in the dialogic, and which is offset by the voices of heteroglossia in the novel, including those of the characters, suggests that there could in theory be an entirely monologic text. If we, at the end of the twentieth century, after many decades of narratological theory have passed, conclude that the author never speaks directly in the text, but that texts are always constructed through the device of the narrator (who may sound more or less 'authoritative', as the case of Tolstoy or Eliot suggests), then we can see that dialogism must always be a property of the literary text. The real-life writer never utters a straightforward word; it is always done at a remove, through another voice: dialogically. This may provide an answer to the problem several commentators on Bakhtin have encountered: does he use the term 'dialogism' prescriptively or descriptively?[36] In other words, if dialogism is always a condition of textual language, then all novels must be dialogic; and if we grant that every novel must have a narrator, then we see why this is so.

Menippean satire and polyphony

Bakhtin discusses Menippean satire in 'Epic and Novel' (26–8), and more extensively in *Problems of Dostoevsky's Poetics*.[37] This genre is a direct descendant of carnivalized folklore, according to Bakhtin (PDP 112); it was and is 'one of the main carriers and channels for the carnival sense of the world in literature' (PDP 113), and a somewhat less direct descendent of the Socratic dialogues which influenced the Dostoevskian polyphonic novel (PDP 109-12). Bakhtin contrasts it with epic, and says that it emerged 'in an epoch when national legend' and 'ethical norms' were in decay. The menippea consists of heterogeneous parts, although possessing generic unity; all the other kindred genres it absorbs – the diatribe, soliloquy, symposium – have in common an internal dialogicality. Bakhtin explains how the soliloquy especially may appear to be monologic – on the face of it, only one voice is present – but is defined by a dialogic relation. Rather than passive self-observation, the soliloquy works by an active dialogic approach to one's self (PDP 119-20).

The menippea is a kind of philosophical novel, in which an idea is tested out in action; philosophical debate is made three-dimensional as the reader follows 'the adventures of an *idea* or a *truth* in the world' (PDP 115). Bakhtin offers as examples various classical satires, Apuleius' *Golden Ass*, and Boethius' *De Consolatione Philosophiae* (PDP 113); the example of Apuleius' work is a revealing one, as the conceit of a man transformed into an ass who travels around is already a version of an idea being tested during its adventures. Bakhtin describes Dostoevsky's story 'Bobok' as 'one of the greatest menippea in all world literature' (PDP 138), and cites Poe's stories as being close to menippea. Many utopian or dystopian fictions could also be termed menippea, including Aldous Huxley's *Island* (1962), Swift's *Gulliver's Travels* (1726), Margaret Atwood's *The Handmaid's Tale* (1985). Other examples of the genre could include Chaucer's works, Samuel Johnson's *Rasselas* (1759), and D. H. Lawrence's *Aaron's Rod* (1922).[38] Bakhtin provides a way of thinking about contemporary works, such as Atwood's novel, which may seem quite divorced from this ancient form; he says of Dostoevsky's works, which bear many menippean features, that 'of course' there is no deliberate menippean stylization on the writer's part, but rather 'one could say that it was not Dostoevsky's subjective memory, but the objective memory of the very genre in which he worked, that preserved the peculiar features of the ancient menippea' (PDP 121). It is as if the genre speaks through Dostoevsky, and Atwood, rather than their consciously adopting it. Bakhtin discusses the fourteen central traits of the menippea in numbered paragraphs, of which the following is a summary:

1 It is a comic genre.
2 Its plot, characters, and setting benefit from a wide-ranging inventiveness, the presence of 'historical and legendary figures',

and the fantastic (PDP 114).

3 The use of the fantastic arises from the menippea's philosophical centre, 'the creation of extraordinary situations for the provoking and testing of a philosophical idea ... embodied in the image of a wise man, the seeker of this truth'.

4 Different generic elements are organically combined: 'philosophical dialogue, lofty symbol-systems, the adventure fantastic, and slum naturalism' (PDP 115).

5 A concern is shown for the 'stripped down' versions of life's ultimate questions (116).

6 There is the appearance of a 'three-planed construction': hell and heaven feature as well as earth.

7 And an 'experimental fantasticality' involving 'observation from some unusual point of view', such as a city from a great height, or, as Bakhtin implies, Swift's use of the device in *Gulliver's Travels* both to enlarge and to shrink everyday human life.

8 Unusual states of mind – insanity, split personality, dreams – are represented, not as 'mere themes' but with a 'formal, generic significance': the subject is no longer a closed, coherent being, possessed of epic or tragic wholeness, but 'ceases to coincide with himself' (PDP 117).

9 Carnivalesque 'scandals and eccentricities' constitute a new artistic category, different from epic events and tragic catastrophes, and again make a breach in the 'epic and tragic wholeness of the world'.

10 Oxymoronic linkages and abrupt transitions characterize the representation of persons – 'the emperor who becomes a slave' – and the plot – 'moral downfalls' (PDP 118).

11 Utopian elements are often present, or the menippea may be a fullblown utopian novel, which often includes the menippea's other features.

12 Inserted genres (letters, speeches, novellas) and poetry appear, usually with a high degree of parody.

13 These inserted genres are an important part of the 'multi-styled' nature of the menippea, and are the beginnings of a new, dialogic relation to the word in the literary text.

14 There is a concern with topical issues; this is clearer in more recent menippea, like *Candide* (1759) or *The Handmaid's Tale*, but Bakhtin points out that it is the '"journalistic" genre of antiquity'.

Dostoevsky and Menippean satire

Bakhtin's analysis of *Notes from Underground* is helpful not only in illuminating that particular text but in showing in action, as it were, the critical use of his categories of menippea, polyphony and dialogism. He says this of his own attention to nineteenth-century novelistic versions of the carnivalesque: his interest is 'the discourse of a *language*, and not its *individual use* in a particular *unrepeatable context*, although, of course, the one cannot exist without the other' (PDP 159). The benefits of concentrating on 'the discourse of a language' become clear if one thinks of applying the same strategies to modern texts which in part resemble *Notes*, such as Ralph Ellison's *Invisible Man* (1952), and even Jenefer Shute's *Life-size*. Dostoevsky's novella is written in the first person, 'as a diatribe (a conversation with an absent interlocutor), saturated with overt and hidden polemic'; its other menippean features include 'abrupt dialogic syncrises, familiarization and profanation, slum naturalism' (PDP 155).

Bakhtin discusses the genesis of polyphony in Dostoevsky's early short story, from his 'Gogol' phase, in *The Double*, where he teases out the three voices which construct the story. The three voices are present for instance in the following extract, where Mr Golyadkin, driven away from a ball, rushes home through a snowstorm and meets a man who later turns out to be his double, the personification of Golyadkin's outspoken side:

> It was not that he feared this might be some bad character, it was simply perhaps ... 'And besides, who knows?' – the thought came unbidden into Mr Golyadkin's mind – 'perhaps this passer-by is – he, himself, perhaps he is here and, what matters most, he is not here for nothing, he has a purpose, he is crossing my path, he will brush against me'. (quoted PDP 220)

In this passage, Bakhtin suggests, are perceptible three different voices 'within the limits of a single dismantled consciousness: that of the narrator ("came unbidden"), and two belonging to Golyadkin, which are barely differentiated although one is in the third person ("he feared ...") and one in the first ("will brush against me")'. There is an almost imperceptible transition between the narration and the hero's speech, a transition represented in the extract above by the ellipses, and, as Bakhtin points out, the voices are so closely merged that the quotation marks which follow ('"And besides ..."') seem unnecessary. The three voices all speak of the same 'word, idea, phenomenon', but in different tones:

The same set of words, tones, inner orientations is passed through the outer speech of Golyadkin, through the speech of the narrator and through the speech of the double, and these three voices are turned to face one another, they speak not about each other but with each other. (PDP 220)

This is an example of rudimentary polyphony within the menippea; the voices, including the narrator's, are all on the same level and converse with one another.

Although Bakhtin claims that this example from *The Double* is not fully polyphonic, he says it is 'no longer homophony'. This seems to be because in *The Double* the separate voices actually split into two, rather than being 'an authentic dialogue of unmerged consciousnesses' within one person, like the kind which appears in Dostoevsky's later novels. Bakhtin's analysis of some passages from *The Brothers Karamazov* (1880) shows how a fully fledged polyphony appears. As a corollary to the increasing degree of polyphony in the following speech of Ivan Karamazov's, telling his brother Alyosha about an encounter with the devil, there is also a much greater degree of dialogism:

He's been teasing me. And you know he does it so cleverly, so cleverly. 'Conscience! What is conscience? I make it up for myself. Why am I tormented by it? From habit. From the universal habit of mankind for seven thousand years. So let us give it up, and we shall be gods'. It was he who said that, it was he who said that! (quoted PDP 221)

This speech follows the structure of the passage from *The Double*, but Bakhtin says here the 'principle for combining voices [...] is deeper and more complex'. In this 'microdialogue' of Ivan's, he 'passes his own personal thoughts and decisions simultaneously through two voices'. Ivan's own ruminations on the human conscience take on the polarized form of two voices, creating tension and eventfulness without being 'dependent on any opposition in content or plot' (PDP 222). As Bakhtin points out, Ivan's self-doubt, reservations, and contradictory experiences all surface as a second, distinctive voice, that of the devil, whose replies to Ivan's words differ from his not in content but in tone. Ivan's consciousness is thus not unitary, but *internally* interrupted and dismantled. Polyphony can come to fruition, as it were, only in tandem with dialogism. Ivan's voice is part of a polyphonic whole in which the narrator's voice does not have precedence; the reason his voice can stand on its own in this polyphonic way is that it is constructed dialogically. Bakhtin explains this in his conclusion to the discussion of Dostoevsky's discourse: both external dialogue (between characters) and internal dialogue (within characters) are 'inseparably connected with the great dialogue of the novel as a whole that encompasses them'. This 'great dialogue' is made possible through polyphony, the establishment of individual, autonomous characters' voices within the text.

In 'Toward a Reworking of the Dostoevsky Book', Bakhtin lists the three central 'discoveries' of the avant-garde artist; the first is polyphony, of which Bakhtin writes here that it is a

> completely new structure for the image of a human being – a full-blooded and fully signifying other consciousness which is not inserted into the finalizing frame of reality, which is not finalized by anything (not even death), for its meaning cannot be resolved or abolished by reality (to kill does not mean to refute). This other consciousness is not inserted into the frame of authorial consciousness, it is revealed from within as something that stands *outside* and *alongside* and with which the author can enter into dialogic relations. (TRDB 284)

In other words, polyphony *makes dialogism possible*; the autonomy of the character's voice provides the conditions for dialogue on equal terms between that character and the narrator (Bakhtin, again, says 'author'), who may interrupt, 'but never drowns out the other's voice, never finishes it off "from himself", that is, out of his own and alien consciousness. This is, so to speak, the activity of God in His relation to man', as opposed to the Dostoevskian Prometheus.

The second discovery of the artist is the depiction of the idea, 'at the level of the human event'; and the third is 'dialogicality as a special form of interaction among autonomous and equally signifying consciousnesses'. The autonomy arises polyphonically, and, as Bakhtin says, '[a]ll three discoveries are essentially one: they are three facets of one and the same phenomenon' (PDP 284).

The construction of polyphony: a case study

In the ten years he spent rewriting *Under the Volcano* (1947), in which time he produced five full draft versions of the final text, Malcolm Lowry was engaged in a process of 'improvement': aiming to write not just 'better' but 'differently'.[39] Not only is statement replaced by rendition; description is replaced by discourse, so that the characters become simply 'images of language', as Bakhtin puts it. One of the consistent changes Lowry makes is to reduce the role of the omniscient narrator, and free up the voices of the individual characters instead. Coincidentally, this is the royal road to polyphony, and is accompanied by an equally fortuitous but marked development of dialogism and heteroglossia, as we will see.

Among the features of the characters of a polyphonic novel are the depiction of how the hero sees the world and how he sees himself, not how the world and he objectively appear; the absence of anything perceptible to a third-person observer, or obtrusive narratorial comment. All these are features of *Under the Volcano*, largely accounted for by the alcoholism of the central character. This is true even to the extent that the Consul's polyphonic view of his own and others' fate is shown to be fine as a principle of construction, where characters can be heard rather than seen, but tragic as a human quality: '"Yes, I can see", he said, only he couldn't see, only hear, the droning, the weeping, and feel, feel the unreality'.[40]

Lowry appears to have conceived of the characters in *Under the Volcano* in a polyphonic way; although the impression given of them in the novel is one of 'completeness', Lowry recognized that the point was precisely to be able to hear rather than see the characters: 'there just isn't *room*: the characters will have to wait for another book [...] The truth is that the character drawing is not only weak but virtually non-existent'.[41] Character drawing may well be 'weak', as this 'drawing' is the opposite of a polyphonic strategy, which might be described as 'listening' or 'transcribing'. Lowry says of the characters in *Under the Volcano* that 'what may look like unsuccessful attempts at character drawing may only be the concrete bases to the creatures' lives without which again the book could not be read at all',[42] acknowledging that their prime function is to widen the range of voices within the text, rather than to offer a species of human verisimilitude. The following example from the drafts of *Under the Volcano* shows this: an accumulation of language adds to the autonomy of the two voices, Hugh's and Yvonne's, and simultaneously to their dialogic properties. In draft, Hugh and Yvonne sound childishly erudite and rather stilted as they look at a Mexican landscape:

> 'Don't you know your Prescott?' [...]
> 'This ought to be the place that made old Diaz' head swim'.[43]

In the published version of *Under the Volcano*, however, although the underlying textual and historical references remain the same, the quotations are made more clearly part of the characters' self-consciousness. Both Hugh and Yvonne are aware of their roles,[44] and Hugh uses the texts he is quoting to keep the conversation off personal matters:

> 'This ought to be the place, if Alcapancingo's over there', Hugh said, 'where Bernal Díaz and his Tlaxcalans got across to beat up Quauhnahuac. Superb name for a dance band: Bernal Díaz and his Tlaxcalans ... Or didn't you get around to Prescott at the University of Hawaii?'
> 'Mm hm', Yvonne said, meaning yes or no to the meaningless question, and peering down the ravine with a shudder.
> 'I understand it made even old Díaz's head swim.'
> 'I shouldn't wonder'.[45]

The words and facts which Lowry valued still get spoken in this new context, transplanted from Prescott's *Historia Verdadera*: Díaz' '"head swam so [...] that he scarcely knew how he got on"';[46] their 'meaninglessness', as Hugh knows it is, apart from a gratuitous contribution to the fabric of the text and to the sense of Mexico's conquered past, is made a full condition of the words' presence. They no longer masquerade as the characteristic utterance of 'ersatz beings'. It is ironic, but only to be expected, that such a transformation in context – the abandonment of an effort at mimesis in favour of collecting as many voices as possible – should make the 'creatures' seem more consistent, more adult and more plausible. This is especially clear in an example where a series of adjectives used in draft to describe Yvonne's reaction to the news of Hugh's visit becomes interminably metonymic in its hopeless effort to describe her emotional state:

> 'What', Yvonne [almost wailed; and] stopped in her tracks. Ths Consul had taken her arm paternally, but her head was buzzing, she felt a strange constriction and a twitching in her temples and she seemed to be floating, rather than walking, sick – this was impossible – outrageous – inconceivable.[47]

As Bakhtin says, 'All direct meanings and direct expressions are false and this is especially true of emotional meanings and expressions' (DN 401). The square brackets above show where Lowry made deletions to this draft version, in what is already a move to omit the voice of narratorial overview – 'almost wailed'. In the published version, this process has gone so far that we have an exemplary instance of dialogized polyphony, in which several voices speak, each autonomous and not subject to an organizing, higher placed voice:

'He's staying with me'.
– BOX! ARENA TOMALIN. FRENTE AL JARDIN XICOTANCATL [...]
'What!' Yvonne stopped dead.[48]

The piling up of words in the earlier version is replaced in the published *Under the Volcano* by a collection of words which evades narration by *symbolizing* conflict and agitation, using a symbol arising from an independent, disinterested voice, the poster for a boxing match. In a late marginal note in the drafts, Lowry tells himself of Yvonne, 'make clear that she's thinking about this deliberately in order to avoid thinking that her ex-lovers are here [...] chart her despairing state of mind – while in the back of her mind – Box!'[49] Even if it is true that the boxing poster offers a distraction for Yvonne, it also ends up expressing the conflict and hurt far better than the omnisciently narrated version of the same scene.

As Bakhtin observes in 'Discourse in the Novel', conventional stylistics does not have a satisfactory way of accounting for the accretive, as opposed to the 'inspired individual', way of writing which is clearly Lowry's: 'the specific tasks involved in constructing this whole out of heteroglot, multi-voiced, multi-styled and often multi-languaged elements remain outside the boundaries of such a study' (DN 265), and indeed in Lowry's case have been given such labels as 'plagiarism'. Bakhtin describes an activity which sounds more like intertextuality; when the influences of an author on another's discourse are 'laid bare', it becomes clear whether this is a 'simple act of reproduction', or the development of the other discourse in 'a new context and under new conditions' (DN 347). Bakhtin quotes approvingly this apt observation of the Russian Husserlian Gustav Shpet: novels '"do not spring from *poetic creativity* but are purely rhetorical compositions"' (DN 268). However, Bakhtin clings to a concept of intentional authorship, which underlies – although is not definitional to – his theory of dialogism. Again in 'Discourse in the Novel', he observes that heteroglossia establishes its own order once it enters the novel, 'and becomes a unique artistic system, which orchestrates the intentional theme of the author'. These two planks of Bakhtin's argument coexist – the perception that literary works come about through following generic and linguistic norms, not through genius; but that an 'author's' intention may be transparently expressed – partly because Bakhtin is contrasting prose and poetry. While the prose author may 'distance himself' from the work's language, and speak (his intention) '*through* language' rather than *in* it, the poet identifies himself *with* his language (DN 299; cf. 311). This is a matter of emphasis rather than a wholesale version of the psychoanalytic idea that language speaks the subject, rather than the other way round.

Lowry observes that the characters in *Under the Volcano* – the Consul, Yvonne, Hugh, and Laruelle, not to mention Dr Vigil, the *pelado*, the pariah dog and various passers-by – are all aspects of a single soul.[50] Bakhtin points out that very strict differentiation among the characters' voices in a text may be a feature of monologism, rather than polyphony. Lowry's rewriting practice suggests this, as he moved utterances from one character to another, and even altered the role of the characters, without radically changing the text and its polyphonic nature as a whole. The characters are shown to be merely the occasions for certain kinds of language to enter the text, and this actually makes their autonomy possible. For instance, in an early version of the bull-throwing episode, Lowry tried several times to fit in a sentence – '"I don't know which you remind me of more, Mithra or John Masefield"' – which never appears in the published version, but obviously had to be said by the Consul of Hugh's antics in the bullring; apart from that, where it appeared during the chapter mattered little. Bakhtin discusses this method of constructing a character's discourse in 'Discourse in the Novel': '*Who* speaks and under what conditions he speaks: this is what determines the word's actual meaning' (DN 401).

Lowry's work on the characters' autonomy, and their lack of dependence on an omniscient narrator, can be seen clearly in his drafts. For the kind of novel he wanted to write, this was the way to 'improve' his work. The place of an Eliotic narrator is parodically taken by the Consul's familiars; he hears sympathetic, omniscient – and illusory – observations on his plight: '"Alas", a voice seemed to be saying also in his ear, "my poor child, you do not feel any of these things really, only lost, only homeless'.[51] He can only hallucinate the absent transcendent viewer of his fate. Like the protagonists of *The Edible Woman* and *The Bell Jar*, the Consul's state of mind is signalled by the formal absence of any narratorial overview: 'the Consul did an odd thing', and 'oddly he had not touched his drink'.[52] These are not fluent, narratorial observations, but testimony to the fact that slipping the postcard from Yvonne under Laruelle's pillow, and indulging in bouts of teetotalism between drinks, are as mysterious in origin to the Consul as they would be to an observer – at whom the latter action at least is partially directed.[53]

Exactly as Bakhtin says, we get an image of how the world looks to the hero, not how the world actually looks, as the Consul's words suggest: 'M. Laruelle, who hadn't noticed a thing, appeared again', and 'Yvonne was laughing, the foregoing bawdry mostly over her head however, the Consul felt, and still she hadn't noticed anything'.[54] The Consul is reassuring himself rather than reporting the facts. This second example is also one worked on by Lowry to turn what was once the 'subject of the author's visualization and representation' into a function of the character's self-consciousness, as Bakhtin puts it in the central paragraph on polyphony quoted earlier (PDP 48). The draft version of this scene in *Under the Volcano* runs: '"I think the spectral chicken of the house would be even more terrific don't you, Hugh?" Yvonne was laughing, although most of the foregoing, unconscious bawdry was above her head'. The comment made by the narrator over the heads of the three diners is replaced in the published version, as we have just seen, where an oblique perception of Yvonne's character trait coexists with a piece of wishful thinking on the part of her ex-husband. The final version is not a piece of information about a pseudo-person but the word of the Consul.

The same shift from description to the rendering of consciousness takes place in relation to the blurring in the text between uttered and silent words; drunk as he is, the Consul cannot always tell whether he has spoken aloud or not, or even whether other people are really present to answer him, and this is a feature which extends to other characters in the text as well. 'Thinking or saying' becomes a refrain, helping to disrupt monologic insistence on a strict division between 'thought as consciousness and voice as speech'.[56]

In the final typescript of *Under the Volcano*, which Lowry sent to Jonathan Cape, and on the publishers' galleys, the last details of this polyphonic novel are altered. Each chapter has its own viewpoint, and strict consistency of viewpoint keeps the omniscient narrator out. As we have already seen, Bakhtin argues that within polyphony, '[n]ot a single element of the work is structured from the point of view of a nonparticipating "third person"' (PDP 18); what is at stake is not the world itself, but the (self-)consciousness of the various protagonists. The following are examples of this process; throughout, italics show pencil additions:

1 who was *she noticed* wearing no socks

The Consul in this chapter is seen through Yvonne's eyes only.

> 2 *he must see her, half jaunty*
> as she knew she must appear, a little jaunty

Yvonne can appeal only to the eyes and awareness of her ex-husband, leaving no suggestion that she 'appears' objectively to narrator or reader.

The amount the Consul points out about Laruelle dwindles:

> 3 ... and it struck the Consul that this imbalance was somehow appropriate to Jacques as denoting the contrast between his life and his ambitions.

becomes in the published version:

> this contrast was somehow obscurely appropriate to Jacques, as indeed was that between the angels and the cannonballs.

The 'obscurely' of the published version stands in for the earlier fuller description, the latter giving with its imprecision a more precise sense of the Consul's subjectivizing everything, even on someone else's behalf.

From Yvonne's chapter:

> 4 *as Hugh described*
> ... the millwheel reflections of sunlight on water, like those this morning on the Cerveceria.

Such apparent examples of fluid sensibility, Yvonne recalling something Hugh originally remarked, must be tidied up in order not to interfere with the times when such a syndrome is important for ulterior reasons. The Consul may be uncertain what he has said about his book, and it turns out that he was heard to say something, as Yvonne later reports their conversation to Hugh; unlike the former instance, ascribable either to carelessness or to an absent, unreported conversation, the latter forms part of the novel's uneasiness with boundaries between inner and outer experience, uttered and silent words.

> 5 Then he gently impelled the Consul before him toward the cantina

becomes

he found himself impelled by the policeman from behind towards
the cantina

The version from the published *Under the Volcano* is made consistently polyphonic – the event is seen from the Consul's point of
view, rather than baldly narrated – simply by a change of voice
from active to passive, which also increases the reader's sense of the
Consul's notorious personal passivity. Again a principle of construction comes to seem like a character trait.[56]

Film and polyphony

It is worth noting in relation to *Under the Volcano* the debt owed by
Lowry to cinema, which may be the origin of his scrupulous attention to the consistency of point of view. Several critics have
discussed Lowry's debt to the techniques of cinema in his textual
practice: his treatment of time, flashback, scenery and setting,
dialogue, printed signs and other eye-catching devices, visual irony
all bear a filmic hallmark.[57] The plot has its own filmic features:
overt references are made to certain films, Yvonne was a child star
and Laruelle a director in Hollywood. The screenplay Lowry wrote
for F. Scott Fitzgerald's *Tender is the Night* bears testimony to his
familiarity with film-making conventions.[58] The opening of *Under
the Volcano* is notoriously similar to the filmic device for introducing
place, the establishing shot, which involves zooming in on an
increasingly detailed map of the film's setting, or, as Seymour
Chatman points out, on a whole city and then a room or building
within it: 'In *Psycho*, the camera starts high above Phoenix, then
glides down into a room where a couple are making love'.[59]
However, in *Under the Volcano* unavoidable heteroglossia and dialogism fracture the textual approximation of this device, as the
introductory voice imitates by turns historical, *Guide Bleu*, literary,
and geographical discourse, even quoting from another text to do
so.[60]

The question of the narrator in film is a vexed one. Inez
Hedges suggests that the 'film narrator [...] is bound up with the
point of view and can therefore usually be identified with the
camera'; and, further, can be assumed to be male.[61] David Bordwell
discusses the idea of a narrator in film in his book *Making Meaning*
as simply a convenient 'anthropomorphic fiction' if ascribed to
every case, since the spectator is aware of being told the story of the
film by 'an entity resembling a human being' only in particular

instances. The narrator – that is, the source of the voice-over – of Orson Welles's *The Lady from Shanghai* (1947), for instance, is the protagonist Michael O'Hara; while Truffaut's *Jules et Jim* (1962) is narrated by an anonymous voice. Bordwell implicitly takes issue with Bakhtin's observation that the source of all textual language is the speaking voice. This is not the case in film: 'we cannot construct a narrator for Vidor's film *War and Peace* with the exactitude with which we can assign attributes to the narrator of Tolstoy's original novel'. Bordwell suggests that, in a reversal of the kind a carnivalesque or polyphonic cast of mind would presumably approve of, instead of a narrator creating narrative in film, it is narrative which creates the narrator 'by appealing to the historical norms of viewing'.[62]

It is significant that the distinction between objective and subjective narration in film, which in fiction often corresponds to monologic and polyphonic construction respectively, works according to its own particular logic. As Bordwell and Thompson point out, objective narration is so often the 'baseline' from which most films briefly depart but to which they invariably return, that even flashbacks, 'usually motivated as mental subjectivity' as the character recalls the past, often include information the character concerned could have no way of knowing.[63] This is true, for instance, in the flashbacks which accompany the individual accounts of Kane's life by the people who knew him, in Welles's *Citizen Kane* (1940); although it is important for the film to show the varying perspectives different people have on Kane, the occasional break in strict consistency of viewpoint does not much matter, or is in some cases essential. In a novel, particularly a polyphonic one like *Under the Volcano*, the whole point is to keep the different viewpoints consistently distinct, even though each viewpoint is partly constructed out of utterances and words from the others.[64]

Seymour Chatman also discusses the difference between narration in fiction and in film, a difference that has implications for the possibility of filmic polyphony. The effect Lowry was aiming for in his avoidance of direct narratorial description of his characters' appearance is basic to film, Chatman argues: 'the camera does not describe at all but merely presents or better, it *depicts*: [...] renders in pictorial form'. Of course what happens in *Under the Volcano* is much more complex than this, as we hardly feel that a 'depiction' as opposed to a description has been given to us of Yvonne. What we have instead is a series of reactions to her, including her own self-consciousness; or, more precisely, further instances of the representation of discourse. Rather than an approach to how she looks, or indeed whether she has been unfaithful to her husband, we get a multiplication of images of language. Chatman cites the 'neutral, "non-narrated" Hemingwayesque fiction – the *camera eye* style', through which events are 'just *revealed*', as the literary approximation to cinematic depiction;[65] such a style is very different from the overloaded, 'chirrugueresque' one of *Under the Volcano*.

One might ask, can a film be polyphonic? and, prior even to that, whether Bakhtin's theories, which are exclusively concerned with the written word, can be of use in discussing film. Several critics would answer the latter in the affirmative, including Robert Stam and R. Barton Palmer; others have clearly assumed the appropriateness of his theories for film, as individual readings show. In an article about the dialogic potential of the image, Palmer points out that film texts 'manifest a systemicity that is linguistic to some degree', and suggests that some of Bakhtin's terms are more useful in considering cinema formally rather than in the institutional terms of more recent film criticism. The impression of filmic narratorlessness is a quality valued by the Russian film-maker Eisenstein, who spoke of cinema's quality of 'directly materializing' reality, rather than having to construct it through the barrier of words. Bakhtin's view, and that of most contemporary critics, would be rather that the words in a text are the reality themselves, neither a means or an obstruction to it. The filmic image is as little genuinely objective as any textual entity; it is not this that distinguishes film and fiction, but the fact that 'cinema, unlike literature, has no corresponding language to objectify and examine in the very process of representation'. In other words, cinema's metalanguage, the way we talk about it critically, is (usually) natural language, not images; on the other hand, literature's metalanguage must be the same as its own language. In the novel, language is both the object and subject of representation, while in cinema there is 'nothing analogous to the Bakhtinian novel ... which takes the natural, populist forces of heteroglossia within living language as both material and theme'.[66]

It seems that, as with the chronotope, film is already such a good exemplar of polyphony that one might say it is polyphonic of necessity. The camera can be only objective, although there are of course ways of giving the audience partial or false impressions. Although it is not the whole story, the issue of fictive versus filmic *description* is a revealing one. In the novel, description is often the site of the monologic narrator, so that any problematizing of this area may suggest the presence of polyphony. Polyphonic construction, that is, where the characters speak for themselves and about each other, rather than being inertly described by a third party, is the most effective means of avoiding direct description. In film, by contrast, description is, arguably, impossible anyway. While an extended rendering of a villain's appearance in a novel will interrupt the plot, in film it would seem simply part of the story-time. As Chatman puts it, 'Once that illusory story-time is established in a film, even dead moments, moments when nothing moves, will be felt to be part of the temporal whole, just as the taxi meter continues to run as we sit fidgeting in a traffic jam.' According to Chatman, even the establishing shot of the kind copied by Lowry at the beginning of *Under the Volcano* for objective effect is not descriptive in film. Objectivity and 'the force of plot' in film obviate any need for a narrator. Perception of a character's clothes, demeanour, and attractiveness, for instance, arises as a side-effect of these other two elements, as Chatman shows in a detailed comparison of scenes from Jean Renoir's film *Une Partie de campagne* (1935) and passages from Maupassant's original story of the same name. Certain kinds of fictional effect – such as the narrator's 'tone', the ambivalent yet innocent self-display of the female protagonist – are replicated in the visual medium by other means, in the latter instance, 'several amusing reaction shots which compensate for the camera's sexless objectivity'. The facility of the narrator makes fiction more flexible than film, according to Chatman, because the former avoids the relatively fixed standpoint of the camera, which suffers from a 'need for placement', and the need to have a 'visual bearing'.[67] The first-person narrator of *Notes from Underground*, for instance, takes a visual bearing only when he looks in the mirror. If a film were made of Dostoevsky's story, the camera would, as Chatman points out, have to orient itself somehow in relation to the protagonist's bodily presence, either in front, behind, or even within it – or all three.

Bakhtin's discussion of one's awareness of one's own, and the other's, external appearance in 'Author and Hero in Aesthetic Activity' provides a partial gloss on this problem. One's own view of one's existence in the world possesses a similar structure to polyphony, in the sense that there is no definitive external definition to be provided of what one looks like: 'Even when I dream about the admiration that my exterior calls forth in others, I do not have to represent it to myself; I represent to myself only the result of the impression it makes on others' (AH 28).

The cost of losing the narrator from the opening of Jane Austen's *Pride and Prejudice* (1813) is described in a review of a film adaptation of the novel:

> Vexingly, Jane Austen's celebrated saw about the single man is
> delivered by the narrator, and is therefore quite unsuitable as the
> opening to a screen adaptation. What to do? In his 1940 screen-
> play, Aldous Huxley's unhappy solution was to award his opening
> line to an olde-worlde draper. In 1980, Fay Weldon gave hers to a
> panting Bennet daughter. [In 1995], in his long-awaited version of
> *Pride and Prejudice*, Andrew Davies brings on Mr Bingley, at a
> gallop, and imagines his reaction to a view of Netherfield Park.
> Instead of a piece of scrupulous, Austenly wit, the audience is
> thereby presented with a show of virility, horseflesh and a corking
> great house [...] If Jane Austen had wanted to begin like an estate
> agent, no doubt she would have done so.[68]

This comment shows in action the need for placement, and embod-
iment, in film, and the contrasting 'flexibility' of the novelistic
narrator. The infamous first line of *Pride and Prejudice* – 'It is a truth
universally acknowledged, that a single man in possession of a good
fortune must be in want of a wife', is quoted in an article by
Morson on Tolstoy's use of extra-novelistic proverbs in his novels,
such as the equally infamous 'All happy families are alike; each
unhappy family is unhappy in its own way', with which *Anna
Karenina* (1873–7) begins. Austen's opening sentence is quite different from Tolstoy's, as it is very clearly double-voiced. It is indirect
discourse, 'and there is clearly a difference in point of view between
the paraphrase and the writer who paraphrases. This sentence does
not make an assertion, it reports one.' Tolstoy's sentence, however,
is also dialogic: 'His absolute sentences polemically assert their
unconditionality and so necessarily enter into dialogue with the
genre whose speech they reject [...] In short, the very refusal to
enter into dialogue is itself both dialogic and dialogizing.' The
difference between these two narratorial statements is that whereas
Austen's participates in two contexts: that of the work in which it
appears, and the context of that work's genre, Tolstoy's is 'dialogized only by the second [generic] context'.[69] Novelization
dialogizes automatically. Volosinov, in *Marxism and the Philosophy of
Language*, makes a point similar to Morson's: 'Any monological
utterance [...] makes response to something and is calculated to be
responded to in turn', and only the 'philologist's' passive understanding of such a 'monument' makes it seem 'isolated' (MPL
72–3).

FILMIC POLYPHONY AND GENDER

Chatman's discussion of *Une Partie de campagne*, the filmic version of a relatively complex story, interestingly plays right into the hands, as it were, of Laura Mulvey's classic essay on so-called 'objectivity' in film, 'Visual Pleasure and Narrative Cinema'. According to Mulvey, the three gazes which constitute filmic narrative – of camera, characters, and spectator – are all masculine, and all objectify the female within the film. Female film spectators will thus find themselves awkwardly split between identifying masochistically with the objectified female on screen and being made to take up a masculine viewing position towards that female, sadistically, as it is the only one available. Chatman repeats each of the three Mulveyan positions: he calls the camera's gaze 'sexless' because it cannot reproduce the tone of the roué's in the Maupassant story, where the narrator calls Henriette '"one of those women who suddenly excite your desire"'. However, the camera has after all chosen to focus on the scene of a young girl on a swing, and because it cannot properly reproduce the desirous tone of the narrator, peoples the scene with a young man, Rodolphe, whose 'voyeurism' even Chatman acknowledges. These are two of the three masculine gazes. The third, that of the spectator, is helpfully clarified by Chatman, who describes one of his 'favourite shots in the film': a column of young seminarians suddenly catches sight of Henriette swinging, and, when they are forced to avert their gazes by their teacher, he 'manages to sneak a glance of his own' before shepherding them on again. Later, dealing with the gender issue in a footnote, Chatman grants that the identification summoned up in the scenes he mentions is a masculine one, but suggests this is just chance: 'Why should female members of Renoir's audience have any more difficulty participating in Rodolphe's lecherous point of view than male members have in participating in the point of view of Molly Bloom?' he asks rhetorically.[70]

It does not seem to be coincidental that the best example of filmic objectivity (polyphony) should be the presentation of a woman's body, nor that it should turn out not to be objective (value-free) at all. This is partly because of the association of the visual with sexual domination, and of woman with the cinematic image, as Mary Ann Doane puts it: 'historically, there has always been a certain imbrication of the cinematic image and the representation of the woman'.[71] The establishing shot at the beginning of *Psycho* (1960) is a case in point: this shot may indeed relate to the plot rather than being descriptive, but it could also be accused of prurience, of seeking out the lovers in their secret tryst, in a manner which will with hindsight seem judgemental. Filmic polyphony under such circumstances might mean giving all the film's protagonists the chance to operate their own signifying systems, and not just be the signifieds of camera, other characters and audience. Henriette's own sexuality may be inferred in *Une Partie*, but it, like her voice and other attributes, is not allowed equal rights with either the camera or the other, male, characters.

Notes

1 See for instance Kate Flint, *Dickens*, Harvester, Brighton 1986, pp. 47–8; Roger Fowler, 'Polyphony and Problematic in "Hard Times"', in Robert Giddings, ed., *The Changing World of Charles Dickens*, Vision Press, Totowa, New Jersey 1983, p. 96, says polyphony is no different from heteroglossia, p. 96; David Lodge claims dialogism and polyphony are 'virtually synonymous', *After Bakhtin*, Routledge, London 1990, p. 86.

2 Fowler, 'Polyphony and Problematic', p. 93; Bakhtin quotes Russian critic L. P. Grossman on Dostoevsky's own acknowledgement of '"his structural system and the musical theory of 'modulations' or counter-positions"', PDP 41.

3 Pam Morris, *Bleak House*, Open University Press, Milton Keynes 1991, p. 26; see also Robert Golding, *Idiolects and Dickens: The Major Techniques and Chronological Development*, Macmillan, London 1985.

4 D. H. Lawrence, 'Morality and the Novel', in *Phoenix: The Uncollected Papers of D. H. Lawrence*, William Heinemann, London 1936; John Bayley, *The Characters of Love: A Study in the Literature of Personality*, Chatto and Windus, London 1960; Wayne Booth, *The Rhetoric of Fiction*, University of Chicago Press, Chicago, Illinois 1961, p. 79.

5 It is worth pointing out Bakhtin's confusing move between 'author' and 'author-as-narrator'. As I observed in the introduction, he means by 'author' the formal dimension of the work, not the historical person; an identifiable voice in the text, as opposed to the 'atmosphere' of the text's structure (PDP 64), is the narrator's.

6 George Eliot, *The Mill on the Floss*, ed. Gordon S. Haight, Oxford University Press, Oxford 1980, p. 12.

7 *Ibid.*, pp. 245, 325, 330.

8 *Ibid.*, p. 331.

9 It is interesting that although it is supposed to be simply a function of the self's or others' consciousness that appearance (of women) is so often at stake.

10 Malcolm Lowry, *Under the Volcano*, Picador, London 1990 [1947], p. 46.

11 *Ibid.*, p. 97.

12 *Ibid.*, p. 72.

13 Malcolm Lowry, *The 1940 Under the Volcano*, eds Paul Tiessen and Miguel Mota, MLR Editions, Waterloo, Ontario 1994, p. 70.

14 Lowry, *Under the Volcano*, p. 48.

15 Jeremy Tambling argues that it is important not to confuse polyphony with free indirect discourse, an aspect of writing itself with a literary technique (*Narrative and Ideology*, Open University Press, Milton Keynes 1991, p. 116 n. 7). Although it is interesting to consider the differences between the two, it seems that Tambling must also be assuming that polyphony is equivalent to dialogism.

16 Lowry, *Under the Volcano*, pp. 71, 72.

17 Chris Ackerley and Lawrence Clipper interpret the phrase 'for Geoff's benefit' rather literally in their astonishing concordance, *A Companion to 'Under the Volcano'*, University of British Columbia Press, Vancouver 1984; they claim the phrase means, 'in that the birds and pyramids have vague neo-Platonic and occult implications, while the Empress [...] is dressed in flowers as a symbol of Venus' (148), but it seems more helpful to see it as part of the book's polyphonic structure. Hugh perceives Yvonne's appearance in terms of its sidewards glance towards her ex-husband, and again the polyphonic structure imitates and constructs jealousy.

18 Lowry, *Under the Volcano*, p. 262.

19 See Lowry, *1940*, p. 50, where Yvonne looks at herself in the mirror.

20 Stephen Spender, 'Introduction', in Lowry, *Under the Volcano*, p. xvii.

21 Lowry, *Under the Volcano*, p. 294.

22 *Ibid.*, p. 341.

23 Betty Friedan, *The Feminine Mystique*, Penguin, Harmondsworth 1965, p. 13.

24 Sylvia Plath, *The Bell Jar*, Faber, London 1966 [1963], p. 194.

25 Elaine Showalter, *The Female Malady: Women, Madness, and English Culture, 1830–1980*, Penguin, Harmondsworth 1987, p. 216.

26 Margaret Atwood, *The Edible Woman*, Virago, London 1980 [1969], p. 64.

27 *Ibid.*, p. 270.

28 Lowry, *Under the Volcano*, p. 181.

29 Ackerley and Clipper, *A Companion*, p. 254.

30 Lowry, *Under the Volcano*, p. 213.

31 On *sobytie*, 'event', see the editorial footnote, PDP 6.

32 Ken Hirschkop, 'Introduction', in Hirschkop and David Shepherd, eds, *Bakhtin and Cultural Theory*, Manchester University Press, Manchester 1989, p. 18.

33 Shlomith Rimmon-Kenan, *Narrative Fiction: Contemporary Poetics*, Methuen, London 1983.

34 Booth, *The Rhetoric of Fiction*, p. 75.

35 Bakhtin does discuss the 'posited author' as a 'compositional device', DN 312; in 'The Problem of Speech Genres', he discusses briefly a prototype of implied reader and author in his consideration of addressivity: 'in addition to the actual author, there are also conventional and semiconventional images of substitute authors, editors and various kinds of narrators' (98).

36 Hirschkop, 'Introduction', p. 6.

37 See also Julia Kristeva, 'Word, Dialogue and Novel', in *Desire in Language: A Semiotic Approach to Literature and Art*, Basil Blackwell, Oxford 1980, pp. 82–6.

38 See F. Anne Payne, *Chaucer and Menippean Satire*, University of Wisconsin Press, Madison, Wisconsin 1981, chs 1–3; James R. Woodruff, '*Rasselas* and the Traditions of "Menippean Satire"', in I. Grundy, ed., *Samuel Johnson: New Critical Essays*, Vision and Barnes & Noble, London and New York 1984, pp. 158-85; Susan French, 'Lawrence and Bakhtin: A Dialogic Reading of D. H. Lawrence's Leadership Fiction', unpublished Ph.D. thesis, University of Sheffield 1993.

39 Michael Worton, 'Michel Tournier and the Masterful Art of Rewriting', *PN Review* 41 (11) 3, 1984, p. 11.

40 Lowry, *Under the Volcano*, p. 197.

41 *Selected Letters of Malcolm Lowry*, eds Harvey Breit and Marjorie Bonner Lowry, Jonathan Cape, London 1967, p. 71.

42 *Ibid.*, p. 86.

43 Lowry, *1940*, pp. 106–7.

44 Spender, 'Introduction', p. xxvi.

45 Lowry, *Under the Volcano*, p. 100.

46 Ackerley and Clipper, *A Companion*, p. 152.

47 Lowry, *1940*, p. 87.

48 Lowry, *Under the Volcano*, p. 60.

49 Comment written by Lowry on a late draft version of *Under the Volcano*, held by the Special Collections Division, University Library of British Columbia, Vancouver.

50 *Selected Letters*, p. 90.

51 Lowry, *Under the Volcano*, p. 354.

52 Lowry, *Under the Volcano*, p. 201, 202.

53 This raises the interesting question of the alcoholic performance in relation to Bakhtinian transgression of footlights: the former imagines the footlights are firmly in place, and that he or she is convincing those around that there is no problem, but their absence in carnival and alcholism undoes him or her.

54 Lowry, *Under the Volcano*, pp. 209, 291.

55 Lowry, *Under the Volcano*, p. 155.

56 These draft quotations are from the same source as n. 49; John Orr, *The Making of the Twentieth Century Novel: Lawrence, Joyce, Faulkner and Beyond*, Macmillan, Basingstoke 1987, p. 152.

57 See for instance Sherrill Grace, *The Voyage That Never Ends: The Fiction of Malcolm Lowry*, University of British Columbia Press, Vancouver 1982; Duncan Hadfield, '*Under the Volcano*'s Central Symbols: Towers, Trees and their Variants', in P. Tiessen, ed., *Apparently Incongruous Parts: The Worlds of Malcolm Lowry*, The Scarecrow Press, Metuchen, New Jersey, and London 1990.

58 Miguel Mota and Paul Tiessen, eds, *The Cinema of Malcolm Lowry: A Scholarly Edition of Lowry's 'Tender is the Night'*, University of British Columbia Press, Vancouver 1992.

59 Seymour Chatman, 'What Novels Can Do That Films Can't (and Vice Versa)', in Gerald Mast, Marshall Cohen and Leo Braudy, eds, *Film Theory and Criticism*, Oxford University Press, New York 1992, p. 409.

60 The book 'quoted' is Domingo Diaz's *Summa Morelense* (1934?), 'a popular

account of the history and geography of the state of Morelos', Ackerley and Clipper, *A Companion*, p. 3.

61 Inez Hedges, *Breaking the Frame: Film Language and the Experience of Limits*, Indiana University Press, Bloomington, Indiana 1991, p. 4.

62 David Bordwell, *Making Meaning: Inference and Rhetoric in the Interpretation of Cinema*, Harvard University Press, Cambridge, Mass. 1989, p. 162.

63 David Bordwell and K. Thompson, *Film Art: An Introduction*, Knopf, New York 1985, p. 67.

64 Perhaps the most striking example of violation of flashback consistency in *Citizen Kane* is our view of two technicians sitting above the stage when Kane's wife Susan is singing in an opera, and holding their noses to show her perfomance stinks: this is not something she could literally have witnessed, although it stands for her awareness of audience dissatisfaction. We have already noted several examples of strict polyphonic consistency in *Under the Volcano*, of the kind: 'who was, she noticed, wearing no socks' (p. 46).

65 Chatman, 'What Novels Can Do', p. 408.

66 R. Barton Palmer, 'Bakhtinian Translinguistics and Film Criticism: The Dialogical Image?', in R. Barton Palmer, ed., *The Cinematic Text: Methods and Approaches*, AMS Press, New York 1989, pp. 307, 332, 334.

67 Chatman, 'What Novels Can Do', pp. 410, 409, 411, 412.

68 Catherine Bennett, 'Hype and Heritage', *Guardian* 2, 22 September 1995, p. 2.

69 Gary Saul Morson, 'Tolstoy's Absolute Language', *Critical Inquiry* 7, 1980–1, p. 674; thanks to Sue French for this reference.

70 Chatman, 'What Novels Can Do', pp. 410, 411, 418 fn. See also Laura Mulvey, 'Visual Pleasure and Narrative Cinema', *Screen* 16 (3), 1975.

71 Mary Ann Doane, *Femmes Fatales: Feminism, Film Theory, Psychoanalysis*, Routledge, London 1991, p. 19.

4

Carnival and the grotesque body

Introduction

In both *Rabelais and His World* and *Problems of Dostoevsky's Poetics*, Bakhtin uses a relatively conventional literary critical approach to introduce his notion of carnival, first discussing earlier critics of a particular writer's work, then using his own theory to show more accurately, as he says, what that writer is about. In the case of Rabelais, Bakhtin emphasizes the forgotten tradition of 'popular humour', which can make sense of his particular discourse; and, in the case of Dostoevsky, Bakhtin sees polyphony's roots in a similar, although more distant, carnival past.[1]

This chapter examines Bakhtin's discussion of carnival as an element of popular history which has become textualized. Carnival is, as Julia Kristeva puts it, 'a signifier, but also a signified': it can be the subject or the means of representation in a text, or both. The carnivalesque may be detected in textual images, plot, or language itself. As carnival 'is a spectacle, but without a stage', in which the participant is 'both actor and spectator',[2] its textualization is not a straightforward matter, because the change of form at once introduces the equivalent of a stage, and a sharp distinction between actor (character and narrator) and spectator (reader). However, Bakhtin's work on representation in the early essay 'Author and Hero in Aesthetic Activity' can make some sense of this problem. Carnival's absence of footlights both encourages and prohibits linking it to drama, which is also considered in this chapter. Bakhtin's notion of carnival includes the literary genre of 'grotesque realism', which centres on the image of the grotesque body. Contemporary interest in the body as a critical category makes this part of Bakhtin's theory particularly compelling,[3] and raises questions of gender, and psychoanalysis, a discipline about which the Bakhtin circle had mixed feelings. The chapter concludes with a look at a critic who has used carnival and the categories of grotesque realism to reassess a modern novel, and a brief example of how this kind of criticism might work in relation to another text.

The origin of carnival's place in Bakhtin's writing is a piece of mythicized literary history: the historical carnivals which characterized the Middle Ages, up to the time of Rabelais in the sixteenth century, live on in 'transposed' (PDP 124)[4] form in literary texts. These carnivals are the precursors of the ones we know today: May Day holidays; the British Notting Hill Carnival; the Brazilian carnivals; New Orleans Mardi Gras; the Mexican Day of the Dead.[5] Bakhtin suggests that in the Middle Ages the carnival played a much more prominent role in the life of the ordinary people, who inhabited a dual realm of existence: one official, characterized by the authority of the church, the feudal system, work, and one unofficial, characterized by reversal, parody, song, and laughter. Bakhtin claims that the carnivalization of literature

> proved remarkably productive as a means for capturing in art the developing relationships under capitalism, at a time when previous forms of life, moral principles and beliefs were being turned into 'rotten cords' and the previously concealed, ambivalent, and unfinalized nature of man and human thought was being nakedly exposed. (PDP166)

However, even here it is obvious that matters are not as straightforward as they seem. The role of the church, for instance, as an oppressive force is used ironically, or double-voicedly, by Bakhtin, Robert Stam suggests, to appear to fit in with Stalinist anti-clericalism, but actually speaking against it. Stam points out that Bakhtin takes favourite Stalinist themes, including '"folk art"', the '"people"' and 'the oppressiveness of the church' and makes them 'boomerang against Soviet officialdom'. In this way, Bakhtin matches his own theory with practice, as he is deploying the 'strategy of subversive co-optation or the "anthropophagic" devouring of dominant discourses'. In a Stalinist atmosphere, this is certainly a carnival exhibiting only 'laughter's footsteps'.[6]

In the Prologue to *Rabelais*, Michael Holquist also suggests that Bakhtin's own historical moment informed his treatment of carnival, and that what has often been thought of as his nostalgic view of a brutal past actually conflicts, or engages dialogically, with a much more oppressive idealism, that of Stalinism (RW xix).[7] Terry Eagleton places a different emphasis on the same point: 'in what is perhaps the boldest, most devious gesture in the history of

"Marxist criticism", Bakhtin pits against that "official, formalistic and logical authoritarianism" whose unspoken name is Stalinism the explosive politics of the body, the erotic, the licentious and semiotic.'[8] Bakhtin's book suffered from this conflict; he submitted *Rabelais* as a thesis in 1940, and it was published in the Soviet Union only twenty-five years later (RW xix). In another reversal, Bakhtin's formulation of grotesque realism is, as Holquist suggests, a point-by-point inversion of categories used in the Soviet Union in the 1930s to define Socialist Realism.[9] It is very tempting to see *Rabelais* as a dangerous joke at the expense of the Soviet authorities, and that it is they who are being lampooned obliquely when Bakhtin describes the medieval culture of *parodia sacra* (RW 14), the Feast of Fools (RW 78), carnival beatings (RW 265), donkeys' masses (RW 78), and Rabelais' complete reversal of the most authoritarian discourse by using it as the template for the 'absolutely gay and fearless talk, free and frank, [...] beyond all verbal prohibitions' of *Pantagruel*'s Prologue. Bakhtin identifies this as a parody of ecclesiastical rhetoric: 'behind the abuses and curses are the Church's intolerance, intimidation, and *autos-da-fé*'. He goes further, and claims that Rabelais' Prologue, written in the manner of a street hawker, by its carnival reversal 'travesties the very foundations of medieval thought, the methods of establishing truth and conviction which are inseparable from fear, violence, morose and narrow-minded seriousness and intolerance' (RW 167). This tone of moral certainty suggests the importance of Rabelais' use of popular culture in his work in a particular context, and perhaps Bakhtin's idea of himself performing a similar role in his own.

Folk humour

Bakhtin describes the 'folk carnival humor' which Rabelais draws upon as a 'boundless world of humorous forms and manifestations [which] opposed the official and serious tone of medieval ecclesiastical and feudal culture'. All the elements of this popular humour – 'folk festivities of the carnival type, the comic rites and cults, the clowns and fools, giant, dwarfs, and jugglers, the vast and manifold literature of parody' – can be categorized under three headings:

1 *Ritual spectacles*: carnival pageants, comic shows of the marketplace.
2 *Comic verbal compositions*: parodies both oral and written, in Latin and in the vernacular.

> 3 *Various genres of billingsgate*: curses, oaths, popular blazons. (RW 5)

These features can, according to Bakhtin, be traced in examples of carnivalesque literature.

In *Problems of Dostoevsky's Poetics*, Bakhtin adds detail to this list in his discussion of the 'transposition' of carnival's 'pageantry' into 'a language of artistic images that has something in common with its concretely sensuous nature' (PDP 122). The following are further characteristics of carnival, some of its literary form only, some of both this and its street form:

> 4 Carnival is 'a pageant without footlights and without a division into performers and spectators' (PDP 122), as its participants do not watch but *'live* in it', with its suspension of 'hierarchical structure and all the forms of terror, reverence, piety, and etiquette connected with it'.
>
> 5 Carnival allows *'free and familiar contact between people'* who would usually be separated hierarchically, and allows for 'mass action' (PDO 123).
>
> 6 Carnival *mésalliances* allow for unusual combinations: 'the sacred with the profane, the lofty with the low, the great with the insignificant, the wise with the stupid'.
>
> 7 Carnival profanation consists of 'a whole system of carnivalistic debasings and bringings down to earth', to the level of the body, particularly in the case of parodies of sacred texts.
>
> 8 Death and renewal are central to carnival, represented most often by the carnival act of 'the *mock crowning and subsequent decrowning of the carnival king'* (PDP 124); the two states are inseparable in the carnival view: crowning entails decrowning (PDP 125).
>
> 9 Carnival laughter is directed at exalted objects, and forces them to renew themselves; thus its debasing results in new life, and it is 'ambivalent' (PDP 126); '[m]uch was premitted in the form of laughter that was impermissible in serious form' (PDP 127).
>
> 10 Carnival parody survives in attenuated form in the 'narrowly formal literary' parody of modern times (PDP 128); in the original kind, '[e]verything has its parody, that is, its laughing aspect, for everything is reborn and renewed through death'.
>
> 11 Carnival in contemporary literature does survive generically, although its influence is usually limited to the work's content (PDP 132); its traces may be detected, for instance in representa-

tions of legends and unofficial history (Toni Morrison's *Beloved*, for instance), and certain kinds of laughter (PDP 165; Malcolm Lowry's *Under the Volcano*), image system (Angela Carter's *Nights at the Circus*), parody; within the individual character's 'ambivalent passions' (PDP 159; Bakhtin cites as examples George Sand's and Victor Hugo's novels).

12 A local carnival feature is its 'sense of a great city', such as St Petersburg (Dostoevsky), Paris (Balzac) (PDP 160), or London (Dickens).

Any list of carnival features should also include a thirteenth category, that of carnival time, which is characterized, as Bakhtin says, by '[m]oments of death and revival, of change and renewal [which] always led to a festive perception of the world'. The monologic authoritarianism of the feudal world explains the omnipresence of carnival, which was 'the people's second life' (PDP 8).[10] Carnival is the opposite of a time of terror or purges, as 'the true feast of time, the feast of becoming, change, and renewal. It was hostile to all that was immortalized and completed' (10). The important point about this is that renewal does not occur within the lifetime of an individual carnival subject, but within the body of the people as a whole: birth is always implicit within death. There are clearly positive elements in this cyclical, rather than linear, model of human life and history.[11] However, the idea of communal (rather than collective) survival, perhaps even at the expense of the individual, is exactly the problem the Russian critic Mikhail K. Ryklin identifies with this theory, in which he sees Bakhtin replacing the Stalinist purges' 'reality of denunciation and convulsions of suffering bodies, confessing their guilt under torture' by 'the coming-into-being of speech body-giants, gazing as if from the sidelines at the suffering of their chance individual incarnations'. In his 1993 article, Ryklin 'chillingly' describes *Rabelais and His World* as 'indirectly dedicated to the terror and dictated by it'. To point to the likely survival of the people as a whole or as an abstraction is, according to Ryklin, a way of blinding oneself to individual deaths – even when these deaths were murders, and suffered by friends and members of one's own circle. Read in such a light, Bakhtin's phrase 'The death of the individual is only a moment in the celebrating life of the folk and of humankind, a moment *necessary for their rejuvenation and completion*' sounds with extra intonation.[12] Bakhtin has allowed his theory to become infiltrated and deformed by Stalinist ideology, according to Ryklin, in contrast to Stam's sense that Bakhtin was manipulating the discourses of that ideology.

However, it is worth noting that Bakhtin sees the carnival-esque view of death as a way of combatting 'real' everyday and religious fears of death in the Middle Ages, conjured up by natural, 'divine and human power'. Such a 'victory over fear' was of course only 'ephemeral', as is the nature of carnival, but from these 'brief moments another unofficial truth emerged'. This suggests at least that Bakhtin sees the 'unofficial truth' of the people's bodily resur-gence as directly proportional to the real threats those people lived under.

Ryklin interprets *Rabelais and His World* as what Caryl Emerson calls 'a requiem' for the individual body, which she says is 'no wonder, for subversion, revolution, and the myth of a collec-tive "body of the people" that never hurts or dies no matter how much you torment it, understandably arouse less rapture in the ex-Soviet-Union than in the West'.[13] Ryklin suggests that Bakhtin has to adopt the theory of 'the life cycle that transcends the individual', to quote Nancy Glazener,[14] precisely because he lived in a regime where individuals were vanishing and being killed in huge numbers. Ryklin sees Bakhtin's attitude to carnival not as an apologia, which for someone who had suffered exile and censorship is unlikely, but as a rationalization based on his own position as a member of the intelligentsia under Stalin, which transformed him into a kind of hostage.[15] 'Only by opposing the ideal and imperishable image of folkness to terror as the catastrophe of the real folk could he survive', Ryklin says. Emerson points out that national history partly accounts for the different aspects of his theories Bakhtin is valued for in the West and Russia. While Western readers value his writings on 'the novel as subversive genre, carnival as permanent revolution, and culture as a battleground where marginal figures endlessly undermine all centers', in Russia his early essays on 'indi-viduation and personality' are more widely read.[16]

The long history of carnival led to the development of a 'rich idiom' of related symbols, which were characterized by the 'pathos of change and renewal' and the 'gay relativity of prevailing truths and authorities', Bakhtin says. The combination of cyclical time with the other significant carnivalesque movement, the 'logic of the "inside out", [...] of the "turnabout", of a continual shifting from top to bottom', leads naturally to parody, as the carnivalesque was a parody of official life. Bakhtin is keen to point out that carniva-lesque parody and travesty are quite different from 'the negative and formal parody of modern times', which only denies without renewing (PDP 10–11). This is a consistent thread in his argument: in modern versions of carnival laughter, 'billingsgate' profanations, and so on, only the downward half of the subverting movement has survived. This is particularly clear in Bakhtin's potted history of the fate of the carnivalesque in the centuries after the Renaissance.

Grotesque realism

Bakhtin describes the literary genre, originally medieval, of 'grotesque realism' as one opposed to all forms of high art and literature.[17] It includes parody and any other form of discourse which 'bring[s] down to earth' anything ineffable or authoritarian, a task achieved principally through mockery: 'The people's laughter which characterized all the forms of grotesque realism from immemorial times was linked with the bodily lower stratum. Laughter degrades and materializes' (RW 20). 'Degradation' is a typical and important operation of the grotesque. Its central trait is an ambivalent act: 'Degradation here means coming down to earth, the contact with the earth as an element that swallows up and gives birth at the same time' (RW 21). This ambivalence, particularly when it involves the new birth implicit in death, or the resurgence implicit in being toppled, is the characteristic principle of both grotesque realism and carnival itself. As well as working on the 'cosmic' level, degradation can be experienced at the level of the human body:

> To degrade also means to concern oneself with the lower stratum of the body, the life of the belly and the reproductive organs; it therefore relates to acts of defecation and copulation, conception, pregnancy, and birth. Degradation digs a bodily grave for a new birth. (RW 24)

Bakhtin points out that the terms 'upward' and 'downward' in grotesque realism do not have simply relative meanings, but 'strictly topographical' ones – and, one might add, what look like strictly gender-related ones. 'Downward' is earth, 'an element that devours, swallows up (the grave, the womb) and [is] at the same time an element of birth, or renascence (the maternal breasts)'; in its bodily aspect, 'the lower part is the genital organs, the belly, and the buttocks'. 'Upward' is heaven; 'the upper part' of the body 'is the face or the head' (RW 21).

Bakhtin suggests that the 'bodily element'[18] of carnival and grotesque realism concerns bodies in general and not bodies as distinguished by gender, which some critics see as transcending, others as succumbing to, the usual gender stereotypes. However, a familiar pattern seems to be described here. Earth and the reproductive body are associated with the feminine; heaven and the rational body with the masculine. Bakhtin concludes, 'Grotesque realism knows no other lower level; it is the fruitful earth and the womb. It is always conceiving'. This semi-metaphorical appropriation of the womb, and other aspects of the feminine, is admired by some critics as a way of retrieving categories which are usually ignored; and deplored by others, who see it as a 'de-femalising' of the female body, and point out that women's 'lives, like their bodies, are melted down into a generalised human existence'.[19] Ruth Ginsburg argues that Bakhtin's interest in pregnancy 'is a metaphoric appropriation of the feminine that has nothing to do with real or fictional females'.[20] The same critical split attends the apparent association of the grotesque itself with the feminine. If grotesque images are associated with the changes of time and 'copulation, pregnancy, birth, growth, old age, disintegration, dismemberment' (RW 25), then they seem to be closer to the feminine than to the masculine. Bakhtin, however, distinguishes the grotesque from its opposite, the classical, in terms of class rather than gender. 'Classic' aesthetics are associated with 'the ready-made [...] the finished, completed man, cleansed, as it were, of all the scoriae of birth and development' (RW 25). Rather than continue the masculine orientation this seems to have, Bakhtin gives a different interpretation of the coexistence of grotesque and classical in Renaissance realism: 'The ever-growing, inexhaustible, ever-laughing principle which uncrowns and renews is combined with its opposite: the petty, inert "material principle" of class society' (RW 24). Adding another dimension, Diane Roberts, in *The Myth of Aunt Jemima* racializes Bakhtin's binary of grotesque and classical within a single gender, and also across gender. The contest over the body was fuelled in the antebellum American South by a Bakhtinian polarity: 'Some bodies are "high", like the statue on the pedestal that so often represents white women in Southern culture, while some, like black women (and black men) are "low", represented by the unspeakable, "unclean" elements official culture would repress'.[21]

    If the Kerch terracottas of laughing 'senile pregnant hags' discussed by Bakhtin (RW 25) are representative of grotesque realism, then Greek and Roman statues are representative of classical aesthetics. In James Joyce's *Ulysses* (1922), when Leopold Bloom visits a museum, he secretly tries to see if the statues of women have any orifices – it is as if he is looking for the grotesque body in the classical one, but cannot find it. Bloom thinks,

> Lovely forms of women sculpted Junonian. Immortal lovely. And we stuffing food in one hole and out behind: food, chyle, blood, dung, earth, food: have to feed it like stoking an engine. They have no. Never looked. I'll look today. Keeper won't see. Bend down let something fall see if she.[22]

Bloom is unable to utter the grotesque word for what he is looking for; and he fails in his quest to find out whether or not these statues have any such attributes, because he is looking for the grotesque in the wrong place – a museum. Bakhtin describes the 'artistic canon of antiquity' in terms that fit Bloom's statues well: '[a]s conceived by these canons, the body was [...] isolated, alone, fenced off from all other bodies', its 'apertures closed'. Bloom is inspired by thoughts of the grotesque cycle of eating and excreting to inspect the statues, but, as Bakhtin points out, 'inner processes of absorbing and ejecting were not revealed' in the classical body. 'The individual body was presented apart from its relation to the ancestral body of the people', a state of affairs symbolized by the divide between Bloom here pretending to drop something on the floor so he can look up at the statues' lower bodily regions, and the statues themselves. We have seen him defecate, and eat offal, and will see him take a bath, and masturbate, while the statues are 'Immortal lovely'; he is a grotesque representative confronting the fact that the 'ever unfinished nature of the [classical] body was kept hidden' (RW 28–9).

Ambivalent carnival festivals

Bakhtin argues that the authoritarian Middle Ages meant that 'every feast in addition to its official, ecclesiastical part had yet another folk carnival part whose organizing principles were laughter and the material bodily lower stratum'. These alternative feasts were important to the people as holiday times, and as times associated with change and renewal. The 'immovable and extratemporal stability of the medieval hierarchy', which had 'eliminated' laughter from 'official cult and ideology', was faced by its other, 'the popular, humorous part of the feast' (RW 82), the second festive life of medieval people (RW 75). The eventual 'disintegration' of such a strict, feudal order contributed to the 'fusion of official and nonofficial', which is a state of affairs more familiar to Bakhtin's Western readers than strict polarization of the two realms. This 'fusion' allowed 'folk humor' to ascend to 'literature and ideology and fertilize it', as Bakhtin sees happening in Renaissance literature. In this new context, Bakhtin argues that Renaissance 'humanist knowledge and advanced literary techniques' combined with carnival forms and humour to produce 'a new free and critical *historical* consciousness', of which Rabelais is the arch exemplar (RW 72–3).

Bakhtin argues that dual images, combining praise and abuse, are characteristic of Rabelais, and of the ambivalence of grotesque realism, which may also blend comedy and tragedy, as the following example of narratorial address from the Prologue to Book 2 of *Pantagruel* shows:

> However, before I conclude this prologue, I hereby deliver myself up body and soul, belly and bowels, to a hundred thousand basketfuls of raving demons, if I have lied so much as once throughout this book. By the same token, may St. Anthony sear you with his erysipelatous fire [...] if you do not believe implicitly what I am about to relate in the present Chronicles. (RW 164)

Praise and abuse here, in this 'billingsgate' invective, are 'the two sides of the same coin', as Rabelais' image of the token suggests. The praise – or, in this case, the excessively servile assurances to the reader with which Rabelais starts out – is already 'ironic and ambivalent', and 'on the brink of abuse; the one leads to the other', and they 'belong to the same body'. Bakhtin sees the 'two-faced Janus' of simultaneous praise and abuse as part of grotesque realism's ambivalence:

> it is based on the conception of the world as eternally unfinished: a world dying and being born at the same time, possessing as it were two bodies. The dual image combining praise and abuse seeks to grasp the very moment of this change, the transfer from the old to the new, from death to life. Such an image crowns and uncrowns at the same moment. (RW 165)

As Bakhtin says, '[i]n the development of class society such a conception of the world can only be expressed in unofficial culture. There is no place for it in the culture of the ruling classes; here praise and abuse are clearly divided and static', because 'official culture is founded on the principle of an immovable and unchanging hierarchy in which the higher and the lower never merge' (RW 166).

Bakhtin observes that the alternative feasts which accompanied each regular feast were officially sanctioned, a fact which has made some recent critics pause over what kind of subversion they could offer.[23] One might also ask how Rabelais managed to get away with his own grotesquely realist treatment of the church, at a time of 'intolerance, intimidation, and *autos-da-fé*'.[24] Bakhtin suggests that this is because of Rabelais' double-voiced discourse, which could not be pinned down as dissent: 'The barker of a show would not be accused of heresy, no matter what he might say, provided he maintained his clownery. Rabelais maintained it' (RW 164). By contrast, Rabelais' friend Etienne Dolet died at the stake, because although his criticisms of the authorities were less damning, they were made seriously: 'He did not use Rabelais' methods' (RW 270) of double-voiced discourse. However, Bakhtin points out that the system of popular festive images adopted by Rabelais was not just a mechanical method of defence against censorship, 'an enforced adoption of Aesop's language'. Freedom was not an exterior right but the inner content of these images.

THE BODY IN BITS AND PIECES

Carnivalesque '"sacrificial" dismemberment' is a novelistic device, in which parts of the body are listed in an irreverent way. This 'dismemberment' is usually primarily linguistic; it unites the levels of language and image in carnival, and raises problems of its own on account of the nature of these particular images. Bakhtin cites an abusive exchange from Dostoevsky's short story 'Uncle's Dream', in which a Prince is abusively 'decrowned' in just such a linguistic dismemberment:

> 'Your *face* is on springs!'
> 'You have no *hair* of your own!'
> 'And the old fool's *moustache* is artificial, too' [...]
> 'At least leave me my *nose* [...]!' cried the Prince. (quoted PDP 161)

A more recent example, Jenefer Shute's novel *Life-size*, includes its own versions of this kind of '"carnival anatomy"'. Shute's novel is a first-person account by Josie, a young anorexic woman, of her hospitalized present and her disordered past. As we will see, Josie's preoccupation with *reducing* her bodily form and *not* eating makes her a Janus-faced version of carnival grotesquerie and excess. In her morning inventory of emaciation, a negative carnival anatomy, Josie omits the breasts, and congratulates herself on the body she has created, in which the only protuberances are bones: 'then I follow the outside of each thigh up towards the hips: no hint of a bulge, no softening anywhere [...] I press each buttock, checking that the bones are still sticking through'.[25]

Bakhtin quotes a passage from Book 1, Chapter 27 of Rabelais' *Pantagruel*, an actual and linguistic 'anatomization' of a casualty in Friar John's 'sausage war', where the Friar commands 154 cooks, armed with kitchen utensils, in battle:

> He brained some, smashed the legs and arms of others, broke a neck here, cracked a rib there. He flattened a nose or knocked an eye out, crushed a jaw or sent thirty-two teeth rattling down a bloody gullet. Some had their shoulderblades dislocated, others their thighs lammed to pulp, others their hips wrenched, others their arms battered beyond recognition. (RW 194)

Carnival is clearly tough for those on the receiving end. It may be comforting to argue that this 'anatomic and culinary treatment' of the body exists at both levels of grotesque realism, signifier and signified or language and image, and is not primarily realistic. By this dismemberment, Bakhtin argues, we are returned to 'the grotesque bodily billingsgate themes: diseases, monstrosities, organs of the lower stratum'. All of these genres, Bakhtin claims, irrespective of 'their literal content', refer to 'the unofficial aspect of the world, unofficial in tone (laughter) and in contents (the lower stratum)' (RW 195). However, Bakhtin's distinction between form and content is not very clear here; if the 'tone' of the Friar John dismemberment is one of 'laughter', then its contents cannot be discarded, and they become even more relevant when we try to recognize the 'lower stratum' in them.

At other times, the relationship between form and content in *Rabelais and His World* is not glossed over so quickly. Interestingly, Bakhtin finds the roots of some of Rabelais' style in the cries of street hawkers, the *cris de Paris*, which offered a realm of 'the proclaimed word', the naming of objects for their own sake. Rabelais' lists of different dishes and utensils (not to mention a list of twelve synonyms for excrement (RW 175)) suggest that the world itself is being offered up for consumption or sale, as it is in 'the cries of the street vendors'. Despite being materially linked to their signifieds by the hope of monetary exchange, these formalized and easily recognized street cries are already signifiers. They 'represent in themselves a noisy kitchen' (RW 182), not just because they advertise food but because of the kitchen-like clatter and confusion their utterance creates. The same double-levelled word-play, which disrupts expectations of both form and sense, is seen in the names of 'joke saints', whose new names suggest either indecencies or feasting (RW 192).

The 'gay thrashing' of the Catchpoles is also, according to Bakhtin, an 'uncrowning' episode typical of carnivalesque ambivalence. The Catchpoles in Book 4 of Rabelais' *Pantagruel* live on their own island and earn their living by letting themselves be thrashed (RW 196), although they also appear as 'slanderers' summoning the Lord of Basché to court (RW 200). In the latter episode, what we are reading is 'time itself', as this is 'the very image of a bodily harvest' (RW 208), and not the very reality. Bakhtin is quick to assure the squeamish, contemporary reader that 'Rabelais does not torture living persons' (RW 214). Again, carnivalesque degradation as a prelude to raising up takes place at the level of signifier and signified. In a carnival reversal, the perpetrators of the Catchpole thrashing act out the parts of victims, each one giving 'an exaggerated description of his injury in incredibly long and complex orations' which 'illustrate by various sounds the nature of the injury':

> The length and variety of the syllables render the number and violence of the blows. When spoken, they cripple the organs of speech, like tongue twisters. [...] Thanks to this method, the unrestrained character of carnival penetrates the *language* of this scene. (RW 204; my italics)

The recitation of injuries in increasing numbers of syllables – '"They were not content to maimanglescotchblemishdisfigurepunch my poor eye, they had to bash in my drum"' – is accompanied by the beating of the wedding drum this 'slanderer' mentions, which, like the 'bridal cuffing' itself, symbolizes 'the sexual act'. This symbolism means that the distressing-sounding fight in fact consists of 'no commonplace blows administered in everyday life. The blows have here a broadened, symbolic, ambivalent meaning; they at once kill and regenerate, put an end to the old life and start the new' (RW 205). Unfortunately for readers wishing to assure themselves that this is the case, Bakhtin rather confusingly adds that 'the thrashing of the Catchpoles has also a fully realistic meaning, as far as the seriousness of the injuries and their final aim are concerned'. Bakhtin means 'fully realistic' partly in the sense that this drama is enacted 'without footlights [...] within life itself' (RW 265). The blows are also 'realistic' in the context of the plot of *Pantagruel* (Lord Basché is freed from his enemies' intrigues by thrashing these

Catchpoles), and as part of carnival regeneration: the Catchpoles' beating is 'a feast of death and regeneration', although they personally do not benefit much from the regeneration.

The scene from Rabelais in which Gargamelle gives birth to Gargantua has also attracted critics' attention as an episode in which the 'literal' meaning of the grotesque, 'ambivalent' violence seems to be glossed over particularly glibly by Bakhtin. In this episode, Gargamelle has eaten too much tripe, and her labour begins 'precisely at the moment when her right intestine [falls] out due to the overeating of tripe, the intestines of fattened oxen' (RW 221). Gargamelle's labour, and the reason for its inception, makes a 'link between the devoured tripe with those who devour them. [...] The bodies [of human and animal] are interwoven and begin to be fused in one grotesque image of a devoured and devouring world'. Gargamelle dies giving birth to Gargantua, but, as Bakhtin cheerily reports, this theme has a renewing ambivalence too: 'The caesarian operation kills the mother but delivers the child' (RW 206). He uses this image as if it were neutral:

> One of the fundamental tendencies of the grotesque image of the body is to show two bodies in one: the one giving birth and dying, the other conceived, generated, and born. This is the pregnant and begetting body, or at least a body ready for conception and fertilization, the stress being laid on the phallus or the genital organs. (RW 26)

However, there is again an implicit gender division here: one gender gives birth, is pregnant, conceives, with its 'genital organs', while the other generates, begets and fertilizes, with the 'phallus'. It is unfortunate for the mother that it is invariably she who represents the 'old' which must give way to the 'new': 'Every blow dealt to the old helps the new to be born' (RW 206) sounds suitably metaphorical, unlike 'Two heartbeats are heard; one is the mother's, which is slowed down' (RW 26).

The Bakhtinian grotesque and the Kristevan abject

Bakhtin says that the ambivalence of grotesque realism is no longer properly understood. Contemporary readers see only the negative pole of billingsgate, 'gay thrashings', and the bodily lower stratum in texts like Rabelais'; and any contemporary version of the grotesque will feature only its downward, not its regenerative, aspect. The reason Bakhtin gives for the current absence of the grotesque is the onset of capitalism and privatized, individual life. A slightly different way to look at the grotesque, and the way in which, as Bakhtin recognizes, it will often be viewed by contemporary readers, is that of Julia Kristeva's 'abjection'.[26] Kristeva's influential essay on Bakhtin's intertextuality and dialogism, 'Word, Dialogue, and Novel', is dated 1966, a year after *Rabelais and His World* was published. In that essay, Kristeva mentions carnival only briefly, but seems to assume that her view of its 'underlying unconscious' structure of 'sexuality and death' is shared by Bakhtin.[27] In *Powers of Horror: An Essay on Abjection*, Kristeva mentions Rabelais and carnival only in passing, but her concept of abjection could be seen as a psychoanalytically inflected development of Bakhtin's grotesque.[28] Even if the link between the two concepts is not that of Kristeva's debt to Bakhtin, Kristeva's model offers a different and more modern way of viewing the same phenomena Bakhtin discusses. Rather than contradicting Bakhtin's theory, hers can be seen as an extension of his.

Kristeva's theory of abjection depends on her theory of the human subject, which at once distinguishes her from Bakhtin, who adheres to a humanist view. Critics suggest that Kristeva's concept arises from a combination of Lacanian psychoanalysis with the Bakhtinian grotesque.[29] According to Kristeva, the child exists at first in the maternal semiotic realm, characterized by the bodily rhythms and pulsions which will later form the basis of language and grammar. The child then enters the symbolic realm, as it becomes socialized and learns to speak; this is the paternal arena of language, law, and gender difference, in which we all exist most of the time. The semiotic, however, is not entirely lost but continues to exert pressure on the symbolic from within, in the form of linguistic or bodily lapses. The mother educates the child in the ways of the symbolic, through social codes of cleanliness, bodily boundaries, how and what to eat, and so on. This educative role means that the maternal must be rejected along with the unacceptable practices the mother has taught the child to reject.

Any lapse from the symbolic code may threaten to cast the human subject back into the unmeaning of the semiotic, to the dismay of that subject. However, Kristeva suggests that the subject's position in the symbolic realm is precariously maintained, and anything that threatens to send the subject back into the semiotic is accompanied by sensations of dread and, more significantly, disgust and revulsion. Sensations of nausea experienced when one is confronted with certain kinds of bodily fluid, for instance, represent one's urge to keep the pollutant out of one's way; bodily fluids, such as blood, mucous, or urine, are signs of health when they are within the body, but signs of a dangerous transgression of boundaries when they are outside. This sense of pollution has nothing necessarily to do with the danger of being literally poisoned; in most cases, the threat to the subject from an unacceptable substance is metaphorical. Kristeva calls the moment in which the subject is confronted by the abyss which opens up when it experiences such nausea, 'abjection'; the subject is 'thrown down', towards a boundary its existence is premised on forgetting.

Many of the images and practices which go to make up grotesque realism also fall under the heading of the Kristevan abject. Both Bakhtin and Kristeva are interested in five central categories: the margins of the body; the maternal; food; death; and the text. Bakhtin's approach to each attempts to reclaim a positive sense of the grotesque. Kristeva, by contrast, tries to explain why the phenomena associated with each of these categories might seem to us 'coarse and cynical', disgusting, or obscene.

I will use Jenefer Shute's novel *Life-size* (1992) in the following discussion of the grotesque and abjection, as it offers a modern perspective on both, from the viewpoint of an anorexic woman. The material bodily principle in *Life-size* is as significant as in *Gargantua and Pantagruel*, but quite differently oriented. Josie, the first-person narrator of *Life-size*, suffers from the dualist thinking Bakhtin identifies in the split between the higher and lower regions in classical canons, and which Kristeva sees as the basis of the subject's fear of a plunge back into the semiotic: the subject does not wish to be reminded of its bodily origins. In Josie's case this takes a Cartesian turn, as she imagines that a 'self' of some kind can exist without its material vessel. Her condition originates in a perception of this dualism as a schoolgirl: 'Buried in this blubbery disguise was my true form; the sharp but delicate articulation of a self'; her approaching death is expressed as the dualism's triumph: '[my brain's] never been purer and less cluttered, concentrated on essentials instead of distracted by a body clamoring for attention, demanding that its endless appetites be appeased'; and approaching health is represented tentatively as the healing of the split: 'Don't say "I have a body", Suzanne tells me, say "I am a body" [...] if I had a body, what would I be?'[30]

I will discuss in turn each category shared by Bakhtin and Kristeva: the margins of the body; the maternal; food; death; and the text.

BODILY MARGINS

Bakhtin emphasizes introjection and expulsion, and transgressing these margins. He says that the open, unfinished nature of the body and its interactions with the world are revealed 'most fully and concretely' in the act of eating, because the 'body transgresses here its own limits [...] Here man tastes the world, introduces it into his body, makes it part of himself' (RW 281). He says of various bodily junctions – mouth, nose, anus, phallus – that 'within them [...] the confines between bodies and between the body and the world are overcome: there is an interchange and an interorientation'. In a central passage, Bakhtin describes the most important events in the life of the grotesque body, which all take place in this realm of 'interorientation':

> Eating, drinking, defecation and other elimination (sweating, blowing of the nose, sneezing), as well as copulation, pregnancy, dismemberment, swallowing up by another body – all these acts are performed on the confines of the body and the outer world, or on the confines of the old and new body. (RW 317)

Each of the activities described here is an example of abjection, according to Kristeva. Of eating and drinking she observes that 'food loathing is perhaps the most elementary and most archaic form of abjection', and describes the revulsion the skin on milk provokes in her: 'When the eyes see or the lips touch that skin on the surface of milk – harmless, thin as a sheet of cigarette paper, pitiful as a nail paring – I experience a gagging sensation, and, still farther down, spasms in the stomach, the belly'.[31] The skin on milk can be revolting, and is grotesque, because it forms the boundary between two elements and two different forms: liquid and solid. It also appears apparently from nowhere, upsetting the idea that milk is an inert substance. Further, as a boundary, it may remind the drinker of her own skin. The effects on the subject are potentially disruptive: 'I spit *myself* out, I abject *myself* within the same motion through which "I" claim to establish *myself*'.

Kristeva's interest in the protuberances and convexities which go to make up the margins of the body takes a different form from Bakhtin's; rather than simply describe their importance, she traces it back to the subject's history. Maternal authority 'shapes the body into a territory having areas, orifices, points and lines, surfaces and hollows, where the archaic power of mastery and neglect, of the differentiation of proper-clean and improper-dirty [...] is impressed and exerted'.[32] The margins, protuberances, and convexities are not predetermined but 'shaped' by the maternal voice with which they are ever after associated, and therefore rendered potential sites of abjection. Bakhtin produces categories of his own to distinguish grotesque bodily zones from those which are not grotesque. For instance, the eyes are not grotesque unless they are protruding; although they may seem like marginal organs, they are usually too associated with the individuality of the face (RW316), which is too 'expressive' a bodily part to be grotesque (unless it is red, with a gaping mouth). Eyes which bulge are grotesque, because the grotesque 'is looking for that which protrudes from the body, all that seeks to go out beyond the body's confines. Special attention is given to the shoots and branches, to all that prolongs the body and links it to other bodies or to the world outside' (RW 317).

Kristeva goes further than Bakhtin, and her explanation of the abject clearly has a psychoanalytic basis; psychoanalysis was a system of thought from which a member of the Bakhtin circle, V. N. Volosinov, had distanced himself. Kristeva criticizes anthropologist Mary Douglas, whose structuralist work influenced *Powers of Horror* quite considerably, for 'naively' rejecting a Freudian framework.[33] The same might be said of Bakhtin, who in *Rabelais* discusses the nose, for instance, and other critics' ignorance of 'the meaning of the grotesque image of the nose: that it always symbolizes the phallus' (RW 316). In *Freudianism: A Critical Sketch*, Volosinov discusses the same cluster of meanings in a tone of astonishment. 'Behind the most innocent-seeming and commonplace of artistic images some erotic object is always decipherable' (F 59), he says, in a stylization of the Freudian thought which is characterized by 'the mighty and fundamental melody of sex'. Volosinov quotes a Russian critic, I. D. Ermakov, on Gogol's story *The Nose* (1836): '[t]he nose in 'Nose' turns out to be, according to Ermakov, a substitute symbol for the penis. Underlying the whole theme of the loss of one's nose [...] is *the castration complex: fear of the loss of one's penis or one's sexual potency*' (F 59). Volosinov dismisses this interpretation on the grounds that it assumes the content of art-works is derived from '*premises in individual psychology*', so that '[n]o room is left for the reflection of objective socioeconomic existence with its forces and conflicts'. Even if images of social and economic reality do appear in art, Volosinov argues that according to a Freudian reading, we have to see them as substitutes: 'behind such images, as behind Major Kovalev's nose, invariably lurks somebody's erotic complex' (F 60). This irony sounds a little odd beside Bakhtin's criticism of the critic Schneegans for his ignorance of the grotesque link between nose and penis. Bakhtin, of course, has in mind a carnival reversal or rotation rather than a crypto-psychoanalytic view, in which nose and phallus more literally substitute for one another, as his description of the 'movements of the clown' suggests: 'the buttocks persistently trying to take the place of the head and the head that of the buttocks' (RW 353). Bakhtin even includes a version (equally non-psychoanalytic, it is true) of castration anxiety in his discussion of the grotesque properties of the nose: as well as the phallus, he observes that '[t]he nose can also in a way detach itself from the body' (RW 317). While Kristeva gives an account of abjection in terms of the psyche, Bakhtin sees the contemporary negative view of the grotesque as part of a historical decline into privatized existence.

In his discussion of other substances which breach bodily boundaries, Bakhtin calls urine and dung 'gay matter', which degrade and transform (RW 335); if they are considered unseemly, it is because of their material, life-giving qualities. They are indeed *qualities* here, as Bakhtin is not interested in the reasons why such substances should have been associated with life. He does give a commentary on the reason why the classical has suppressed the life-giving aspect of the bodily lower stratum and its products. He says that, when food and labour stop being collective, the grotesque element in them dies: 'Work triumphed in food [...] If food is separated from work and conceived as a private way of life, then nothing remains of the old images: man's encounter with the world and tasting the world, the open mouth, the relation of food and speech' (RW 281). This is why the image of corpulence, for example, leads a split life. 'The soul of the people as a whole cannot coexist with the private, limited, greedy body', and images of 'heroic popular gluttons', like Gros Guillaume, are quite different from 'the insatiable simonist abbot' (RW 292). Bakhtin says the same of the 'radically changed' meaning of the body's 'sexual life, eating, drinking, and defecation' in the modern image: 'they have been transferred to the private and psychological level [...] torn away from the direct relation to the life of society and to the cosmic whole' (RW 321). Volosinov argues that psychoanalysis itself might be seen as a symptom of the modern era. He attributes to all decadent movements, including the contemporary decline of the bourgeois world and the attendant rise of psychoanalysis, a 'fear of history, a shift in orientation toward the values of personal, private life, the primacy of the biological and the sexual in man' (F 11).

Robert Stam claims that 'Bakhtin's vision exalts the "base"

products of the body: feces, urine, sperm, menstrual flow'. Bakhtin also suggests that each stands in for the other, in an unhierarchized way. Kristeva, by contrast, distinguishes these fluids by dividing them into two types, excremental (which includes 'decay, infection, disease, corpse, etc.') and menstrual; while '[n]either tears nor sperm [...] have any polluting value'. Excrement and death stand for an external threat, but menstrual blood represents 'the danger issuing from within the identity (social or sexual)'.[34] In *Life-size*, food is as polluting to Josie as these 'products', as her comparisons of food with excrement, mucous and urine suggest.[35] The emanations of sexual difference, however, come in for special scorn: 'Who, given the choice, would really opt to menstruate, invite the monthly hemorrhage – a reminder that the body is nothing but a bag of blood, liable to seep or spatter at any moment?'[36] What Josie fears here is exactly what Bakhtin would praise: the body capable of transgressing its own boundaries, of mixing up inner and outer realms, recognizing its composition out of the 'gay matter' of blood and urine.

An internal battle between classical and grotesque has led Josie to her anorexic mind–body divide. She aims for classical deletion of the 'sprouts and buds' of the grotesque and, in this case at least, female body, and any evidence of its lower bodily stratum. Josie is keen to construct an absolute boundary between her body and everybody else's; she thinks, 'Other people: bodies you can't control'.[37] The grotesque, according to Bakhtin, draws the confines between 'the body and the world and between separate bodies' quite differently from 'classical and naturalist images' (RW 315). Josie is also keen to maintain the body–world distinction criticized by Bakhtin. As well as insisting on a rigid distinction between self and body, she insists on a division between surface and substance. She wants to avoid exactly the grotesque permeability and interactiveness described by Bakhtin: 'the artistic logic of the grotesque image ignores the closed, smooth, and impenetrable surface of the body and retains only its excrescences (sprouts, buds) and orifices, only that which leads beyond the body's limited space or into the body's depths' (RW 318).

The avoidance of the grotesque becomes a complex expression of Josie's sickness. She wants to attain bodily closure, for instance, by using a *Vogue* cover to shield her face because the model's skin is a 'sealed and poreless stretch of pink'. As an economics postgraduate, she reads a topology textbook, 'the study of those properties of figures that remain unchanged [...] so long as no surfaces are torn', and wishes to lick its lollipop-red cover rather than open it.[38] It appears that her anorexia is partly a symptom of her fierce allegiance to intactness. The imagined intrusion of a catheter for force-feeding is little different from the intrusions of intercourse or admitting the desire to eat: 'my frenzy led me to seek something to cram into myself, while [men] crave something into which to cram themselves'.[39] Kristeva also speaks of food's potential to 'penetrate' the self's 'clean and proper body'.[40] All these features go against Bakhtin's postive emphasis on consumption and ejection, merging and uncertain boundaries, excess and licence; Kristeva's darker view of the same categories fits Josie's eating disorder better.

THE MATERNAL

In the second of Kristeva's categories, Bakhtin criticizes the classical body which bears no sign of its origin;[41] and claims that 'There can be nothing terrifying on earth, just as there can be nothing frightening in a mother's body' (RW 91). He does point out that, from the point of view of the classical, the womb is seen as 'the earthly element of terror', while the grotesque sees in it simply 'new life'. According to this view, the classical has historically superseded the grotesque.

Kristeva starts from the premise that the womb and the maternal *are* seen as terrifying, and tries to explain why this is so. In her view, the symbolic, with its classical outlook, supersedes, if imperfectly, the grotesquely oriented semiotic in every individual. Kristeva emphasizes the threat of the abject to the already unstable symbolic 'in its most significant aspect – the prohibition placed on the maternal body'. Devotees of the abject, Kristeva argues, keep looking for 'the desirable and terrifying, nourishing and murderous, fascinating and abject inside of the maternal body'.[42] Bakhtin describes a similar-sounding body: 'the body that interests [Rabelais] is pregnant, delivers, defecates, is sick, dying, and dismembered'. However, although it may be implicitly female, hidden in this body's sickness is only the surprise of regeneration, not of horrified desire. Kristeva describes the fascination the link between childbirth and death held for her literary exemplar, novelist Louis-Ferdinand Céline, as 'the height of bloodshed and life, scorching moment of hesitation (between inside and outside, ego and other, life and death)'.[43]

As we saw in the case of real death-threats, and the resulting appearance of carnival images of 'laughing death' in the Middle

Ages, according to Bakhtin there is a causal link between the two: the stronger the threat, the more important are 'unofficial' images. In the case of the grotesque and its apparent ignorance of the fear-inspiring and violent underpinnings of its own images, Bakhtin proposes a similar link. Carnival versions of death and abject bodily terror are 'droll and monstrous'; the 'symbols of power and violence [are] turned inside out', into 'comic images of death and bodies gaily rent asunder'. The grotesque itself *exists only as a carnival form*: its real-life original is everything that is 'terrifying', but, within the culture of medieval laughter, '[a]ll that was terrifying becomes grotesque' (RW 91). Bakhtin is not concerned here with the 'real' terror, only with the carnival version which we see represented in Rabelais' work: hence Bakhtin's silence on the former (and hence Ryklin's discomfort). Thus it could be argued that it is knowledge, and not ignorance, of something like the Kristevan abject that is the reason for the 'falsely cheerful' imagery of the grotesque. The two realms, in this reading, are not alternatives but Janus-faced versions of each other.

In *Life-size*, Josie links pregnancy with food. Ostensibly, this is a link which should draw her closer to Bakhtin, who dwelt on the labour of Gargamelle precisely because it confused devourer with devoured, and the different functions of belly and womb, which are often spoken of in *Rabelais and His World* as if they were one organ. Bakhtin says that in Gargantua's birth-scene, '[t]he limits between animal flesh and the consuming human flesh are dimmed, very nearly erased [...] One dense bodily atmosphere is created, the atmosphere of the great belly.' As we saw in relation to Kristeva's rejection of the skin on milk, from the viewpoint of the abject, confusing devourer and devoured can be a moment of horror rather than a moment of 'generating and growing superabundance' (RW 221). In *Life-size*, food and the body threaten to merge in a way which revolts Josie, and gives her reason to reject that food. Strawberries are 'scabrous' while scabs are 'mulberry'; a tomato has a 'woody navel'; the vegetable attributes of an 'ear of corn' disappear under its metaphorical associations: 'an ear, a hunk of muscle, thick brown blood: something dismembered'.[44] Clearly, the overlap between body and food is also linguistic here, and critical explorations have been made of the links between self-starvation and either a reduced or an abundant language.[45] Josie's suspicion of a baked potato, 'completely sealed in its papery skin. I cannot decide where to slit it, stab it, spill its mealy guts',[46] is based partly on abjection at the signified, the potato – like her, it has a skin which may be 'stabbed' – but also partly on the signifier, as her use of the emotive word 'guts', and alliteration of the verbs of assault, suggest.

Josie has no time for idealizations of pregnancy, which she sees simply as super-fatness, caused by over-eating or an analogous appetite. After taking great pains with an apple and a cube of cheese, she describes herself as 'palming my belly to gauge the swelling there. I'm pregnant already, pregnant with matter that will soon be me'.[47] Again, Josie fears exactly what Bakhtin praises in the scene of Gargantua's birth during the 'feast of cattle slaughter': 'Gargamelle's labor and the falling out of the right intestine link the devoured tripe with those who devour them' (RW 221).

The realm of the maternal raises once more the issue of femininity within the grotesque, although, as we have noted, Bakhtin's theory depends on the moment of 'interchange', as he puts it (RW 317), where the body 'transgresses its own limits' (RW 281), rather than separate bodies or their genders. This is the 'impersonal' body' (FTC 173), as the grotesque image 'never presents an individual body' (RW 318). The lists Bakhtin gives of 'apertures [...] and offshoots', and ways in which the body exceeds its own limits (RW 26), cite together male and female attributes and activities. Some critics have suggested that this makes the grotesque an 'androgynous' or gender-free realm, in a positive way;[48] or, on the other hand, as we have seen, that its adoption of feminine bodily functions writes actual women out of the picture. Ruth Ginsburg says of Bakhtin's treatment of maternity that 'pregnancy is a metaphoric appropriation of the feminine that has nothing to do with real or fictional females', and Pam Morris observes that Gargamelle's death while giving birth to a boy may not be a particularly ambivalent event for female readers in any positive way. Mary Russo says that Bakhtin 'failed to incorporate the social relations of gender in his semiotic model of the body politic',[49] in her discussion of the Kerch terracotta figurines of 'laughing' and 'senile pregnant hags'. This is Bakhtin's description of them:

> This is a typical and very strongly expressed grotesque. It is ambivalent. It is pregnant death, a death that gives birth. There is nothing completed, nothing calm and stable in the bodies of these old hags. They combine a senile, decaying and deformed flesh with the flesh of new life, conceived but as yet unformed. (RW 25)

From the point of view of classical aesthetics, Bakhtin continues, the pregnant hags are 'ugly, monstrous, hideous', but, as grotesque, they are 'ambivalent', representing 'a death that gives birth'. Ann

Jefferson argues that Bakhtin's discussion of the pregnant hags offers a completely new evaluation of 'death, the feminine, and degradation in general';[50] that is, he reverses the negative connotations of excessive femininity.

As Russo says, contrary to Jefferson's positive view, Bakhtin's interest in these hags glosses over exactly how the image is 'more than ambivalent'. It is an image remarkable not only as an example of irreverent old age producing life but as one 'loaded with all of the connotations of fear and loathing around the biological processes of reproduction and of aging' in women.[51] This is another example of the difference between Bakhtin's and Kristeva's approach: while Kristeva starts with this fear and loathing, and bases her analysis of the non-classical body upon it, Bakhtin looks back to a mythic age in which the communal pleasures of feasting and drinking, giving birth and excreting, were unproblematically recognized. Kristeva argues that '[w]e are envious of the renascent mirth of Rabelais who give himself up, trustfully, to the pleasures of a palate where mankind becomes intoxicated, thinking it has found guiltless flesh, mother and body'.[52] According to her, and *pace* Bakhtin, there never was a time of guiltless flesh, or filth without defilement. It is only by ignoring the 'fear and loathing' implicit in the figurines of pregnant old women that Bakhtin can see them as ambivalent in a positive way.

THE EDIBLE

The third category, food, links, for Bakhtin, the idea of community (it is eaten at feast times) with bodily margins, as it is an obvious example of a healthy transgression of the body's confines and the enlargement of the individual's self. Through the mouth, 'man tastes the world, introduces it into his body, makes it part of himself [...] The limits between man and the world are erased, to man's advantage' (RW 281). Bakhtin discusses various specific kinds of food and drink, including sausages and tripe, in a way which notably ignores their abject potential. Tripe represents the belly which eats and the belly which is eaten; it is linked with other 'stomachic' processes, including both defecation and birth, and with death, since 'to disembowel is to kill'. It thus sets in 'play the merging of 'the upper with the lower sphere', in usual grotesque fashion. Bakhtin also draws attention to the punning surrounding the word 'tripe' (RW 163), which shifts the grotesque to a linguistic level: the word refers to the food consumed and to the consumer's own intestines. Kristeva, as one might expect, describes the fantasy of confusing bowels and womb in abjection, links it to the subject's incorporation of a 'devouring and intolerable mother' whose interior is associated with excremental decay, and to the subject's attempt to give birth to themselves.[53] Kristeva's interest in food is in the construction of food taboos and the distinctions between what is considered edible and what is not. She discusses its polluting properties, and the efforts of clean and proper subjects to avoid excessive contact between the social and the organic repre- sented both by food and by excrement. Again, in Kristeva's view, it is as if grotesque and classical are not diachronically arranged, separated from each other in time, as Bakhtin suggests, but coexist synchronically within each individual subject. As she puts it, 'abjec- tion is resorbed in the grotesque: a way of living it from the inside'.[54] The subject must constantly negotiate between its exis- tence in the symbolic order and the pull to semiotic chaos threatened by abjection.

As we have seen, Kristeva argues that food abjection is a widespread phenomenon. Her disgust at the skin on milk is the modern counterpart to Bakhtin's enthusiasm for tripe, and an example of the kind of 'common domestic abjection', as Allon White calls it,[55] well known from anyone's experience of either eating or reading. As milk is food offered by mothers, refusing it altogether may amount to a phobic 'disintegration of the taboo barring contact with the mother', Kristeva says.[56] This is almost what happens in Gargantua's birth-scene, which is also Garga- melle's death-scene; although she is not literally consumed by her newborn son, Gargamelle dies so that he might live. Kristeva argues that 'abjection dread' can 'explain the incest dread of which Freud speaks'; it protects one from the 'temptation' to return to the maternal semiotic. Abjection, she argues, preserves the 'immemor- ial violence with which a body becomes separated from another body in order to be'.[57] In the birth-scene from Rabelais, the 'immemorial violence' is represented in almost fantasied form, but no anxiety.

Bakhtin observes that 'in the image of tripe life and death, birth, excrement, and food are all drawn together and tied in one grotesque knot' (RW 163). At the '"feast of cattle slaughter"', Gargamelle '"eats too abundantly"' of tripe, with the result that her '"right intestine (you call it the bumgut")' falls out, and is mistaken for a child; the child, however, is born through her left ear, as the overeating has enlarged a vein leading from her 'matrix' to her head (RW 220–6).[58] Bakhtin observes:

The dividing line between man's consuming body and the consumed animal's body is once more erased [...] the right intestine that fell out, the consumed ox tripe, the womb that is giving birth (the mother's intestine is mistaken for the baby) – all these elements are indissolubly interwoven. (RW 225)

The erasing of a dividing line in all the cases Bakhtin describes would result in a psychotic crisis for the Kristevan subject, rather than an image of the Bakhtinian 'ever-regenerated body of the people' (RW 226). Kristeva argues that such divisions are maintained by religious, and other, 'rituals of defilement', which function 'to ward off the subject's fear of his very own identity sinking irretrievably into the mother'. It is possible to read the scene of Gargantua's birth in this light. In the absence here of any 'rituals of defilement', anything can be eaten and boundaries merge both within and between bodies, human and animal: 'The abject confronts us [...] with those fragile states where man strays on the territories of *animal*'.[59] Gargamelle symbolically devours, and then is devoured by, her own son; nothing has prevented either of them succumbing to the abjection of incest.

DEATH

The fourth category, death, is never an isolated event for Bakhtin, but a hybrid process which includes birth. Morson and Emerson, who are unhappy with many of the implications of carnival, observe that for the carnivalistic self, death is 'like cell division [...] there are no dead bodies'.[60] This image captures neatly the idea that, although the original 'cell' or 'self' has died 'in a sense' (RW 19) by disappearing, there is a 'body' which carries on; and its method of reproduction knows no gender difference. As Bakhtin says, continuing the amoebic slant, in the grotesque body 'death brings nothing to an end, for it does not concern the ancestral body, which is renewed in the next generation' (RW 322). Thus '[i]n Rabelais' novel the image of death is devoid of all tragic or terrifying overtones [...] It is the other side of birth' (RW 39). Carnival 'degradation' is regenerative as well as destructive – it 'digs a bodily grave for a new birth' – in contrast to contemporary degradation, which enacts only the downward movement.

'The combination of birth and killing is characteristic of the grotesque conception of the body and bodily life' (RW 248), Bakhtin observes, though a modern reader in the era of what he calls 'degenerated' carnival might think it more characteristic of violent misogyny. Of his comment quoted earlier, 'The caesarian operation kills the mother but delivers the child' (RW 206), Bakhtin says that this is a Rabelaisian image of fixing the moment between old and new. Again, why this particular old and new should be an appropriate image is not examined; as Ruth Ginsburg puts it, Bakhtin follows Rabelais in seeing 'the old as the mother and the new as the son'.[61] The very combination of death and birth for a 'degenerated' reader might be a potent moment of abjection: it confuses important boundaries, and brings to the fore any fear the subject might have that the counterpart to the mother's life-giving abilities are the ability to take life away again.

Kristeva sees death as a site of abjection: 'refuse and corpses show me what I premanently thrust aside in order to live'; and, 'If dung signifies the other side of the border, the place where I am not and which permits me to be, the corpse, most sickening of wastes, is a border that has encroached upon everything'. While most waste products affirm the subject who has converted them into objects, in the case of the corpse a subject has itself become waste and been thrown out. This is not death as part of a life-giving process, as in the grotesque, but death which threatens the foundations of life in the symbolic order: 'The corpse, seen without God and outside of science, is the utmost of abjection. It is death infecting life.'[62] For Bakhtin, the reverse is true, and life infects death: 'Death is included in life' (RW 50). As in the case of all the other categories, it seems that abjection is the grotesque of modernity, its darker version: it is equivalent not to the classical, which turns its back on the organic, but to a frightening grotesque.[63]

In the case of Josie in *Life-size*, death is the narrative and bodily ending that is avoided, as the title suggests. There is no carnivalesque ambivalence about the avoided end. Death is the logical conclusion to Josie's separation of mind and body, and to the anorexic trajectory: Josie is not in stasis but in decline. Josie's declaration, 'One day I will be pure consciousness, traveling unmuffled through the world; one day I will refine myself to the bare wiring, the irreducible circuitry that keeps me alive', is later replaced by her perception that, 'the more I reduced [the body], the less I found'.[64] There is little ambivalence here.

THE TEXT

Finally, the text may be the most appropriate site for either the grotesque or the abject, as it is for the carnivalesque. Kristeva says of abjection that its 'signifier, then, is nothing but literature': literature is the sign of its presence, and its best expression.[65] Bakhtin pointed out that in the case of Rabelais' descriptions of the Catchpoles' thrashing, and the wedding-feast beating, language is the central factor in grotesque realism. He argues that familiar blows are the tangible equivalent of improper speech, as in both cases 'freedom and equality' are expressed. Of Rabelais' banquet imagery he says that the images themselves, in their excess and display, resemble the giant buns and sausages of carnival processions (RW 278).[66] Two out of the three carnival features which Bakhtin lists are verbal manifestations: parodic compositions, and billingsgate oaths. The grotesque has its own realm, in which signifiers construct a grotesque layer of interchange and interorientation. For instance, listing for its own sake is a grotesque textual attribute, as Bakhtin points out of Book 4 of *Pantagruel*, which features 'the longest list of foods of all world literature' (RW 280).[67] The same could be said of the abject; the shock of suddenly changing subject positions, and the vivifying of objects by unexpected use of verbs or adjectives, can occur most clearly within a text.

Life-size also suggests that the truly grotesque body is that of the text itself. Josie may be anorexically reduced, starved in body and mind, but – or rather therefore – the text in which she appears is paradoxically abundant, substantial, voluminous and rich in its verbiage. The text is dialogic, both in the way its character is polyphonically constructed and in its own heteroglot form, as Shute's acknowledgements page at the end of the book suggests. She cites the texts out of which her novel is constructed, including clinical accounts and first-person narratives about anorexia, 'insights from which are woven throughout Josie's story' and 'without which *Life-size* might never have grown to just that'.[68] This is not a sleek, classical text placed on a pedestal but one with multiple protuberances and buds, characterized on the most general level by a consciousness of its own possible fictiveness,[69] and by Josie's irony, without which carnival tone the story could hardly be read. As Bakhtin says, the 'new world outlook' of 'folk humor' in the postmedieval age could grow untrammelled only by moving into 'the world of great literature' (RW 96); carnival must enter literature in order to be politically effective, and to enter into dialogue with official forms and with a wide range of readers.[70]

The trouble with Rabelais

It has become increasingly commonplace to observe that Bakhtin's writings are gender-blind, and either to discuss the implications of this, or, more usually, to produce a feminized Bakhtin by reading his theories with gender added.[71] In the carnival realm, the problem is increased, but also made much clearer, by Bakhtin's reliance on Rabelais' works, which draw on a cultural and literary tradition used to having women as its object. Bakhtin values Rabelais for the scatological and parodic elements of his work; it is hard to imagine the former in particular in a way which does not disparage the feminine. Even Freud observed that a 'dirty joke' is always constructed at the expense of a woman.[72] François Rigolot suggests that the same is true of parody: he writes of 'the particular brand of misogynous cliché that loomed large in various satires written in France and Italy from the thirteenth to the fifteenth century', and in various other medieval genres, compounded by the revival of Platonism in Rabelais' time.[73] Carol Bellard-Thomson suggests that it is possible to separate subversive grotesquerie from misogyny, and that not all Rabelais' comedy is sexual, even when it involves women:

> There is as much satirical comedy in the presentation of a filthy old [male] academic [...] as there is in the sight of a proud and fickle woman being pursued through the streets by packs of dogs, following the scent of a bitch with which her gown has been sprinkled.[74]

This seems a little like claiming that Jonathan Demme's film *Silence of the Lambs* (1990) is feminist because it represents a serial killer who is not sexually motivated in the usual sense, although all his victims are women. Bellard-Thomson may be calling upon the difference between the 'innocent' and renewing nature of Rabelaisian obscenity and the Freudian dirty joke, which must be exactly the kind of thing Bakhtin had in mind when observing that '[o]bscenity has become narrowly sexual, isolated, individual, and has no place in the new official system of philosophy and imagery' (RW 109).

Bakhtin's own methodology can be used to reclaim gender within his own work, and then to use his work for feminist analysis. This is the case with Bakhtin's criticism of the carnival-blindness of critics of Rabelais, who are so out of touch with the tradition of popular humour he draws on that they interpret his imagery as a complex series of political allusions. Bakhtin sees the argument against this 'historical-allegorical method' as clinched by his observation that every image has 'its own aesthetic logic independent of the allusion', using the example that even if the episode of 'Gargantua's swabs is correctly interpreted, it offers us nothing for the understanding of the symbol itself'. (For instance, Bakhtin describes the episode where Gargantua uses a 'March cat' as a swab, and is scratched as a result; some interpret this as a contorted reference to Francis I's bout of venereal disease and his mother's sympathy for him during his sickness, ignoring the carnival tradition this image comes from, which makes a purely historical interpretation monologic (RW 112–15).) One could say the same of the images of women in Bakhtin's use of Rabelais' texts (and in his own examples). This aesthetic logic is based on a tradition of its own, of 'woman's physiological and theological inferiority', resulting in Rabelais' 'text in which women scarcely feature, except as mothers dying in childbirth, as old hags, as caricatures of soothsayers – always as object[s] of comic ridicule'. Bellard-Thomson's defence of Rabelais relies on her rather breathtaking belief that his subversiveness 'challenges the Church and the law; it does not challenge patriarchy because that was not the controlling power'.[75] This position is at odds with that taken by Nancy Glazener, who criticizes overly simple feminist appropriations of carnival which celebrate it, and femininity, for an inherent subversion; carnival offers only a temporary suspension of class and not of patriarchy, and 'subversion never accomplishes a clean break or an unambiguous negation'.[76] Terry Eagleton, while agreeing that carnival is 'a *licensed* affair in every sense', links carnival's subversive potential to its textualization: carnival 'is, in effect, a kind of fiction: a temporary retextualizing of the social formation that exposes its "fictive" foundations'.[77] This is a very important point; carnival does not not lose out, or become denatured, by its transfer to the novel but fulfils its potential in this form; this idea is explored further below in the section on carnival and representation.

It is further revealing that the incident from *Pantagruel* which Bellard-Thomson refers to, of the degradation of the proud Parisienne who is followed about town by 'six hundred thousand and fourteen' urinating dogs, has become something of a test case in feminist approaches to Rabelais, and, by extension, to Bakhtin. Wayne Booth's early article on Bakhtin and feminism deals with this episode, which he sees as 'sexist' because the Lady of Paris is punished as much for resisting Panurge's advances as for being a haughty upper-class person. Clearly the two identities in her case are not easily separable: she is a haughty upper-class woman. With brave honesty, Booth reveals that once he found the scene very funny, and 'was transported with laughter' to the extent that he had to share it with his wife, so he read it aloud to her 'as she did the ironing (!)'. He gives feminist criticism the credit 'for vexing me out of laughter and into thought', thought which produces the notion that, for all Bakhtin's talk of dialogue, he ignores the most conspicuous instance of monologue in Rabelais' text: all the voices are men's.[78] Bakhtin is similarly guilty of this monologism; there are plenty of women in *Rabelais and His World*, but they are invariably the objects of Bakhtin's own commentary, in a non-polyphonic fashion.

François Rigolot similarly sees Panurge as the Lady of Paris's 'sexual harasser', but his analysis of the episode as a rerun of the Passion narrative, with Panurge as the satanic tempter, and the Lady as an abused Christ figure, gives some weight to his reference to 'Rabelais' complex staging of Panurge's misogyny'.[79] The complexities here include the fact that there is clearly a difference between Rabelais and his characters, but, even if it is only Panurge's misogyny we see represented, we may not find it as funny as he, or the implied reader, does. Similarly, the intertextual point relies on the reader's familiarity with a tradition of misogynist writings.

Bakhtin himself says of another infamous and often-cited example of Panurge's misogyny, his plan to build walls from the genitalia of women (interleaved with those of men, however, Bellard-Thomson points out[80]), that this simply shows that 'grotesque imagery' has a 'special concept of the body as a whole and of the limits of this whole' (RW 315). Of the Lady of Paris, he is more concerned that the episode is a 'parody of a religious procession on the day of *Corpus Christi*', but that readers need not fear sacrilege, as 'extremely free, grotesque images of the body were quite usual on these occasions and were consecrated by tradition' (229). Like Rigolot, Bakhtin perceives a kinship between the Lady and Christ, although as her followers are dogs she seems to suffer from the reversal as much as does the son of God. It seems that Bakhtin is doing himself a disservice in concentrating on the formal presence of carnival imagery at the expense of the imagery's precise content, as he does in his discussion of the chronotope. As Booth says, Bakhtin misses out a particularly silenced voice from his heteroglot conception of the world, misses an opportunity to imagine a particularly startling power-reversal (however unhelpful such a strategy may turn out to be), and does not apply his own theory that meaning is constructed by repetition in different contexts: what of the interesting class and gender context for a religious carnival here? Where women are mentioned as part of a scheme of grotesque carnival reversal, the reversal they undergo is always related to their sexual function in a way men's reversal is not, as the example Bakhtin gives from *Don Quixote* (1605–15) suggests: 'The gay principle of regeneration can be seen [...] in the [...] flocks of rams and sheep (armies of knights), innkeepers (lords of the castle), prostitutes (noble ladies), and so forth' (RW 22).[81]

RABELAIS AND FOLK HUMOUR

Bakhtin's defence of Rabelais on a smaller scale is more effective. He produces an exemplary, proto-deconstructive reading of A.N. Veselovsky's tolerance of Rabelais' 'cynicism', his use of billingsgate and the indecency of his imagery. Bakhtin quotes from Veselovsky's analysis of Rabelais:

> 'If you like, Rabelais is cynical, but as a healthy village boy who has been let loose from a smoky hut into the spring air; he rushes madly on, across the puddles, besmirching passersby with mud and laughing merrily when lumps of clay cover his legs and face, ruddy with springlike, animal gaiety.' (RW 146)

Veselovsky displays the lack of understanding Bakhtin claims Rabelais' particular humour is often confronted with, by critics ignorant of the tradition of popular humour (combined with Renaissance learning, RW 72) from which he springs. Veselovsky's image of a village boy is not quite right, as Rabelais' 'cynicism' belongs rather 'to the city marketplace, to the town fair and the carnival square'. Nor is individual gaiety a correct characterization of Rabelais, whose interest rather is in 'the collective gaiety of the people gathered at the fair'. Although Veselovsky has the season in his image right – Rabelais' is 'a truly springlike carnivalesque, Paschal laughter', though this can also include death (RW 81) – the boy's youth is inappropriate to a 'cynicism' emanating from 'the most ancient stratum' of Rabelais' novel. Most interesting, perhaps, is Bakhtin's treatment of Veselovsky's image of the boy '"besmirching passersby with mud"', which is 'a far too tame and modernized metaphor'. Grotesque debasement and degradation, as we have seen, bring pretension down to 'the material bodily lower stratum, the zone of the genital organs'. 'Therefore debasement did not besmirch with mud but with excrement and urine.'

Such debasing gestures, which are commonplace in Rabelais' work and in carnival events such as the '"feast of fools"', are of course ambivalent. They are not simply indecent, 'coarse and cynical', or 'trivial', as they would be today, when a 'stylistic abyss' has opened up between lower bodily acts and higher matters, such as religious discourse, or indeed most kinds of printable discourse (RW 147–50). The abyss is the result of losing the sense of ambivalence attending the lower bodily stratum. '[A]mbivalent improprieties' became mere 'erotic frivolity' (RW 103), degenerating in the nineteenth century into 'alcove realism', a genre of eavesdropping and peeping into private life, although even here a 'tiny spark' of carnival flame remained (RW 106). As 'the lower stratum is not only a bodily grave but also the area of the genital organs, the fertilizing and generating stratum', a link with 'birth, fertility, renewal, welfare' is preserved in the images of urine and excrement (RW 148) in Rabelais' work. Without ambivalence, and if the 'positive and negative poles of becoming (death–birth) are torn apart and opposed to each other', then images of the bodily lower stratum retain only their negative meaning and lose their ambivalence. This loss of ambivalence explains why the following episode from Rabelais, quoted by Bakhtin as an example of the 'regeneration' implicit in his lower bodily images, may seem to the modern reader, with their 'limited and reduced aesthetic stereotypes' (RW 224), disgusting rather than renewing: 'In Rabelais [...] all the warm medicinal springs of France and Italy were generated by the hot urine of the sick Pantagruel' (RW 150). Similarly, Bakhtin's observation that '[d]eath and death throes, labour and childbirth are intimately interwoven', seems from a contemporary perspective indicative of the fear and revulsion experienced by modern subjects towards the feminine and reproduction, rather than revealing these images' combined ability to 'debase, destroy, regenerate, and renew simultaneously' (RW 151).

Carnival and representation: author and heroine

A comment made by Josie at the end of *Life-size* – '"Live?" I say. "What a novel idea!"' – raises the issue of absent footlights in true carnival.[82] Josie seems to be uttering the idea of novelizing her experience, or even that her anorexic past has an intimate connection with writing: the smaller she gets, the larger the text. In carnival as social event, the absence of footlights means that there is no difference between actors and spectators: everyone is a participant. However, there is a transcendent observer in cases where carnival is transposed into fiction, and where the author may choose to place 'himself above or beyond the scene of carnival', becoming a spectator rather than a participant. Not only does authorship thus becomes a decarnivalizing force, but so does any commentary on or awareness of carnival, including historical or sociological studies, and Bakhtin's own work on Rabelais. Jefferson reverses the usual link between carnival and representation, in which the former precedes the latter, by suggesting that, in terms of Bakhtin's own intellectual career, concerns with representation came first, in the form of his essays 'Art and Answerability' and 'Author and Hero', but were succeeded by carnival:

> Crucially, what carnival reveals is that relations of representation can be reconstituted as relations of participation, or at the very least that the specular basis of classical representation can be transformed into one which implies an involvement with representation, its objects and its recipients.[83]

The problem in 'Author and Hero' of the former having ascendency over the latter is resolved in those texts, particularly *Problems of Dostoevsky's Poetics*, where Bakhtin theorizes carnival; as we have seen, Bakhtin's term for this democratic construction of a character is 'polyphony'.

Jefferson's formulation, however, offers a different way of looking at grotesque versus classical: if carnival is process, while representation makes a product, then this suggests that there is every danger of even the grotesque body becoming complete and closed when it is represented rather than enacted. As one would expect, the most productive relation between the two aesthetics is a dialogic one; the grotesque may become closer to the classical by the fact of its appearance in a text, but it also gains by this transposition of medium. Jefferson says that 'the body of Bakhtin's hero, [...] the body of representation is a *finished* construction, whereas the body of carnival and the grotesque is by definition *unfinished*'.[84] However, Bakhtin's conception of the hero in 'Author and Hero' by no means has the final word on the matter, so that the fact that 'carnival is a process, representation makes a product' does not mean that there cannot be represented carnivals, nor that they cannot include representations of grotesque bodies. The two states are in tension, and one could not exist without the other, as the case of the pregnant senile hags shows: they are valued by Bakhtin (and by Jefferson) because as figures of birth within death they are in process, but, as statues, they are also product.

To return to Josie's arch metafictional comment, it is more interesting to look at the links between the grotesque body represented in *Life-size* and its grotesque textual form, than to try to work out whose utterance this is. It is perfectly plausible to read

Life-size as a *Künstlerroman* (i.e. the history of an artist, particularly how they came to write the present work), whose conclusion is the point at which the protagonist can begin writing the very story we have just read; James Joyce's *Portrait of the Artist as a Young Man* (1915) is an example of this genre. In *Life-size*, at first it seems as if we are simply reading a stream of consciousness, that of an underground woman in a hospital room; later on, it becomes clear that Josie is narrating her memories not only to us but to Suzanne, the nurse, and this has become the reason, the motivation, for us to hear them. Suzanne's voice intrudes quite startlingly the first time we hear it, as Josie pauses during her account of a sexual encounter as the prelude to a binge: "'Tell me more about him'". Later, one among the multitude of voices which assails Josie commands:

> Next, draw an image of your own body (life-size) on the blank paper provided for you. The therapist will then ask a bystander to draw his or her image of you, next to yours. Finally the therapist will stand you against the wall, arms outspread, while he traces your actual outline with a crayon. These three depictions – the patient's, the stranger's and the rapist's – will provide material for analysis and for subsequent Body Image Awareness Exercises.[85]

This is a metafictional conceit: what Josie draws on the blank paper is the text we read, called *Life-size*. She has ironically obeyed the therapeutic instruction, and produced the expected inaccurate outline, inaccurate in being too big and too wordy, just as in the mirror she has seen herself as too big.

This extract from a therapeutic instruction is clearly infiltrated by Josie's typically deflating, carnivalesque narration, as she divides, *à la* Mary Daly, the word 'therapist' up to suggest a false etymology. She is also satirizing, however, the kind of relation between 'author' and 'hero' which Bakhtin portrays in his essay of that name, and which Ann Jefferson discusses. Jefferson suggests that Bakhtin's theory of the dependence of self on Other is the basis for his discussion of the relation between hero and author; neither the self nor the fictional hero can be self-determining, because both are 'subject to the grip and grasp of the gaze of the Other' – the near homophony in English of 'other' and 'author' is a 'nice bonus' for this link. As Jefferson points out, 'one does not see oneself as one is seen by others, and this difference in perspective turns on the body'; only the Other sees the self's body as a whole, while to the self the body is composed of 'sensation and fragment'.[86] Clearly, such an approach has great potential for a text which represents a disorder founded on the dichotomy between what the subject sees of herself and what she imagines others see. It is as if anorexia becomes the textual symbol of this aesthetic dilemma: how to get the balance between author and hero right, so that the former's commentary does not, undialogically, submerge the latter's psychological and physical appearance. The footlights issue also becomes relevant: is the subject being watched, and by whom? This is a particularly pressing question in Josie's case, as in her first-person narrative she is both author and 'hero'. She imagines herself watched, spied upon, criticized, as a symptom of her anorexia and because she is a textual character. Alone in a flat at a moment of crisis, she bites her hand to stop herself doing worse to her body: 'a familiar cold tingle wormed over me, and I heard someone laugh through the wall and then laugh again and then applaud. I stood up and took a bow and the room was very large'. Josie's sense of being seen on stage provokes a crisis in the balance between being author and hero, as she realizes she is one of the objects in the room: 'I understood that I could be both *here* and *there* at the same time and wondered why I had never noticed this before. I wanted to stare at myself in the bathroom mirror to reflect on this (and also to check for insects in my hair)'. A potential moment of realization – that one can have an author's view of oneself, even if only mirrored or in images – becomes self-destructive, as Josie can only wish to whittle away what she sees of herself. This crisis was initiated by her glance at her own body, which, rather than being reassuring, and a corrective to her idea that 'No one had looked at me (I think) for weeks; a body that isn't looked at doesn't exist', ruins her determination to 'stay invisible, undefined in space' by avoiding self-regard in the shower, and leads to further self-destructiveness.[87]

The urge to see oneself from the outside, and the constant exhortations Josie has internalized to do so ('*Stand tall, glance down. If you see your navel, you need tummy firming*'), becomes in her case a stark example of a false introduction of footlights. The weighing scale is Josie's stage; she will eat only when the curtains to her bed are drawn, as if the performance has not yet begun.[88] In her mind is Kafka's Hunger Artist, who displayed his starving form to the public: 'I'm somewhere else – an empty cage, a pile of straw'; at school, her refusal of food 'became the daily spectacle [...] and I, the hunger artist, rarely disappointed my audience'.[89] Josie's pose, positioning herself as audience as well as object, transforms the ugliness of starvation ('in the dark glass I catch sight of a face, haggard in the harsh fluorescence, its dull, wispy hair like that of a cheap doll [...] I realize it's me') into a different sign ('Automatically, I adjust the tilt of my head ... now it's a face of exquisite delicacy, ethereal, haunting').[90]

This seems to be why the text *Life-size* is a therapeutic one, ending not in death but with a question about the relation between self and body, or between the author and the hero in oneself. The ability to see oneself in some way as whole as well as fragmentary, to narrate a coherent life history, as Josie starts to do with Suzanne, represents a solution to the problem both of anorexia and of self-authoring first-person narrative. Jefferson points out that there are four possible 'hiccups' in the relation between author and hero (and self and other) as Bakhtin describes it, which may confuse the boundaries between the two: the hero may not like the authorial judgement passed on him; he may 'internalize an image of his external self'; desire may bring the partners fatally close; the hero's death may form a part of the author's image of him.

In Josie's case, gender adds enormous extra significance to these hiccups, especially the second and last ones. As Jefferson points out, Bakhtin uses the analogy of active male lover and passive female loved one for his theory, although both figures are referred to as male.[91] In Josie's case, both narrator and character are female, uniting author and 'hero' in one figure; for this reason, and because it is the concern of her narrative, she provides both internal and external perspectives on herself. Rather than internalizing an image of her external self – Jefferson uses the revealing example that the beloved hero 'cannot have access to his own beauty' – Josie does the opposite, trying to impose an internal image on to her external bodily form. The process partakes of both the metaphorical and the literal senses of inner and outer in Josie's case, suggesting again that the image of an anorexic is also the image of the author's effect on the hero. As Jefferson asserts, the Other creates an 'external shape and form for the subject's body', which makes it hard to imagine that Other and subject do not enter into some kind of dialogical image-construction: does the subject not see any of the Other's estimate reflected back? Josie is obviously both Other and subject, or 'subject and tyrant', as she puts it; the Other does not just reveal but aesthetically produces the subject's body,[92] in her case quite literally: 'What lover, in his urgent rush to ram himself into me, could properly appreciate what I have created here – the lean skid of the flank, the poignant ridging of the rib cage, the tiny bones of the feet?' After the shock of seeing herself in the shower, Josie thinks, 'I would have to start over, drawing the bounds again, etching the skeletal self again from that blurred mass bleeding at the edges (bad color, cheap funnies – but no joke, no punch line, the last frame's missing, printer's mistake)'.[93] Josie sees herself already as a representation, as her metaphor of a newspaper cartoon suggests, and confuses having a pure inner being with having an emaciated body, as the phrase 'skeletal self' shows – she uses it not as a metaphor but as a description.

Bakhtin suggests that self-regard, an attempt to author oneself, can be fatal, as the consequences of Josie's downward glance in the shower suggest, but this also shows the problem with Bakhtin's conception of author and hero. It should be possible to look at oneself without precipitating hospitalization, and a reciprocity of Other and self, which Jefferson sees in Sartre, would consign the self less thoroughly to naivety and passivity.

The possibility of death entering into the relation between author and hero is clearly implicit in Josie's narrative, symbolized by the idea of a 'skeletal self'; perfection for her would be total fleshlessness, in a literal version of the aesthetic problem that 'for the authorial picture to be complete, the hero must be as if dead'.[94] Jefferson's phrase, 'as if dead', suggests that representing the hero as subordinate, non-polyphonically in an undialogic setting, amounts to a dead image; again, in Josie's case, the death which may be suffered for the sake of completion is a real one.

The problem of drama

As we have seen in relation to poetry and epic, Bakhtin's exclusion of drama from his delineation of the dialogic does not mean that critics have not taken issue with his estimate, and used his categories to discuss dramatic texts.[95] In the criticism of contemporary texts, the carnivalesque is usually considered together with dialogism; and carnival is a markedly dialogic form, in which high and low interact.[96] Some critics of drama have concentrated on carnival more autonomously, because of the issues carnival raises in relation to spectacle and spectatorship.[97] Part of the reason for this examination of carnival outside its dialogic framework is that Bakhtin considers only novelistic genres, and, as well as omitting film, he suggests that epic, poetry and drama are genres which are necessarily outside his delineation of the dialogic. In *Problems of Dostoevsky's Poetics*, Bakhtin discusses critics who praise Dostoevsky's novels for their dramatic qualities, and why non-dialogic dialogue is not the same as dialogism:

The whole concept of a dramatic action, as that which resolves all dialogic oppositions, is purely monologic. A true multiplicity of levels would destroy drama, because dramatic action, relying as it does upon the unity of the world, could not link those levels together or resolve them. In drama, it is impossible to combine several integral fields of vision in a unity that encompasses and stands above them all, because the structure of drama offers no support for such a unity. (PDP 17)

Drama cannot be dialogic, according to Bakhtin, because it possesses no scope for the fictional narrator – 'a unity that encompasses and stands above'. In the novel, it is the whole which is dialogic, while, in a play, dialogue cannot accumulate into Bakhtinian polyphony; the voices do not interact, in the way that those in *Crime and Punishment* do, but simply speak one after the other. As Bakhtin claims in 'Discourse in the Novel', '[i]n drama there is no all-encompassing language that addresses itself dialogically to separate languages' (266); and, 'A speaking person's discourse in the novel is not merely transmitted or reproduced; it is, precisely, *artistically represented* and thus – in contrast to drama – it is represented *by means of* (authorial) discourse' (DN 332). Bakhtin is prepared to make a partial exception in the case of mystery plays, which are 'truly multi-leveled, and to a certain extent polyphonic', but these qualities are small-scale and do not 'permit the full development of a plurality of consciousnesses and their worlds'. Drama is, at best, an example of 'ordinary dialogic form', that is, 'an unfolding of material within the framework of its own monologic understanding and against the firm background of a unified world of objects' (PDP 17–18).

DRAMA AND CARNIVAL

Although Bakhtin uses dramatic categories when discussing carnival, which he identifies as a form characterized precisely by its absence of footlights, it is clearly in its differences from drama that the carnival becomes a subversive force: 'carnival does not know footlights, in the sense that it does not acknowledge any distinction between actors and spectators. Footlights would destroy a carnival, as the absence of footlights would destroy a theatrical performance' (RW 7). In the carnival, there is no such thing as a spectator or audience member, 'the viewer who would objectify an entire event according to some ordinary monologic category' (PDP 18), such as theatre. The whole point of carnival, and equally the dialogic novel, is that 'the viewer [is] also a participant'. One can imagine the phenomenon of audience participation in plays, particularly pantomime, being cited as a counter-example, but presumably Bakhtin would maintain that such limited transgression of theatrical footlights simply draws attention to their presence. He argues that the particular ambivalence of medieval carnival can no longer be reproduced. In the medieval culture of humour, clowns and fools 'were not actors playing their parts on a stage, as did the comic actors of a later period, impersonating Harlequin, Hanswurst, etc.'. This is a question not of a play-within-a-play but of characters on 'the borderline between life and art, in a peculiar mid-zone' (RW 8).

Bakhtin points out that Renaissance writers are the sources of carnival 'reincarnated' (PDP 157) in literary form; he cites particularly Boccaccio, Rabelais, Shakespeare, Cervantes, and Grimmelshausen. It is of course immediately striking that Bakhtin himself cites a playwright as an example of carnivalesque literature. Even if drama cannot be fully dialogic, it may represent carnivalesque images. Bakhtin's quotations from the nineteenth-century critic Chernyshevsky on a 'new structural form of an "objective novel"', as he calls it', which Bakhtin admits comes 'very close indeed to the idea of polyphony', suggest that such objectivity may be possible even in drama, as an aspect of character representation. Bakhtin continues,

> This new 'objective' authorial position (whose realization Chernyshevsky finds only in Shakespeare) permits the characters' point of view to unfold to their maximal fullness and independence [...] 'each says for himself: "the full right is on my side" – you judge these conflicting claims. I do not judge.' (PDP 66–7)

However, although Bakhtin sees the rudiments of polyphony in Shakespeare's plays, he also unequivocally states that 'to speak of a fully formed and deliberate polyphonic quality in Shakespeare's dramas is in our opinion simply impossible'. (As we saw in Chapter 3, 'polyphony' means the independence of characters' voices from the judgements of a narrator; in a polyphonic novel, the characters speak on the same level as a narrator.) Bakhtin summarizes this impossibility under three headings: first, drama may be multi-levelled, but it cannot represent multiple world-views; second, as each of Shakespeare's plays contains only 'one fully valid voice', that of the hero, it would make sense to talk of Shakespearean polyphony only if one was referring to all Shakespeare's works; and third, Shakespeare's heroes are not 'points of view' or 'ideologists' in the same, highly distinctive way they are in Dostoevsky (PDP 34).

Contemporary carnival: two case studies

In this final section, I look briefly at two examples of contemporary carnival. One is an example from fiction, the other uses carnival for literary-critical ends.

CARTER AND THE CARNIVALESQUE

Various critics, including Mary Russo, have pointed to elements of the carnivalesque, and grotesque realism, in Angela Carter's works.[98] It is perfectly possible that these elements were knowingly added by Carter, of whose writing one might well say, with Bakhtin: 'the entire field of realistic literature of the last three centuries is strewn with the fragments of grotesque realism, which at times are not mere remnants of the past but manifest a renewed vitality' (RW 24). Carter's short story 'The Kitchen Child', from the collection *Black Venus* (1986), reproduces many of these fragments on a small scale. In this story, the lower orders of a great house are the ones with real refinement and feeling, in a carnivalesque reversal: 'I tell you, the English country house, yes! that's the place for grub; but, only when Sir and Madam are *pas chez lui*. It is the staff who keep up the standards'. This is a permanent reversal, however, not the kind of 'queen for a day' format of Bakhtinian carnival. Its permanence is typified by the fact that, at the end of the story, the illegitimate kitchen boy who narrates the story reveals that he has become a 'duc's stepson'. His mother, the cook, has been carried off to 'the duc's very own regal and French kitchen' not to work there but as his wife.[99] This is not the ending we have expected, as Lorna Sage points out: the kitchen child 'resolutely refuses to recognize his father', and, as in Carter's novel *Wise Children*, the 'anti-moral is that illegitimacy must be the higher vocation'.[100] None the less, the ending is more like the one-way reversal of fairy-tale than the multiply changing positions of the novel.

The plot of 'The Kitchen Child' is from a different genre to grotesque realism, more similar to a 'pastiche folk-tale', as Sage puts it, although the story's images owe something to the grotesque. Its language is a mixture of the vernacular and the literary: 'And the very first soufflé that ever in her life as cook me mam was called upon to make, ordered up by some French duc, house guest of Sir and Madam, me mam pleased as punch to fix it for him since few if any *fins becs* pecked their way to our house'. The narrator emphasizes individual grotesque traits to undercut the housekeeper, who 'elocutes' in 'ladylike and dulcet tones': '"What are the – hick – lower ordures up to?"' A reminder of the grotesque activities of the body interrupts both pretensions to high-class utterance, and attempts to use the 'new bodily canon' of disgust at such substances as 'ordures' against the people.

Food and reproduction are linked verbally: 'the housekeeper is pricked perpetually by the fancy for the importation of a Carême or a Soyer with moustaches like hatracks to *croquembouche* her and *milly filly* her as is all the rage'. They are also linked within the plot, as the narrator is conceived during the preparation of a soufflé. Like the war of the cooks in Rabelais, here kitchen utensils, in a grotesque reversal, become weaponry, although not in as systematized a way: 'my mother wields her wooden spoon like a club, brings it, smack! down on to the duc's head with considerable force'. These utensils also become musical instruments, as the kitchen child's birth is heralded by 'a veritable fusillade of copper-bottom kitchen tympani'.[101]

The kitchen itself, as a public meeting-place, is by turns a barracks occupied by a 'kitchen brigade', a nursery in which the child bathed 'in a big tureen' and slept in a 'copper salmon kettle', and a church-like, 'holy' place with 'the range like an altar [...] before which my mother bowed in perpetual homage. At his birth, the kitchen-child was part of a debased nativity scene, in which featured

> My mother, wreathed in smiles, enthroned on a sack of spuds with, at her breast, her babe, all neatly swaddled in new-boiled pudding cloth, and the entire kitchen brigade arranged around her in attitudes of adoration, each brandishing a utensil and giving out therewith that merry rattle of ladles, yours truly's first lullaby.[102]

The narrator adds, 'Raphael might have sketched it, had he been in Yorkshire at the time', giving to the image of madonna and child, and Renaissance high art, the kind of debunking of epic which Bakhtin observes in the representation of Hecuba changing diapers (RW 304). Like Gargantua, the Kitchen Child is born amid food and feasting, but the extreme mingling of bodies and the mother's death are absent.

It could be said that 'The Kitchen Child' represents not the 'modern canon' of the classical body and text but the 'reduced'

remnants of grotesque realism in its food imagery and its irrever-
ence. As Sage points out, it offers 'ironical praise of the domestic
arts (including the very art of tale-telling we are being treated to)'.
Calling it 'carnivalesque' helps place it generically, rather than
calling it, for instance, an example of magic realism.

CRITICISM AND THE CARNIVALESQUE

Apart from more accurate labelling, however, one might ask how
using Bakhtin's categories of grotesque realism and carnival can
change one's view of a particular text. Bakhtin reveals that Rabelais
has been misunderstood, his grotesque images misread as simple
political allegories or as obscenity and 'cynicism'; replacing him in
the tradition of popular humour gives a quite different dimension to
his aesthetic. A pioneering article on Malcolm Lowry's *Under the
Volcano* attempted to do the same for that novel, using Bakhtinian
notions of carnival and Menippean satire. Jonathan Arac notes that
Lowry's novel is a 'confusing' mixture of 'gestures of generaliza-
tion' with 'fanatically precise attention [to] locale', but that carnival
offers a way of recognizing 'these differences and eccentricities'
within the novel without abstracting them into a false unity. As
usual, carnival exists in this novel at the level of both form and
theme. Arac goes through a list of Menippean features, and notes
that Lowry's novel is characterized by the 'reduced laughter' of
seriocomic complexity; by 'specialized' and various uses of
language; unexpected transitions and meetings; sequences of 'scandals' accompanying the 'emergence of seriousness from farcicality';
and concern with the 'ultimate questions'. The Mexican setting of
Under the Volcano is part of its Menippean form: 'stretching from the
bottom of the barranca to the top of the mountains, [it] clearly
follows this principle [of a heaven above and a hell below] and
concretely gives significance to the pervasive moral language of
falling and rising'. This is accompanied by an interest in 'threshold
states', as the text is set literally and metaphorically on the edge of
an abyss. Both the 'prologue-epilogue' of the novel and the time of
its central action are the Day of the Dead, 'the day that living and
dead can meet briefly on the threshold that usually separates
them'.[103]

Arac sees carnival as a force uniting the many elements of
Menippean satire, and proceeds to identify in *Under the Volcano*
various carnivalesque images. Characters assume the masks of
confected identities; doubled roles, such as those of 'the tragic
clown or the wise fool', occur; even emotion is carnivalized 'in the

grotesque mixture of opposites' and ambivalence, which we see in each of the characters, particularly the Consul; and, set as it is on the Day of the Dead, 'a fiesta of return', Lowry's form is 'concretely rooted in carnival life'. Arac uses Bakhtin's definition of carnival as 'the very process of replaceability' to account for the form of *Under the Volcano*. Carnival is 'functional, not substantive, in its emphasis and is thus hostile to any final ending'. He quotes Lowry's remark in a letter that '"when you get to the end [of the book], if you have read carefully, you should want to turn back to the beginning again"'. The space of reading can heal the losses of time, Arac argues, although without mentioning Bakhtin's notion of chronotope. Carnival, Arac concludes, can show how this novel, 'for all its copious variety', goes round 'in one smooth circle in a carnival path of loss and return'.[104]

Clearly, Arac's article does not exhaust the potential of reading *Under the Volcano* in a carnivalesque light, nor the relevance of Bakhtin's other concepts to it; as well as the chronotope, Arac omits dialogism, heteroglossia, and polyphony. Although he says that carnival is a relational, not a substantive, phenomenon, he gives no account of the dialogic interaction of its elements. Allon White discusses *Under the Volcano* briefly in his article 'Bakhtin, Sociolinguistics, and Deconstruction', as an example not of 'the carnivalesque spirit' – Joyce's *Ulysses* and Pynchon's *Gravity's Rainbow* (1973) get this accolade – but as a 'cacophony of voices [which] indicates not a robust debunking of powerful groups but a chaos of competing voices'. He argues that the setting of *Under the Volcano*, in the midst of real carnival, and its self-conscious polyphony (by which he means 'polyglossia'), do not necessarily make it carnivalesque: 'the fiesta is the Day of the Dead and the polyphony is that of Babel'. It is as if we are in the Kristevan realm of modern, 'degraded' carnival. Polyglossia here is 'pressed back into the service of romantic pathos, recuperated through its evocation of alienated misunderstanding and irreducible foreignness', above which clamour Yvonne's plea for '"*our* speech"' can hardly be heard. Her plea is read by White as an example of 'the use of polyglossia so as to reinforce the authority of high languages'. The episode in which the Consul reads her words, which are in a letter he carries about with him, is one in which he is surrounded by what White sees simply as a 'chaos' of different languages, 'the cacophony of the bar', ranging from a Spanish radio programme, the Consul's drunken ramblings, and the words of a Mexican. To be fair to Lowry, Yvonne's invocation of a privileged discourse is a small instance of such special pleading, while constructions of meaning out of apparent 'cacophony' are much more widespread in the novel.[105]

White claims that *Under the Volcano* presents a 'religious and Faustian myth of a fall without resurrection', although the 'buffoonery' in quotations from Marlowe's *Dr Faustus* (1604) is used by Arac as evidence for the novel's adherence to 'reduced laughter'. Arac of course sees the Consul's fall as more ambivalent than White does; if the text is as circular as Lowry suggests, then the Consul does achieve an ironic kind of 'resurrection' on each reading of the text. It is true that Pynchon's carnival, which White compares with Lowry's, has a more populist depth and a more authoritarian height, and these two poles are represented by low-life discourses 'from the locker-room, the sewers (in *V*), the jazz club and cabaret, New York Yiddish, student fraternities, and GI slang', versus the high languages of 'technology, psychoanalysis, business, administration, and military jargon'.[106] However, as we have seen in the chapter on polyphony, Lowry enlists carnival as part of a polyphonic enterprise which does probe 'power and authority', even if not as part of a Pynchonesque rejection of both high and low language, which involves 'setting them off against each other in hilarious scenes which unnervingly flip over into sinister intimations of death and apocalypse'.[107]

Notes

1 Bakhtin published a revised version of *Problems*, with a new chapter 4, in 1963; see Gary Saul Morson and Caryl Emerson, *Rethinking Bakhtin: Extensions and Challenges*, Northwestern University Press, Evanston, Illinois 1989, pp. 160–1. Ken Hirschkop points out that the English translation of *Rabelais and His World* translates the Russian adjective *narodnyi* as 'folk', but 'popular' is probably more appropriate; I have altered my own practice as a result. (I am grateful to Sally Eames, Anne Grigson and Isobel Wilson, students on the Sheffield University MA in Information Studies, who conducted bibliographical searches for works linking Bakhtin and Kristeva; to the British Academy, who partially funded my attendance at the Seventh Biennial Bakhtin Conference in Moscow, June 1995, where I gave a version of part of this chapter; and to David Shepherd and the Bakhtin Centre at the University of Sheffield, where I gave another version.)

2 Julia Kristeva, 'Word, Dialogue, and Novel', *Desire in Language: A Semiotic Approach to Literature and Art*, Basil Blackwell, Oxford 1980, p. 78.

3 See for instance Carroll Smith-Rosenberg, 'The Body Politic', in Elizabeth Weed, ed., *Coming to Terms*, Routledge, London 1989, pp. 101–21.

4 This is the translator's term, naturally.

5 See Peter Jackson, 'Street Life: The Politics of Carnival', *Society and Space* 6, 1988, pp. 213–27; I am grateful to Professor Jackson for this reference.

6 Robert Stam, *Subversive Pleasures: Bakhtin, Cultural Criticism and Film*, Johns Hopkins University Press, Baltimore, Maryland 1989, p. 158.

7 Michael Holquist, 'Introduction', RW xix.

8 Terry Eagleton, *Walter Benjamin, or Towards a Revolutionary Criticism*, New Left Books, London 1981, p. 144.

9 Holquist, 'Introduction', pp. xix, xvii.

10 Clair Wills, 'Upsetting the Public: Carnival, Hysteria and Women's Texts', in Ken Hirschkop and David Shepherd, eds, *Bakhtin and Cultural Theory*, Manchester University Press, Manchester 1989, p. 133.

11 See Wills, 'Upsetting the Public' on history as crisis, pp. 131, 133: and Ken Hirschkop on carnival and history, 'Introduction', in Hirschkop and Shepherd, *Bakhtin and Cultural Theory*, pp. 33–5.

12 Mikhail K. Ryklin, 'Bodies of Terror: Theses Toward a Logic of Violence', *NLH* 24 (1), winter 1993, pp. 54 (Bakhtin's italics), 56. Ken Hirschkop suggests a source for Bakhtin's emphasis on the collective which is different from Ryklin and Emerson's: the researches of Brian Poole suggest that this is 'the neo-Kantian Hermann Cohen's contrast of the "mortal individual" with the "immortal people" (the latter alone being the true subject of historical progress and ultimate redemption)'. Cohen is discussed in AA 240–1, n. 73.

13 Caryl Emerson, 'Preface' to Ryklin, 'Bodies of Terror', pp. 48, 46.

14 Nancy Glazener, 'Dialogic Subversion: Bakhtin, the Novel and Gertrude Stein', in Hirschkop and Shepherd, *Bakhtin and Cultural Theory*, p . 113.

15 Ryklin, 'Bodies of Terror', p. 55. This is an issue which has exercised critics: Sergey Bocharov quotes a conversation with Bakhtin, in which Bakhtin says the only way to have avoided betraying his homeland and culture would have been '"By perishing. I began writing an article to be called 'On Those Who Failed to Perish' [...] of course I destroyed it later"' (Bocharov, 'Conversations with Bakhtin', *PMLA* 109 (5), October 1994, p. 1020). Morson and Emerson reply to Wall and Thomson's review: Bakhtin, who 'spent much of his life eluding purges, who barely escaped what amounted to a death sentence, and who saw his friends (including Medvedev) arrested and disappear', could only have disapproved of Stalinist practices. (Medvedev was shot probably in early 1938; Volosinov was also a victim of Stalinist terror, but precise details of his fate are not known.)

16 Ryklin, 'Bodies of Terror', p. 55; Emerson, 'Preface', p. 46.

17 See for instance Ilkka Joki, 'David Mamet's Drama: The Dialogicality of Grotesque Realism', David Shepherd, ed., *Bakhtin, Carnival and Other Subjects, Critical Studies* 3 (2)–4 (1/2), 1993, pp. 80–98.

18 Ann Jefferson, 'Bodymatters: Self and Other in Bakhtin, Sartre and Barthes', in Hirschkop and Shepherd, *Bakhtin and Cultural Theory*, p. 166.

19 Jefferson, 'Bodymatters', and Mary Russo, *The Female Grotesque: Risk, Excess, and Modernity*, Routledge, London 1994, are more positive than Ruth Ginsburg, 'The Pregnant Text. Bakhtin's Ur-Chronotope: The Womb', in Shepherd, *Bakhtin, Carnival*, p. 168, and Jane Miller, *Seductions:*

Studies in Reading and Culture, Virago, London 1990, p. 149: see her discussion pp. 139–50.

20 Ginsburg, 'The Pregnant Text', p. 169.

21 Diane Roberts, *The Myth of Aunt Jemima: Representations of Race and Region*, Routledge, London 1994, p. 2.

22 James Joyce, *Ulysses: The Corrected Text*, ed. Hans Walter Gabler *et al.*, Penguin, Harmondsworth 1986, 8.928–32. Thanks to J. S. Bernstein for discussing this episode with me.

23 Kristeva says, in 'Word, Dialogue, and Novel': 'Carnivalesque discourse [. . .] is a social and political protest. There is not equivalence, but rather, identity between challenging official linguistic codes and challenging official law', p. 65.

24 See Holquist's 'Prologue', RW xiii–xxiii.

25 Jenefer Shute, *Life-size*, Secker and Warburg, London 1992, p. 10.

26 Kristeva, 'Word, Dialogue, and Novel', p. 78.

27 *Ibid.*

28 Julia Kristeva, *Powers of Horror: An Essay on Abjection*, Columbia University Press, New York 1982, pp. 138, 205.

29 See Peter Stallybrass and Allon White, *The Politics and Poetics of Transgression*, Methuen, London 1986, p. 175; Russo, *The Female Grotesque*, p. 10; and Sue Vice, 'Grotesque Body, Abject Self: Bakhtin and Kristeva', in C. Adlam, R. Falconer, V. Makhlin and A. Renfrew, eds, *Face to Face: Bakhtin in Russia and the West*, Sheffield Academic Press, Sheffield 1997.

30 Shute, *Life-size*, pp. 123, 7, 231.

31 Kristeva, *Powers*, pp. 2–3.

32 *Ibid.*, p. 72.

33 *Ibid.*, p. 166, *pace* Ginsburg: 'It seems quite obvious that for Bakhtin the mother's body is "uncanny" in the Freudian sense', 'The Pregnant Text', p. 172.

34 Kristeva, *Powers*, p. 71.

35 Shute, *Life-size*, pp. 165, 173, 78, 17.

36 *Ibid.*, pp. 5, 159.

37 *Ibid.*, p. 211.

38 *Ibid.*, pp. 14, 35.

39 *Ibid.*, pp. 45, 185.

40 Kristeva, *Powers*, p. 75; in *Marxism and the Philosophy of Language*, Volosinov takes *hunger* as his example of the 'simplest' kind of feeling, 'not outwardly expressed', which none the less cannot escape 'some kind of ideological form' (pp. 87): Josie's case is this point taken to an extreme. See the rest of his discussion, pp. 87–9.

41 'The body must bear no trace of its debt to nature', Kristeva observes in her discussion of Biblical taboos against deformity or decoration (*Powers*, p. 102).

42 *Ibid.*, pp. 14, 54.

43 *Ibid.*, p. 155.

44 Shute, *Life-size*, pp. 105, 42, 23, 109.

45 See Mark Anderson, 'Anorexia and Modernism, or How I Learned to Diet in All Directions', *Discourse* 11.1, fall/winter 1988–9; Maud Ellmann,

Hunger Artists, Virago, London 1993; Sue Vice, 'The Well-Rounded Anorexic Text', in Tim Armstrong, ed., *American Bodies: Cultural Histories of the Physique*, Sheffield Academic Press, Sheffield 1997.

46 Shute, *Life-size*, p. 126.

47 *Ibid.*, p. 47.

48 Stam, *Subversive Pleasures*, pp. 159–63; Jefferson, 'Bodymatters', p. 166.

49 Ginsburg, 'The Pregnant Text', p. 169; Pam Morris, 'Carnivalizing the Gargantuan Mother', paper delivered at the Sixth International Mikhail Bakhtin Conference, UNAM, Mexico, July 1993; Russo, *The Female Grotesque*, p. 12.

50 Jefferson, 'Bodymatters', p. 166.

51 Russo, *The Female Grotesque*, p. 63.

52 Kristeva, *Powers*, p. 205.

53 *Ibid.*, pp. 102, 101.

54 *Ibid.*, p. 165.

55 Allon White, 'Bakhtin, Sociolinguistics, Deconstruction', in *Carnival, Hysteria and Writing: Collected Essays and an Autobiography*, Oxford University Press, Oxford 1994, p. 168.

56 Kristeva, *Powers*, p. 64.

57 *Ibid.*, pp. 63, 10.

58 Bakhtin is quoting Rabelais here.

59 Kristeva, *Powers*, pp. 63, 12; Kristeva discusses the Biblical prohibition on eating a calf in its mother's milk as an incest prohibition, p. 105; and defilement as incest, p. 85.

60 Gary Saul Morson and Caryl Emerson, *Mikhail Bakhtin: The Creation of a Prosaics*, Stanford University Press, Stanford, California 1990, p. 226; see also their debate with Wall and Thomson on this matter, 'Cleaning Up Bakhtin's Carnival Act', *Diacritics* 23 (2), summer 1993, pp. 47–70, and Morson and Emerson's reply, 'Imputations and Amputations: Reply to Wall and Thomson', *Diacritics* 23 (4), winter 1993, pp. 93–9; and their sponsorship of Ryklin.

61 Ginsburg, 'The Pregnant Text', p. 173.

62 Kristeva, *Powers*, pp. 3, 4.

63 Kim Newman's review of the film *Kingpin* (Peter and Bobby Farrelly, 1996) contrasts its attitude to the body with that of the same directors' *Dumb and Dumber* (1994), as if the former is of the classical canon, the latter grotesque: 'Physical humour should play on our recognition that we all have bodily functions, bringing us into communion with the lowest of comics. *Kingpin* is more the equivalent of a freakshow: it delights in being disgusting and appalling, but it prompts an uncomfortable silence, not raucous laughter' (*Sight and Sound*, August 1996, p. 58).

64 Shute, *Life-size*, pp. 7, 231.

65 Kristeva, *Powers*, p. 5.

66 See Bakhtin's discussion of 'edible metaphors', RW 299; and 162.

67 Anorexic variants of such lists feature in Shute's *Life-size*, as Josie obsessively recounts the contents of her post-coital binges.

68 Shute, *Life-size*, p. 232; the intertext of Sylvia Plath's *The Bell Jar* (e.g. p. 133) goes surprisingly unmentioned.

69 *Ibid.*, pp. 55, 102.

70 Wills, 'Upsetting the Public', p. 131; Hirschkop disagrees, 'Introduction', in Hirschkop and Shepherd, *Bakhtin and Cultural Theory*; Wills, p. 140.

71 Carol Adlam identifies three separate areas of Bakhtin-influenced feminist research, in 'Ethics of Difference: Bakhtin's Early Writings and Feminist Theories', in Adlam *et al.*, eds, *Face to Face*; see also Glazener, 'Dialogic Subversion', in Hirschkop and Shepherd, eds, *Bakhtin and Cultural Theory*.

72 Sigmund Freud, *Jokes and their Relation to the Unconscious*, trs. James Strachey, Norton, New York 1960, p. 60.

73 François Rigolot, 'Rabelais, Misogyny, and Christian Charity: Biblical Intertextuality and the Renaissance Crisis of Exemplarity', *PMLA* 109 (2), March 1994, p. 225.

74 Carol Bellard-Thompson, 'Rabelais and Obscenity: A Woman's View', in Helen Wilcox *et al.*, eds, *The Body and the Text: Hélène Cixous, Reading and Teaching*, Harvester Wheatsheaf, Hemel Hempstead 1990, pp. 173, 172.

75 Rigolot, 'Rabelais, Misogyny', p. 225; Bellard-Thompson, 'Rabelais and Obscenity', pp. 171, 174.

76 Glazener, 'Dialogic Subversion', p. 111.

77 Eagleton, *Walter Benjamin*, p. 149.

78 In Rigolot, 'Rabelais, Misogyny', p. 232; Wayne Booth, 'Freedom and Interpretation: Bakhtin and the Challenge of Feminist Criticism', in Gary Saul Morson, ed., *Bakhtin: Essays and Dialogues on His Work*, University of Chicago Press, Chicago, Illinois 1986, pp. 160–1, 168, 165–6.

79 Rigolot, 'Rabelais, Misogyny', p. 233.

80 Bellard-Thompson, 'Rabelais and Obscenity', p. 172.

81 See also Bakhtin on the ambivalence of women when turned into ambiguity, RW 240–2.

82 Shute, *Life-size* p. 231; the construction of discourse with a loophole also does away with footlights: PDP 237. Wall and Thompson suggest that carnival 'is not a mere game, as the latter is always cut off by semiotic framing devices: a mechanism of memory, carnival is an active process of renewal', whose 'cyclical reapparitions are equivalent to mechanisms of collective storage', 'Cleaning up Bakhtin's Carnival Act', pp. 58–60.

83 Jefferson, 'Bodymatters', pp. 165, 164. Ken Hirschkop points out the close connection Bakhtin assumes between 'bodiliness' and the aesthetic. The body is significant as the 'essence' of any aesthetic act, and as 'that which must be redeemed – by art, and, ultimately, by God – which goes part of the way towards explaining [Bakhtin's] otherwise apparently casual dismissal of individual death'.

84 Jefferson, 'Bodymatters', pp. 168, 167.

85 Shute, *Life-size*, pp. 171, 218.

86 Jefferson, 'Bodymatters', pp. 153, 154.

87 Shute, *Life-size*, pp. 219, 218.

88 *Ibid.*, p. 63.

89 Note also Josie's description of other anorexics, using carnival vocabulary, where the lack of a regenerative movement is very clear: she sees these women as a Hallowe'en toy (p. 48), and 'a hunched gargoyle on a stick' (p. 72).

90 *Ibid.*, p. 70.
91 Jefferson, 'Bodymatters', pp. 156, 161.
92 *Ibid.*, p. 154, 155.
93 Shute, *Life-size*, pp. 42, 218.
94 Jefferson, 'Bodymatters', pp. 157, 156, 161, 158.
95 Critics who have used Bakhtinian categories to discuss drama include Robert Cunliffe, in his 'The Architectonics of Carnival and Drama in Bakhtin, Artaud, and Brecht', in Shepherd, ed., *Bakhtin, Carnival and Other Subjects*, and also in his 'Monologism, Drama: Bakhtin, Derrida', in Adlam *et al.*, eds, *Face to Face*; see also the curious case of the Polish theatre company Gardzienice, who work under the sign of Bakhtin: his photograph hangs in the troupe's dressing-room (Halina Filipowicz, 'A Polish Expedition to Baltimore', *Drama Review* 31 (1), spring 1987, pp. 137–65; I am grateful to Rachel Newman for this reference). As Ken Hirschkop points out, Bakhtin considered Shakespeare's plays to be full of carnivalesque features, as is made clear in the 'Supplements and Amendments to *Rabelais*', concentrating on *King Lear*, *Macbeth*, and *Othello*. This section of 'Supplements' appears in translation in a forthcoming book on Shakespeare edited by Alfred Arteaga.
96 White, 'Bakhtin', pp. 125, 131; Wills, 'Upsetting the Public', p. 126.
97 Carnival features prominently in works by Renaissance critics, for instance Jean-Christophe Agnew, *Worlds Apart: The Market and the Theater in Anglo-American Thought 1550–1750*, Cambridge University Press, Cambridge 1986; Michael D. Bristol, *Carnival and Theatre*, Methuen, New York 1985; Thomas Healy, *New Latitudes: Theory and English Renaissance Literature*, Edward Arnold, London 1992; Steven Mullaney, *The Place of the Stage: License, Play and Power in Renaissance England*, Chicago University Press, Chicago, Illinois 1988; Leonard Tennenhouse, *Power on Display: The Politics of Shakespeare's Genres*, Methuen, London and New York 1986; Peter Stallybrass, 'Reading the Body and the Jacobean Theatre of Consumption: *The Revenger's Tragedy* (1606)', in David Scott Kastan and Peter Stallybrass, eds, *Staging the Renaissance: Reinterpretations of Elizabethan and Jacobean Drama*, Routledge, London 1991, and Stallybrass's 'Patriarchal Territories: The Body Enclosed', in M. Ferguson *et al.*, eds, *Rewriting the Renaissance*: University of Chicago Press, Chicago, Illinois 1986. Media studies has also taken up both carnival and Bakhtin's concept of genre: see John Fiske, *Television Culture*, Routledge, London 1987, pp. 241–8, and John Caughie, 'Adorno's Reproach: Repetition, Difference and Television Genre', *Screen* 32 (2), summer 1991, pp. 139–52. I am grateful to Erica Sheen for these references; see also Lynne Pearce on drama criticism, *Reading Dialogics*, Edward Arnold, London 1994, p. 87 n.
98 See essays by Marina Warner, and Kate Webb in Lorna Sage, ed., *Flesh and the Mirror: Essays on the Art of Angela Carter*, Virago, London 1994, although the latter repeats the point that carnival works better for men than for women, p. 301.
99 Angela Carter, 'The Kitchen Child', in *Black Venus*, Picador, London 1986, pp. 62, 69.

100 Lorna Sage, *Angela Carter*, Northcote House Publishing, Plymouth 1994, p. 45.
101 Carter, 'The Kitchen Child', pp. 62, 64, 63, 68, 63 respectively.
102 *Ibid*., pp. 65, 64; I am grateful to Jayna Brown for drawing the nativity connotations to my attention.
103 Jonathan Arac, 'The Form of Carnival in *Under the Volcano*', PMLA 92, 1977, pp. 481–6.
104 *Ibid*., pp. 487, 488.
105 White, 'Bakhtin', pp. 146–8.
106 *Ibid*., p. 148; see Hirschkop's discussion of the Lukácsian idea that 'proliferating specialised languages are a symptom of reification, the separating off and technicisation of human powers', 'Introduction', Hirschkop and Shepherd, eds, *Bakhtin and Cultural Theory*, p. 19.
107 White, 'Bakhtin', p. 149.

5

The chronotope: fleshing out time

Introduction

Bakhtin's concept of the chronotope comes by analogy from Einsteinian mathematics, he says (FTC 84), and its etymology from the Greek, 'chronos', meaning time, and 'topos', meaning space. Its literal sense, 'time-space', conveys the inseparability of the two elements in any work of art. Bakhtin's use of a metaphor from Einstein's theoretical physics conveys the intellectual shift in perceptions of history and geography which relativity ushered in. Bakhtin discusses the chronotope mainly in the essay 'Forms of Time and Chronotope in the Novel', in *The Dialogic Imagination*, and in sections of 'The *Bildungsroman*', in *Speech Genres and Other Late Essays*. In 'Discourse in the Novel', Bakhtin describes the textual representation of the Renaissance in terms of its scientific shift from a medieval Ptolemaic view of the world, in which the sun revolves around the earth, to a modern Galilean view, in which the earth revolves around the sun (DN 415). In contrast to the centralized Ptolemaic world-view, where the world makes sense from a single vantage-point, this modern view necessitated a particular kind of plural, relativizing discourse:

> Languages of heteroglossia, like mirrors that face each other, each reflecting in its own way a piece, a tiny corner of the world, force us to guess at and grasp for a world behind their mutually reflecting aspects that is broader, more multi-leveled, containing more and varied horizons than would be available to a single language or a single mirror. (DN 414)

Both Galileo and Einstein 'shifted the boundaries of the old geographical world', and, while the former is the presiding scientist for Bakhtin's discussion of dialogism, the latter is for the chronotope.

Bakhtin describes the chronotope as the means of measuring

how, in a particular genre or age, 'real historical time and space' and 'actual historical persons' are articulated, and also how fictional time, space, and character are constructed in relation to one another.[1] In some chronotopes, mainly those of travel, and uprooted modern life, time may take precedence over space; in the more idyllic, pastoral chronotopes, space holds sway over time.[2] Although the chronotope can be useful in discussing both painting and film,[3] Bakhtin's concern in 'Forms of Time and Chronotope in the Novel' is with the literary text, in which, he says, 'spatial and temporal indicators are fused into one carefully thought-out, concrete whole' (FTC 84). The particular way in which these indicators intersect in a text is what constitutes its characteristic chronotopes, which are also affected by historical factors such as attitudes to nature, geographical knowledge, and conceptions of the human subject's interior life.

The concept of the chronotope may be puzzling or hard to grasp because it seems omnipresent to the point either of invisibility or of extreme obviousness. Bakhtin quotes Kant at the beginning of his essay: 'space and time [are] indispensable forms of any cognition' (FTC 85 n. 2), and adds in his own Conclusion: 'Without such temporal-spatial expression, even abstract thought is impossible. Consequently, every entry into the sphere of meanings is accomplished only through the gates of the chronotope' (FTC 258). Bakhtin here uses a kind of critical chronotope to discuss the chronotope, that of the door which opens on to knowledge; as we will see, he is often conscious of the everyday use of chronotopic expressions. However, what is suggestive about Bakhtin's essay is his historical and generic charting of the chronotope. The subtitle to his essay, 'Notes towards a Historical Poetics',[4] shows that his interest is in how texts relate to their social and political contexts, rather than in simply drawing up a typology of how time and space relate to each other within different texts.

Bakhtin also shows how particular aesthetic forms, including conceptions of human subjectivity, come about at certain times; as he says in 'Toward a Reworking of the Dostoevsky Book', for instance, 'Capitalism created the conditions for a special type of inescapably solitary consciousness. Dostoevsky exposes all the falsity of this consciousness, as it moves in its vicious circle' (288). The relations between time and space, and the human figures which populate them, alter according to the text's setting in both literary and wider history. The chronotope operates on three levels: first, as the means by which a text represents history; second, as the relation between images of time and space in the novel, out of which any representation of history must be constructed; and third, as a way of discussing the formal properties of the text itself, its plot, narrator, and relation to other texts. When discussing the particular suitability of film as a chronotopic form, Robert Stam mentions both its own formal properties, which very clearly 'fuse' both 'temporal and spatial indicators', and its material representational properties: 'the cinematic chronotope is quite literal, splayed out concretely across a screen with specific dimensions and unfolding in literal time (usually 24 frames a second), quite apart from the fictive time/space specific films might construct'.[5]

History and the chronotope

Although every text has its own chronotope or set of them, which interact dialogically with other chronotopes within and between texts, some texts are more fruitful to approach in this way than others, for instance those which are set at a particularly fraught historical moment, which set out to represent a historical event, or which adopt one of the forms where relations between time and space are especially clear, such as the road movie, or tales of time travel.

The three central layers of Alain Resnais' film *Hiroshima mon amour* (1959) can be analysed using the notion of the chronotope in its three forms: external history as represented in the film; the film's own images of space and time; and the film's formal construction. Within the film, Hiroshima is both a place and a time; it is the city of the film's post-war present, and the moment of the atom bomb. This is made clear in the dialogue between the lovers: 'Were you there, at Hiroshima?' the French woman asks the Japanese man. Such a phrasing of the question only makes sense if 'Hiroshima' is seen chronotopically, and in a particularly charged way, as a location in both time and space. The woman wants to know whether the man was there the day the bomb was dropped, rather than whether he was simply in the city at some time in the past, which is why she says 'at' rather than 'in'.

The three aspects of the chronotope are interlinked in the film, as is often the case. Resnais was unable to fulfil his commission to make a short documentary film on the atom bomb, until Marguerite Duras provided a fictional structure for this 'false documentary', as she called it.[6] The film is about the making of a documentary on the bomb, which provides a narrative reason for the French woman, who is a film actor, to be in Japan. The chrono-topic representation of history in the film is that of film-making, which includes both false and real documentary footage, and footage of the various war museums in Hiroshima and its Peace Garden. This intersects with the romance narrative, which is chronotopically charged because the lovers are from different coun-tries – separated by space – and meet with the knowledge that they will have to part. Their awareness of time threatened by space is balanced by an awareness of space representing time, as the lovers do not call each other by their names, but by the towns which constitute their respective histories: the man is called Hiroshima by the woman, and she is called Nevers by him. The film's own time and space is constructed according to the logic of flashback as a chronotopic representation of memory; the posture of the Japanese man sleeping reminds the woman of the German soldier she loved during the Second World War, who was shot just before the liber-ation. Her flashbacks begin as unexplained moments, but become more protracted and act more as narratives in their own right as the film progresses.[7]

As for the third category, the film's own formal chronotope is that of metafiction, as it is about film-making. Narratively, it has a double plot: the present of the love affair, and the unravelling of the past, which proceed together. Both elements of this third cate-gory are so deeply caught up in the politics of the film, and its two other chronotopic categories, that it is almost impossible to separate them. The film thus unites what Bakhtin sees as a split in the chronotope, between human public and private existence: the public, historical events of the dropping of the atom bomb on Hiroshima, the occupation of France, and the Second World War in general are shown as inescapably part of the protagonists' personal histories and subjectivity. The film is, as its title suggests, a story of desire between countries, between tragic fates, or even between historical events, rather than simply between two individ-uals. Its link with Michael Curtiz's 1942 film *Casablanca* is signalled by a scene in a bar of that name in Hiroshima, but this intertextual hint also shows that whereas in *Casablanca* the war is subordinated to the love story, in *Hiroshima* they are equally weighted. In his discussion of the Greek romance, Bakhtin observes that, '[c]harac-teristically it is not private life that is subjected to and interpreted in light of social and political events, but rather the other way around – social and political events gain meaning in the novel only thanks to their connection with private life' (FTC 109). While this does seem to be true of *Casablanca*, which is after all remembered as a great love story in which war is a backdrop and obstacle, it is not the case with *Hiroshima*, where 'private life' gains its meaning only through political events. The war is not an obstacle but what draws the lovers together, an inevitable condition of life even fifteen years on.

Bakhtin's regret at the passing of certain kinds of chronotope is clearest when he discusses what he sees as the decline of the chronotope from a communal to a more privatized, bourgeois form. For instance, he describes the gradual loss of the chronotope of the public square (FTC 135), which characterizes carnivalesque literature, and its replacement by domestic spaces, which characterize the novel from the eighteenth century onwards: 'the forms of *drawing-room rhetoric* acquired increasing importance, and the most significant form was the *familiar letter*' (FTC 143). Thus, in a famous scene in Homer's *Iliad*, Achilles weeps so noisily about the death of Patroclus that he is heard throughout the Greek camp from his tent; as Bakhtin points out, there are many rival explanations for this striking event, but in chronotopic terms it fits perfectly with the contemporary conception of human nature, the 'complete exteriority of public man' (FTC 134). In this chronotope, 'every aspect of existence could be *seen* and *heard*', which bears testimony to 'the spirit of the Greek public square [...] upon which the self-consciousness of European man first coalesced' (FTC 135), as Bakhtin rather grandly puts it.

In contrast with this, one might think of Jane Austen's 'new private and drawing-room world' (FTC 143), in particular the scene from *Persuasion* (1818) in which Captain Wentworth overhears a conversation between Anne Elliot and Captain Harville, which prompts him to write her a letter declaring his love. This fits exactly with Bakhtin's observation about the transformation of the public declaration in the square into a letter read in a drawing-room, a chronotopic move which accompanies a change in conceptions of subjectivity. Far from uttering anything audible, Wentworth's passion is silently read by Anne (and by the 'snooping' reader). As Bakhtin puts it, 'The human begins to shift to a space that is closed and private, the space of private rooms where something approaching intimacy is possible, where it loses its monumental formedness and exclusively public exteriority' (FTC 144). He suggests that this shift is accompanied by a changing attitude to nature itself, which is also drawn into the 'new private and drawing-room world', and survives only as 'landscape', 'setting', a 'view' (FTC 143–4, 217). Bakhtin contrasts this with earlier literary approaches to nature, such as the pastoral idyll or georgic, both of which are concerned with nature as a force humans are contained by, or, more significantly, work in. In 'Discourse in the Novel', Bakhtin offers a more generic view of the novel's spatial layout; he suggests that the Sentimental novel is 'associated with the intimacy of one's own room [...] the zone of the letter, the diary' (FTC 397); one of the examples Bakhtin gives is Samuel Richardson's epistolary novels. The private room, the home and the 'more house-like Protestant church' are contrasted with the public square, palace and (Catholic) cathedral.

The nostalgia which Bakhtin clearly feels for the earlier kinds of chronotope, and therefore for the more communal kinds of society these chronotopes refract, is not as explicit here as in his discussion of carnival, but none the less his history of the chronotope charts a progressive decline, a regrettable move away from open spaces to the parlour. However, as Ken Hirschkop has pointed out, this real-life decline is compensated for by the 'developmental' nature of narrative technique: it 'gets better at depicting the spaces that are available'.[8] Bakhtin makes a link with his work on Rabelais by arguing that Rabelais' work inaugurated a new kind of chronotope, and a new exterior image of humanity, a change made possible by the waning of the Middle Ages and its dark world-view. Rabelais replaced this with a chronotope of a 'generative time [...] measured [...] by creative acts, by growth and not by destruction' (FTC 206). Bakhtin suggests that such a chronotope could arise only from 'a collective, work-oriented agricultural base' structured according to a calendar of 'social everyday time [...] connected with the agricultural labor cycle' and its clearly defined seasons, times of the day, stages in the lives of crops and livestock.

It is interesting to read, for instance, Thomas Hardy's *Tess of the D'Urbervilles* (1891) in this light, as Tess's decline is set against, and associated with, the increasing industrialization of rural England. The 'natural' calendar of her life as a milkmaid is replaced by a hellish, exploitative timetable dictated by new agricultural machinery. Hardy's regret is comparable to Bakhtin's own, and he implicitly likens Tess to a natural phenomenon, like the moon, which is blighted by a move into a new, unnatural chronotope, by naming the seven parts of the novel 'Phases'. The high point of privatized, individual existences occurs, Bakhtin claims, 'when financial relations develop in slaveholding societies under capitalism' (FTC 215). This certainly seems to be confirmation that the move of the chronotope away from collective, public spaces to personal ones is not to be recommended. However, Bakhtin writes admiringly of writers who skilfully deploy their particular chronotopes even in the modern age; he notes Balzac's 'extraordinary' ability to '"*see*" time in space', and observes that he and Stendhal (one could add one's own list of authors here, including for instance Jane Austen) do not limit themselves to the parlour and salon. He adds, '[w]e need only mention Balzac's marvelous depiction of houses as materialized history and his description of streets, cities, rural landscapes at the level where they are being worked upon by time and history' (FTC 247). This is a materialist criticism which focuses particularly upon the relations between time and space in people's lives, as these are given meaning by their background of work, suffering, travel, war, and death.[9]

Bakhtin also links increasing privatization of the chronotope with a certain kind of narration, and the appearance of certain kinds of characters in fiction. The implication of the withdrawal from fields and roads to boudoirs and parlours was that life lived in the latter was secret; this contradiction '*between the public nature of the literary form and the private nature of its content*' meant that both narrator and reader are placed in the position of spies and eavesdroppers. 'The literature of private life is essentially a literature of snooping about, of overhearing "how others live"' (FTC 123). Narratorial developments such as free indirect discourse, epistolary novels, and first-person narrative can be seen as a result of this, as can more obvious devices such as the instance of a character in Alain Lesage's eighteenth-century novel *Le Diable boîteux* who lifts the roof off a house in order to expose what is going on inside (FTC 127). The presence of prostitutes and courtesans, Bakhtin says, is functionally similar to that of servants in novels (though the resemblance may not end there, as contemporary critics have suggested[10]), as all these groups are in good positions to find out the 'secrets and intimacies' of private life (FTC 125). This is a particularly good example of the shift, imperceptible in some cases but all-important, between the chronotopes of the real world and those of the represented world; in the latter, particular kinds of characters and settings appear for structural reasons as much as for mimetic ones. The solutions mentioned above to the problem of a public form like the novel trying to narrate the private actually have a dialogic function: there is a logical, if unlikely, reason in these instances why one person knows more than another, and it is not simply because they are a classical narrator. The Lame Devil in Lesage's novel reveals 'personal life at those moments when a "third person's" presence would not be permitted' (FTC 127). This is exactly how the dialogic novel operates: nothing is narrated which could be known only to a 'non-participating third person' (PDP 18) or impersonal narrator, and in the case of Lesage's novel this principle is actually dramatized.

THE CHRONOTOPE AND PLOT

In *Problems of Dostoevsky's Poetics*, Bakhtin discusses Dostoevsky's 'artistic conception of time and space' in the context of carnival, although the word 'chronotope' does not appear. Dostoevsky's representation of space matches his representation of time. Both are concerned with *'points of crisis [...] turning points and catastrophes'*, which in the case of time means leaving out 'uninterrupted historical or biographical time', and, in terms of space, concentrating action

> on two 'points' only: on the threshold (in doorways, on staircases, in corridors, and so forth), where the crisis and the turning points occur, or on the public square, whose substitute is usually the drawing-room (the hall, the dining-room), where the catastrophe, the scandal take place. (PDP 149)

The concept of a domestic equivalent to the public square of carnival is clearly an important one, and Bakhtin sees Raskolnikov as a contemporary version of a carnival king in the process of being decrowned (PDP 168–9). He adds to the list of household spaces which 'substitute for the *public square*', 'the third-class railway car' (PDP 174) and 'streets, taverns, roads, bathhouses, decks of ships' (PDP 128). In *Crime and Punishment* (1866), however, the typical spaces of the novel are even more constricted; there is no representation of interiors typical of biographical life, and events occur at '[t]he threshold, the foyer, the corridor, the landing, the stairway, its steps, doors opening onto the stairway, gates to front and back yards, and beyond these, the city: squares, streets, façades, taverns, dens, bridges, gutters' (PDP 170[11]). The time of crisis which interests Dostoevsky has its corresponding subjective state, typically a version of the '"final moments of consciousness" before execution or suicide', or a time of penal servitude or of gambling (PDP 172).

It is clear that the chronotope is such an elastic category that it can be made to do duty in a variety of different roles. It can be used to analyse local effects in a text, such as the asylum in *Jane*

Eyre;[12] it can be used to discuss a whole genre, such as film noir.[13] Bakhtin suggests that both author and reader inhabit their own chronotope (FTC 252–3), so that the term comes also to have a reader-response element; and, perhaps most commonly, it can be used to analyse local images in a text which are based upon a link between time and space. Bakhtin points out that everyday phrases such as the 'path of life' (FTC 120) or the 'threshold' (FTC 248) have a clear chronotopic basis. In all of these phrases, time passed means distance covered. (The plays of Samuel Beckett, notable for their static sets and plots, suggest that time passed does not necessarily mean distance covered.) Other common novelistic devices can be categorized chronotopically. The tendency for texts which follow the form of the Greek adventure novel to consist of events which are not related consistently or psychologically is the result of their particular chronotope. Events occur 'suddenly', out of the blue; non-human forces intervene to cause change; one thing follows after another, but without logic (FTC 92–5). This adventure time requires large amounts of space in which its chronotope can be played out, hence the adventure novel's plot-line of abduction, parting, pursuit, escape (98–100), often set in arbitrarily chosen foreign locations. Most eighteenth-century Gothic fictions, such as *The Castle of Otranto* and *Vathek*, fit this description very closely. Transformation scenes and metamorphosis in such texts also have chronotopic resonance; they represent personal alteration in a sudden, unmotivated way, as a series of crisis points and not as internal evolution (FTC 112–15). The magical changing of a person into another form – Bakhtin gives the example of Lucius being turned into an ass in Apuleius' text (FTC 122) – shows a kind of collapsing of time and space. Instead of gradual change, it happens on the spot. Dystopian and utopian novels also have a particular chronotopic identity, depending on their particular attitude to their own present and how they project a future based upon it (FTC 147). In novels where unity of place is maintained throughout generations, Bakhtin identifies the 'idyllic chronotope', in which *'unity of place'* is so strong that time again appears to collapse upon it: 'unity of place brings together and even fuses the cradle and the grave', contributing to a 'cyclical' rhythm (FTC 225).

It is tempting to see the idyllic as an ambivalent chronotope; while Bakhtin has expressed admiration elsewhere for a cyclical chronotope based on stasis, notably in his discussion of the grotesque carnival body, it also carries connotations of property-owning inheritance, primogeniture, and other features of capitalist society. It might be more helpful to see Bakhtin's categories as descriptive, rather than prescriptive, even where he appears to offer an evaluation of them; chronotopes of this 'idyllic' kind are often most interesting at the point where change starts to occur, where the cyclical rhythm is disrupted and its chronotopic construction is laid bare. For instance, constancy of location in *Tess of the D'Urbervilles* has quite varied meanings – Tess's family has worked in the same village for generations, although time does not stand still there. Tess, who can read and has been to a village school, is a representative of a new generation and the future, but she is dragged backwards by her father's fixation on a false genealogy, represented by the artefacts that have been collected in her home. They are concrete embodiments of a dangerous spatialization of time. Alec D'Urberville, however, who has bought the right to the house and name he sports, is a sham. Even though true aristocratic heritage is by no means endorsed, his *nouveau riche*, rootless status is an index of his moral shallowness.

To use a filmic example, in Ingmar Bergman's *Wild Strawberries* (1957) the central character Isak Borg finds some kind of peace of mind when he is near death through a vision of his parents beckoning to him from the place where his father used to fish. Although Borg no longer lives in the same place, this hint at a possibility of psychic continuity is best represented by a shared location which persists through generations. Borg's case actually unites at least two different chronotopes, as the occasion for his memories is a car journey to Stockholm, an example of the road chronotope in which, as Bakhtin says, time and space markers are very clearly linked (FTC 98). In Borg's case, he journeys forward into the past: 'Isak can only come to terms with his egocentricity by traveling back in time to his earliest youth, finding there the seeds of his failure as husband, lover, and father', as Peter Cowie puts it.[14] The relation here of personal time and space, that of memory, regret and peace of mind, to historical time and space, in which the human subject is on a car journey and soon to die, are complex and perhaps most interestingly unravelled using the concept of chronotope.

In the examples which follow, it is clear that Bakhtin's insistence on a social and political reading of time and space can be extended beyond his own uses of the term. He allows a loophole for possible extensions in his essay, by saying that other work will 'in its further development eventually supplement, and perhaps substantially correct, the characteristics of novelistic chronotopes offered by us here' (FTC 85). In the Conclusion to the essay, written in 1973, Bakhtin adds 'Whether the approach taken in this present work will prove fundamental and productive, only the further development of literary research can determine' (258). These comments are useful in paving the way, to speak chronotopically, to using Bakhtin's work as something which can be built upon using contemporary categories, such as gender, or analysing works whose chronotopes are more up-to-date than those of the Greek adventure novel.

The chronotope of the road

The clearest textual expression of the link between time and space is probably the road narrative, in which time spent means ground covered, and pages turned. However, Bakhtin's account depends on the traveller along the road being a (heterosexual, white) male, which would seem to make his theory unsuitable for considering recent narratives which do follow the road pattern but in which the travellers are not as Bakhtin imagined them.[15] A Bakhtinian reading of Ridley Scott's *Thelma and Louise* (1991) shows that, if the element of gender is introduced, the chronotope becomes a fruitful critical category for feminist and queer theory.

When *Thelma and Louise* was released it was greeted with critical suspicion as well as acclaim in both Britain and the USA, because it seemed merely a reversal of male buddy-movies complete with their violence and anonymous sex, only this time enacted by women.[16] As an example of the usual kind of road narrative, this is Jack Kerouac's description in *On the Road* (1957) of Sal Paradise deciding to go travelling with Dean Moriarty:

> Although my aunt warned me he could get me into trouble, I could hear a new call and see a new horizon, and believe it at my young age; and a little bit of trouble or even Dean's eventual rejection of me as a buddy, putting me down, as he later did, on starving sidewalks and sickbeds – what did it matter? I was a young writer and I wanted to take off.
>
> Somewhere along the line I knew there'd be girls, visions, everything; somewhere along the line the pearl would be handed to me.[17]

This passage is an archetypal version of what Bakhtin describes as a feature of the Greek adventure romance in 'Forms of Time and Chronotope in the Novel'. He says,

> Of special importance [in such narratives] is the close link between

the motif of meeting and the chronotope of the road ('the open road'), and of various types of meeting on the road. In the chronotope of the road, the unity of time and space markers is exhibited with exceptional precision and clarity. (FTC 98)

This 'unity' is suggested, for instance, in Sal Paradise's phrases 'a new horizon' and 'along the line', which operate in both space and time, and at both a literal and a metaphorical level.

The ways in which Kerouac's novel fits Bakhtin's definition of the road chronotope are not, however, limited to its structure of meetings and adventures; as the quotation suggests, this is a *man's* chronotope, in which the unfinalizable quest represented by the road is not only a quest for knowledge, in the 'Platonic' form of biography, as Bakhtin puts it (FTC 130), or for 'the pearl', as Sal Paradise says. Women are also a goal of such a quest, to be 'met' and bypassed along the way ('I knew there'd be girls', Paradise thinks), which implies a certain, proprietorial attitude to the land covered as well. This is represented, for instance, in Dennis Hopper's *Easy Rider* (1969), one of the precursor texts cited by *Thelma and Louise*, where encounters with women are as integral a part of the journey as the tabs of acid and camp-fires.[18]

In other words, Bakhtin assumes that the person doing the travelling in the road chronotope, and thus the central consciousness of the narrative, is male; as he puts it, 'The image of man is always intrinsically chronotopic' (FTC 85), and the point here is precisely that for 'man' we cannot also read 'woman'. The apparently 'neutral' elements of 'the high road' which Bakhtin cites turn out to be gender-blind rather than genuinely neutral. He says, 'The road is a particularly good place for random encounters [...] People who are normally kept separate by social and spatial distance can accidentally meet; any contrast may crop up, the most various fates may collide and interweave with one another' (FTC 243). For women on the high road, these 'random encounters', collisions, and interweavings transcend their status as simply structural elements, and become filled with political meaning: in *Thelma and Louise* they include encounters with a barmaid whose efforts to protect them get sidetracked; a fatherly detective; a thieving cowboy; attempted rape, and sexual harassment.

What is striking about Bakhtin's omission of gender is that it would have fed particularly aptly into his own theory; the meaning of encounters, and the way in which the road-narrative begins (that is, the reasons why people are on the road in the first place), are both clearly quite different when women are involved. The reasons Thelma and Louise, or Marian Crane in *Psycho* (Alfred Hitchcock, 1960), who also takes to the road, do so is because they are women. Callie Khourie, who wrote the script for *Thelma and Louise*, explains: 'I just got fed up with the passive role of women. They were never driving the story, because they were never driving the car'.[19]

The difference such redescription of Bakhtin's comments on the road chronotope makes to the reality it forms is something emphasized within the film itself. The spectator of the film sees different discourses clash on the road; according to one distinctive linguistic universe – one which depends on grunts and gestures as much as words – the women are 'bitches from hell'. According to others, they are quite the opposite. As several instances in the film show, it is characterized rather by a dialogic repetition-with-difference than by a 'dialectic' reversal. Thelma robs a store by re-enacting J.D.'s performance, although with significant differences of her own, and this time she is repeating the words of a man, who has just robbed her. Simple role reversal does not account for the complexity of the apparently blank, abstract space of the road becoming full of a charged meaning when gender enters the picture. The credit sequence of *Thelma and Louise* suggests this: it presents a landscape of plains and peaks, then the camera pans to show an empty road leading to a mountain. This is the first and last time in the film that we see such a spectacle: anonymous, empty open space, a road suggesting simply forward movement, which is what a road free of the implications of sexual difference, of the kind Bakhtin describes, would look like.

Film as chronotopicity

Bakhtin emphasizes the fact that the road chronotope is a metaphor made real; he describes this process, which is true of all chronotopes: 'Time as it were, thickens, takes on flesh, becomes artistically visible; likewise, space becomes charged and responsive to the movements of time, plot and history' (FTC 84). This description seems tantalizingly close to a recasting of Christian Metz's formulation of cinema's construction in terms of the 'imaginary signifier', where the very illusion of the three-dimensionality of space depends precisely on its absence. Metz says that 'voyeuristic desire, along with certain forms of sadism, is the only desire whose principle of distance symbolically and spatially evokes this fundamental rent' – that is, the Lacanian rent of the subject, post-mirror stage and having acquired language, hopelessly desiring an unattainable object.[20] Indeed, Stam has suggested that the power of cinema depends on the fact that involvement in a spectacle increases in inverse proportion to the 'representational adequacy' of the medium.[21] We imagine we see the double of reality precisely because there is a lack to be filled, the screen representing unreality in a way the stage, for example, does not.

Although particular films, like *Thelma and Louise*, make this very plain, time and space in cinema are not gender-free terms to start with. Mary Ann Doane, following Laura Mulvey's classic essay 'Visual Pleasure and Narrative Cinema', points out that particular cinematic techniques are typically used to film women as flattened out iconic figures, whose presence interrupts the narrative trajectory. Deep focus, on the other hand, often characterizes the representation of the male figure on screen (hence perhaps Orson Welles's fondness for using a deep field of focus); the female figure is treated to 'certain practices of imaging – framing, lighting, camera movement, angle. She is thus [...] more closely associated with the surface of the image than its illusory depths, its constructed three-dimensional space which the man is destined to inhabit and hence control.'[22] Lynda Hart cites Teresa de Lauretis's argument that traditional narrative is governed by an Oedipal logic, in which every spectator or reader is limited to two positions '"of a sexual difference thus conceived: male-hero-human, on the side of the subject; and female-obstacle-boundary-space, on the other"'.[23] In *Thelma and Louise* the traditional associations of women with space of these kinds – geographical, narrative, and cinematic – are defamiliarized.

Bakhtin points out how the parlours, salons, and boudoirs of Stendhal and Balzac where plots and affairs are conducted make the epoch 'not only graphically visible [space], but narratively visible [time]' (FTC 247); the same could be said of the typical spaces of *Thelma and Louise*, which include bars, service stations, diners, motels, and women's rooms.[24] As Bakhtin says, things which are static in space cannot be statically described: narrative forces them into three-dimensionality, on to the road. He typically undoes the neutrality of his own description, however, by taking as his example the beauty of Helen of Troy, which can take on meaning only by becoming 'the subject of a dynamic story' (FTC 251); to paraphrase Callie Khourie, Helen herself, unlike Thelma and Louise, certainly had little part in driving the warships of her own story.

Bakhtin points out that meanings 'must take on the form of a sign that is audible and visible' (FTC 258). As Robert Stam argues, this seems to suggest that film *is* chronotopicity (or the chronotope's fullest expression is film), exactly the 'temporal-spatial expression' of a sign which Michael Gardiner defines as 'the system of interacting time and space indicators that are necessary for any kind of artistic visualization',[25] in a formulation which might apply equally to film as to the chronotope. Again *Thelma and Louise* demonstrates the paucity, or even meaninglessness, of this definition if it is restricted to the simply formal. The sign itself affects the means of temporal-spatial expression, as the difference between the meaning of the diners in *Thelma and Louise* and those in other films shows, for instance that in Barry Levinson's *Diner* (1982), a patriarchal space.

Near the end of 'Forms of Time and Chronotope in the Novel', Bakhtin discusses the 'adventure novel of everyday life', in which the life of the central character corresponds both to that character's wanderings and to the form of the plot: these elements are indistinguishable (FTC 111). Fabula and sjuzhet are one (that is, to use the Russian Formalists' distinction, story and plot are the same: 'story', or 'fabula', is the chronological sequence of events from which the artistic rearrangement of 'plot', or 'sjuzhet', is constructed). This seems to be true of *Thelma and Louise*, as the ambiguity of whether we are referring to the film or to the protagonists suggests. In the film, the plot and the road become synonymous; causes take effect a little further on, often in a 'snowballing' way, as Louise puts it. Time equals distance which equals safety as the women flee from the police and the past; when they drive away after Thelma holds up the store, she advises Louise to slow down, to which the latter replies that she is trying to put 'some distance between us and the scene of our last goddamn crime!'

An interesting example of the clash between contingent and necessary plot progress in this road narrative – the FBI agent asks whether the women's apparent success is due to luck (contingency) or brains (necessity) – is Thelma's encounter with the young man J.D. Is she robbed because she has sex with him, as in *Psycho* it seems that Marian is killed by Norman Bates *because* she stole some money to fund an extra-marital relationship? Or is there no causal relationship suggested between the events, which simply follow one after the other?[26] One way to see the robbery is as a reminder of the atypical nature of this particular road narrative; instead of Thelma being one of the 'girls along the line' mentioned by Sal Paradise,

J.D. is the boy 'along the line' of her road narrative who is encountered and then bypassed; the continuing imbalance of the genders as they travel, however, is registered by his theft and the fact that he flees first.

There are other, non-linear devices, apart from the 'snowball' of one event following (and compounding) the other, which also tell the time and chart its passage in the film.[27] The maps the pair use to plot their journey are materially emphasized ('We don't need the east coast any more', says Thelma, stuffing the map into the back of the car): maps chart space, but they also represent time. The police want Louise to speak for long enough on the phone to find out where she is, and stop the road narrative in its tracks; they use time to pinpoint space. The episode where the women watch sunrise over a desertscape and then trap the policeman in his car is accompanied by clear indications of time through the movement of sun and shadows: time is represented in spatial terms. The film is constructed by alternations of scene to show what is happening in the investigative trajectory of the story which parallels the road narrative: while Thelma and Louise are passing the trucker for the first time, for instance, Hal Slocum is visiting Jimmy back home, and we are shown one after the other. The forces which aim to stop the road narrative are interleaved with its progress; over the phone Hal says to Louise he feels as if he knows her, to which she reasonably replies he doesn't, which is a measure of the distance between the two plots at this point. Their closest moment of contact is probably when the two lines – one forward-moving and unplanned, the other circuitous and interpretive – appear within the same frames at the end of the film, especially when Hal runs in slow motion after the fast-disappearing car.

The characters themselves are intermittently aware of the symbolic nature of their journey. When Louise first telephones Jimmy, he says to her ambiguously, 'Where the hell you at? Are you out of town?' Louise suggests that she is, both literally and metaphorically: 'I'm in deep shit, Arkansas … I did it, and I can't undo it'. This description of her position seems to conform exactly to Bakhtin's words about time taking on flesh in the chronotope; the place Louise is in is both brutally material and intangibly moral. She did commit the crime in Arkansas (Hal belongs to the Arkansas State Police), although the name may sound mythic for various reasons including its reference to the interminable episodes of the children's cartoon Wacky Races, the end-point of which was indeed Arkansas. At the same time, her phrase, 'I did it, and I can't undo it', points exactly to the road which follows: you cannot retrace your steps down a road or a narrative and wipe out the earlier journey. This may be implicit in Louise's refusal to travel through Texas, on account of a past trauma which remains a diegetic mystery.[28]

Thelma also shows awareness of the symbolic importance of the spatial in her realization that she has gone too far: 'Something's crossed over in me and I can't go back – I just couldn't live'. This remark corresponds closely to what Bakhtin says of the 'chronotope of the *threshold*', which can be 'combined with the motif of encounter, but its most fundamental instance is as the chronotope of crisis and break in a life' (FTC 248). Thelma's 'break' in life has certainly been combined with, if not instigated by, a particular encounter. Her remark shows awareness of what Bakhtin describes as the fact that the 'word "threshold" itself already has a metaphorical meaning in everyday usage', and although again he continues to a masculinist conclusion – 'In Dostoevsky, for example, the threshold and related chronotopes [...] are the main places of action in his works, places where crisis events occur [...] decisions that determine the whole life of a man' – clearly the threshold has particular resonance for the construction of a gender-aware chronotope. Its metaphorical meaning derives from the boundary between private and public space, just as Thelma realizes she cannot cross back from the journey with Louise into the house she shared with Darrell. Cathy Griggers notes that critics of the film claimed it was unrealistic because it represented domestic anxieties taken outside the domestic scene to the road,[29] but this transgression or crossing over is exactly the point in a chronotope of the feminine.

Finally, Louise's farewell to Jimmy – 'I'll catch up with you later; further down the road' – again demonstrates that chronotopicity resides even (or especially) in common phraseology, which clearly recognizes that life is a path. In this case, 'the road' has several alternative identities. It is the Route 81 to Dallas we see in the mise-en-scène, saturated with unreal colour and bristling with phallic symbols, according to Lynda Hart, and also the anonymous road where herds of cattle churn up dustclouds.[30] The women follow secondary roads to Mexico, and sometimes drive off-road, for safety and also in acknowledgement that this is not usually the kind of story which takes the high road. Even a comparison between the charms of Darrell and J.D. is expressed in terms of road discourse: Thelma says her husband is not cute at all, as 'You could park a car in the shadow of his ass'. At the end, Thelma can only express her resolve in the same terms of forward movement which the women have already experienced: 'Let's not get caught ... Let's keep going ... Go!' Cathy Griggers suggests that this, combined with the replay of earlier clips from the film which run for the duration of the end credits, creates a circular narrative out of a linear one, 'a loop in time, a return to the moment before loss'.[31]

Thelma and Louise fail at first to recognize the Grand Canyon when they come upon it, and it is this cleft in the land which is the end of the road and of the narrative. It becomes literally a place where a 'line is overstepped' (PDP 169), a massive threshold from which there is no turning back. Critics have pointed out that the women cannot be at the Grand Canyon when they say they are there, and Hart terms the depiction of space in the film in general 'incoherent geography'. Travelling to Mexico from Oklahoma City avoiding Texas would take them not to Arizona, where the canyon is, but to New Mexico (which is where the scenes were filmed: the chronotopes of space within the film and of the film's material construction are united).[32] The most specific journeys may turn out to be so in a way other than the mimetic.

The chronotope and gender

Bakhtin makes gender into a formal property of narrative in 'Forms of Time and Chronotope'; he mentions women only as narrative devices or functions (prostitutes and courtesans, FTC 125) or as narrative objects in male-centred action (he describes 'circular' time, in which the same events repeat themselves: 'people eat, drink, sleep, have wives, mistresses', 248). These women are not driving any cars. However, introducing gender into Bakhtin's own categories becomes a particularly fruitful way to approach a text which, as Thelma and Louise does, brings sexual difference to the fore partly by emphasizing the posturing involved in the cinematic clichés, such as male bonding, of which they offer feminized versions;[33] to quote Kimberly Devlin on Molly Bloom, whose behaviour has similarly been criticized as a kind of female patriarchy, they undo ideology by doing it.[34]

Michael Holquist points out that a particular chronotope is defined by the 'way in which the sequentiality of events is "deformed"',[35] and in terms of the road movie it could be suggested that the deformation consists in sequentiality masking causality; in Thelma and Louise, the 'chance' which Bakhtin discusses imperfectly

217

conceals a narrative drive constructed by the imperative of gender relations. Holquist also observes that 'fabula' is a historical concept, and that conceptions of how time and space relate depend on a precise historical moment;[36] this seems particularly true of the road movie, and also of the new version of it which *Thelma and Louise* constitutes. Narrative forms are always historical, as Holquist says, and the film shows this both in its implicit reference to recent male road narratives, and in its dependence on contemporary constructions of femininity.

To conclude, a chronotope of the feminine would take account of gender as a third element of the fleshing-out process: not only would time become spatial, and space historicized, but the emptiness of these terms would be filled with an account of how different open spaces, and domestic spaces, are for women and men. The distinction Bakhtin makes in relation to *Crime and Punishment* springs to mind: the spaces he describes as carnival moments of change, suited to Dostoevsky's interest in crisis time, are all 'masculine' ones – gutter, bridge, tavern. The spaces associated with women are the ones Bakhtin describes as spaces of biographical time, the household interior of drawing room, boudoir, and salon, although in 'Discourse in the Novel' even the most intimate space is given a male occupant. In certain novels 'the arena of man's experience' is narrowed down 'to his very own room' (DN 397).

The chronotope and the Holocaust

In Ida Fink's novel *The Journey* (1992), the first role of the chronotope in a literary work, its mediation between real historical events and their appearance in the text, seems to be paramount. The events – the Second World War and the Holocaust – are clearly recognizable, if not named. However, the novel's title highlights the chronotope's second role, that of establishing a text's own fictional balance between time and space, and it is this chronotope which unexpectedly takes precedence in the narration of the story. The title is deliberately misleading; this is not a road-narrative, and the two young women protagonists are not journeying so much as forced out and pretending to journey innocently. Greater generic flexibility is achieved by allowing the first chronotope to combine with the second, as is shown by imagining how it would sound if the novel had a more explicit, historicized title, like *Return to Auschwitz*, which would signal the precedence of the first chronotope and that the text is clearly autobiographical.[37] *The Journey*, by contrast, is presented as fiction.[38] The precedence of the second type of chronotope explains why this narrative fits Bakhtin's category of adventure novel, but each feature is filled with a meaning that makes Bakhtin's sense seem almost ironically benign.

Bakhtin says that the reader will be struck by

> the enormous role played by such devices as recognition, disguise, temporary changes of dress, presumed death (with subsequent resurrection), *presumed betrayal* (with subsequent confirmation of unswerving fidelity) and finally the basic compositional (that is, organizing) motif of a test of the heroes' integrity, their selfhood. (FTC 105)

All these features are present in *The Journey*, but, again, full of a meaning which is considerably more significant than the plot-serving devices listed here. In this fictionalized autobiography, two Jewish sisters escape Nazi-occupied Cracow in 1942 by masquerading as gentiles 'volunteering' for forced labour; they are unmasked, and the rest of the text chronicles their success in getting jobs as unpaid servants in Nazi Germany by pretending to be simple non-Jewish Polish girls. 'Recognition' is constantly feared, and depends on more than simply finding out someone's real name: the narrator reports of another Jewish woman, Marysia, 'Nothing about the way she looked would arouse the slightest suspicion [...] But I recognized her immediately, and she recognized me too'; and 'disguise' is essential for survival, as the 'savage' and 'foreign' narrator's use of the third person about her fictive German self suggests: 'When I'd escaped, I'd remembered to bandage the brave German girl's finger because nowadays, in brave German households, potatoes were peeled by savage foreigners from the East'.[39] Similarly, 'temporary changes of dress' bear a meaning far more significant than than the trivial trickery implied by Bakhtin; this is because, as with all these adventure features, it exists in two chronotopes at once, that of real history and that of the text's own plot, whereas, in the novel Bakhtin is concerned with, changes of dress exist only in the latter. In *The Journey*, hats and gloves are life-preserving signals of legitimacy and disguise for one train trip. Neither presumed death nor presumed betrayal is a disappointment: Marysia really does vanish – 'Walenty's words, prophetic and ominous, that we were saying goodbye as if we would never see each other again. Why never? I knew: never'; and real betrayal takes place.[40] Finally, the novel is a test of selfhood or integrity only if that also means a

literal preservation of the self and of the body's integrity. The intersection of the two chronotopes fills these abstract categories
Bakhtin enumerates with the kind of meaning, at once personal and
political, he regrets the ancient adventure novel can never achieve
(FTC 110) – but which the *Bildungsroman*, where the hero(ine)
emerges in conjunction with the age, can (B 23).

The time which characterizes this kind of 'novel of ordeal'
(FTC 86) is that of '*random contingency*', as Bakhtin explains:
'[s]hould something happen a minute earlier or a minute later, that
is, should there be no chance simultaneity or chance disjunctions in
time, there would be no plot at all, and nothing to write a novel
about' (FTC 92). Looking back on moments which are clearly
pivotal, and without which there would indeed have been 'nothing
to write a novel about', the narrator of *The Journey* comments on
meeting an old friend who gives her money: 'A miracle had
occurred. If I had walked that way a few minutes earlier, or a few
minutes later, if that insistent gaze hadn't driven me from the
streetcar'; and of a much later incident, when a call to the Gestapo
is interrupted: 'He dialed the number, and at that very moment, the
station commander opened the door. Sheer chance, the perfect
concurrence of two events. The policeman put down the
receiver.'[41] The chronotope of chance makes it hard to determine
which are the important events, but the narrator chooses the latter
one: 'Later she used to say: The place where everything almost
ended [...] But why that place? After all, there were other places
equally, if not more deserving of that description.'[42]

In the case of *The Journey*, 'the normal, pragmatic and premed-
itated course of events' has indeed been interrupted, which Bakhtin
says is also characteristic of the adventure novel, as the narrator
explains of the time just before the journey out of the ghetto
begins: 'we watched the work in the garden, familiar rites and
routines that now seemed to us strange and even comical'.[43] As
Bakhtin puts it of the adventure novel, 'there is no implied native,
ordinary, familiar world [...] against whose background the otherness and foreignness of what is foreign might be clearly projected'
(FTC 101). This is what *The Journey* is about, the loss of any 'home'
and the identity that goes with it.

The two functions of the chronotope are almost chillingly
united in the moments of apparently 'random contingency' in *The
Journey*, as they are throughout the novel, with the second kind
remaining uppermost, perhaps because this is exactly how historical
events and places appear to human witnesses, and how this novel

can be described as a 'high-grade thriller', as if the 'inevitability and fluke' have only a narrative meaning.[44] It is why the book attracts the kind of comment reprinted on its cover: 'The distance travelled by the author in *The Journey* is formidable', in which the chronotope of the road is used figuratively, to suggest literary progress and talent. The first kind of chronotope, that of actual events, is not visible from the ground, but the second, a local disposition of time and space, is just how public events are perceived by their victims. If 'everything' had ended in that place where a policeman rang the Gestapo, then the novel would have ended too. The story ending there would have meant that the tale would have no beginning either, no one to narrate it. It almost comes to another kind of halt when Halinka, after the first stage of the girls' journey, offers the narrator somewhere to hide; but, as Halinka will not also take the narrator's sister, the two continue on their way, and the narrative carries on. However, what looks like random chance or 'the intrusion of non-human forces' (FTC 95) in this novel of ordeal is not really that simple, as events are dictated in a very definite, incontrovertible manner, by Nazi policy. As the young women have little chance of altering their own fate under such a policy, anything which makes possible their continuing to live looks more like chance than agency.[45]

The precedence of the second, formal chronotope over the first in *The Journey* is not uncommon in novels about overwhelming historical events. In this case, the gap between the two chronotopes is sometimes a knowing one: 'Elzbieta had dark hair and an olive complexion. Before, people used to say she looked Italian', the narrator reports of her sister.[46] The preposition 'Before' is made to do a large amount of chronotopic work, and is not glossed with specific labels or dates. It draws a line before and after the 'new era', also unnamed, during which even train timetables are disrupted: it 'had brought about nocturnal departures not listed on any schedule'.[47] The train is *The Journey*'s chronotopic figure, its characteristic space in the way that salons and boudoirs characterize Balzac and Stendhal. Bakhtin says of the adventure novel, 'all the character's actions in Greek romance are reduced to *enforced movement through space* (escape, persecution, quests); that is, to a change in spatial location' (FTC 105); in this case, it is hardly a reduction but the story's whole meaning. The train links the periods spent by the sisters in different work-camps or farms, and comes to represent the forward motion of the two women and of their story, as the narrator thinks at a threshold moment on their journey 'south, down to the lake, close to the border', when they are about to adopt new identities for the third time:

> But just then I didn't want to think about the guards at strange train stations; the dim lobbies with their little ticket windows; the huge timetables from which we would randomly choose our destination and our time of departure; the moment when we would have to say where we were going, casually, our accents flawless, and with gloved hands, the gloves that hid rough skin and fingers black from peeling tons of potatoes, pick up our tickets from the brass plate. Most of all, I didn't want to think about the stares of the other passengers on the train, which, with every mile would bring us close to the birth of Barbara and Maria, to the moment when we would be asked our names and have to say them aloud, the moment from which there would be no turning back.[48]

The train will take the women closer to their geographical 'destination', and closer to the time when they will have to fictionalize themselves again. Its forward movement is contrasted to claustrophobic stasis; working on a field, the narrator sees a train go by in the distance and 'felt – very clearly, very palpably – the proximity of danger and the futility of my desperate scrambling, my frantic efforts to break out of this closed circle. It was as if a metal band was suddenly squeezing my ribs'.[49] To the reader the train may have a more general association with the events of the Holocaust, with the kind of journey, 'shorter and with no return' which the narrator knows is an alternative to the one she does embark upon. However, because the text is working most of the time at the level of the second, locally textual chronotope, rather than the first, historically aware one, this effect is limited to the reader's chronotope (FTC 252). The absence of the first chronotope from the text reflects the narrator's ignorance at the time of these events of what they signified, of the label which would later come to be applied to them, and even to such details as the name of the death camp where her boyfriend is killed: 'She knew: Auschwitz, Treblinka, Belzec. She knew: Bergen–Belsen, Mauthausen, but not Majdanek. She had never heard of Majdanek.'[50] Bakhtin describes the uniting of public and private histories in his essay on the *Bildungsroman*: in certain novels, which are set 'on the border between two epochs, at the transition point from one to the other', the character is forced to become 'a new unprecedented type of human being' (B 23).[51] The character in these kinds of novel 'emerges *along with the world* and [...] reflects the historical emergence of the world itself'. This is obviously the case in *The Journey*, where the end of the war means the end of the journey, the possibility of life elsewhere, and also the end of the narrative.

THE CHRONOTOPE OF MEMORY

Time in *The Journey* has a personal significance, divorced from either the ordinary calendar or the seasons, as the narrator describes before the journey begins: 'Time and again we stood on the porch looking for the signs. It was early spring when we first stood there, our coats still wet from the hours we'd spent lying under the bushes [...] That night they took away the elderly, the sick, and the disabled'.[52] The signs they are waiting for are not known in advance, come from an agenda which works according to its own timetable, and is not perceptibly linked to the wider events which are forming it. The relative terms of the second chronotope have absolute meanings in this context, such as '"You set out too late"',[53] as if a coherent calendar were in operation. Even the seasonal calendar gets drawn into the underlying, deforming one; in one forced-labour farm, the narrator reports, 'In the basement, lined up on shelves like books in a library, were jars of pickled pork. Every jar was numbered and marked with the date of the slaughter. Currently they were eating the year 1940'; and in spring while thinning beets in a field: 'They needed room – *Lebensraum!* – to grow into large, fat beets which would be taken to the cellar in the fall. In the fall! What would happen in the fall? Who knew?'[54] The land itself becomes a historical document, uttering a threatening meaning. This is a very clear example of a shift in chronotopic emphasis, from time to space; space is infected with the ideology of a 'time out of joint'.[55] Both the agricultural and seasonal calendars are thus distorted by an underlying chronotope which tends toward the end of the journey and death, rather than the usual, and carnivalesque, cyclical renewal.

The Journey is constructed according to the chronotope of memory, by means of the formal chronotopes of prolepsis (flashforward) and analepsis (flashback).[56] The way in which these two deviations from a narrative present work imitates the logic of memory, so that the reader's 'journey' towards the end of the text does not always proceed straightforwardly. Although sometimes the narrator says she will not relate events out of order, predictive phrases such as 'I didn't know that Pola would betray Zosia' are frequent. She describes her project: 'All the bits and pieces must be assembled into one continuous whole, and the task is difficult, and above all painful',[57] but the whole is that of repetitive, incomplete memory rather than a strictly chronological history. A comment made at the narrator's last meeting with Marysia is told three times, the first time when we are introduced to Marysia and have no idea yet who Walenty is: '"Why is she hugging and kissing you as if you two were never going to see each other again?" Walenty asked mockingly, after she left'.[58] Beginning and end are collapsed on to each other, in a chronotope which fits not the orderliness of plot, but the vagaries of personal recall. The narrator is at times aware of this herself:

> So this is the background to our 'affair', which is about to begin, that first evening, without delay, as if there were nothing more urgent. It will start during supper, over a bowl of rutabaga soup, which is tasteless, slightly sweet, and hard to swallow [...]
>
> Just a minute, just a minute. First Schmidt has to deliver his welcoming speech.[59]

The inevitability of plot and of a known history become indistinguishable as they are told; the 'affair' is about to start again, like a play which shows every night, but also with the dread repetition of a trauma which cannot be put aside,[60] so that 'has to deliver' is double-voiced. It has to happen so the narrator, in the present, can set the record straight; and it had to happen in the past because it was part of a chain of events allowing no leeway. Later, it is the gap between plot and history which concerns the narrator; she describes how the location she recalls is different from the place she visits after the war: 'For thirty years the policeman had led us through the circular plaza with thick trees to the building on the right. From now on, was he going to lead us in a different direction? And through which plaza? Circular or rectangular?[61]

What *The Journey* suggests is that the different roles of the chronotope in relation to texts are not fixed, nor hierarchically arranged, but rather, as Bakhtin says of chronotopes in general, in dialogic interaction with one another. It is also true that, although Bakhtin's descriptions of particular kinds of chronotope may seem to be missing some crucial elements, particularly that of gender, they can act as templates into which more specific, political meaning may be placed. Rather than being irredeemable because of their omissions, Bakhtin's categories can generate meaning in the way he claims meaning is always generated: by a repetition of a structure or utterance in a new context, or with altered content.

Notes

1 Anthony Wall and Clive Thomson discuss the 'more flexible' idea that 'chronotopicity [can be] said to lie in the very event of representation', 'Cleaning Up Bakhtin's Carnival Act', *Diacritics* 23 (2), summer 1993, pp. 47–70, p. 48.

2 Critics have debated the political implications of whether time or space has priority. Wall and Thomson criticize Morson and Emerson for claiming, in *Mikhail Bakhtin: The Creation of a Prosaics*, that time is more important than space, which means 'the unclean space of laughter and the body must be wiped away', 'Cleaning Up', p. 58. See Gary Saul Morson and Caryl Emerson's reply, 'Imputations and Amputations: Reply to Wall and Thomson', *Diacritics* 23 (4), winter 1993, pp. 93–9.

3 See for instance D. J. Haynes, *Bakhtin and the Visual Arts*, Cambridge University Press, Cambridge 1995.

4 See Michael Holquist, 'Introduction', DN xviii. Ken Hirschkop points out that the title and subtitle were devised by its compiler, Sergey Bocharov, although Bakhtin may well have assented to it.

5 Robert Stam, *Subversive Pleasures: Bakhtin, Cultural Criticism and Film*, Johns Hopkins University Press, Baltimore, Maryland 1989, p. 11.

6 Margaret Duras and Alain Resnais, *Hiroshima mon amour*, Grove Press, New York 1961, p. 4.

7 See Maureen Turim, *Flashbacks in Film: Memory and History*, Routledge, London 1989.

8 Ken Hirschkop, 'Is Dialogism for Real?', *Social Text* 30, 1987, p. 110. In his comments on the *Bildungsroman*, Bakhtin traces an opposite trajectory from the one I mention here: the chronotope is gradually perfected and 'becomes truly historical with the appearance of Goethe'.

9 See for instance Marilyn Butler on Jane Austen, in *Jane Austen and the War of Ideas*, Clarendon Press, Oxford 1975; Judith Lowder Newton on George Eliot, in *Women, Power and Subversion: Social Strategies in British Fiction, 1778–1860*, Methuen, London 1981.

10 See Jane Gallop, 'Keys to Dora', in *Feminism and Psychoanalysis: The Daughter's Seduction*, Macmillan, London 1982, in which she links the interchangeability of women within marriage and the family with the more explicitly monetary exchanges of service and prostitution.

11 See Ken Hirschkop, 'Introduction', in Ken Hirschkop and David Shepherd, eds, *Bakhtin and Cultural Theory*, Manchester University Press, Manchester 1989, on the importance for Bakhtin of the 'public square' as a place where different contexts, or their representatives, can meet, p. 16.

12 Suzanne Rosenthal Shumway, 'The Chronotope of the Asylum: *Jane Eyre*, Feminism, and Bakhtinian Theory', in Karen Hohne and Helen Wussow, eds, *A Dialogue of Voices: Feminist Literary Theory and Bakhtin*, University of Minnesota Press, Minneapolis, Minnesota 1994, 152–70.

13 Vivian Sobchak, '"Lounge Time": Post-War Crises and the Chronotopes of Film Noir', cited in R. Barton Palmer, 'Bakhtinian Translinguistics and Film Criticism: The Dialogical Image?', in R. Barton Palmer, ed., *The Cinematic Text: Methods and Approaches*, AMS Press, New York 1989, p. 307.

14 Peter Cowie, *Ingmar Bergman*, André Deutsch, London 1982, p. 157.

15 As a relatively random sample, see Janice Galloway's novel *Foreign Parts*, Minerva, London 1994, about unconventional voyagers; films *Messidor* (Alain Tanner, 1977), *Truck Stop Women* (Mark Lester, 1974), *The Adventures of Priscilla, Queen of the Desert* (Stephan Elliott, 1994), *My Own Private Idaho* (Gus Van Sant, 1990), *Two for the Road* (Stanley Donen, 1967), *Mad Love* (Antonia Bird, 1995), all make gender and sexuality an integral part of the journey – and therefore part of the chronotope.

16 See Sharon Willis's summary of the American press reception of *Thelma and Louise*, 'Hardware and Hardbodies, What Do Women Want?: A Reading of *Thelma and Louise*', in Jim Collins, Hilary Radner, and Ava Preacher Collins, eds, *Film Theory Goes to the Movies*, Routledge, New York 1993, pp. 120–3; Lynda Hart, *Fatal Women: Lesbian Sexuality and the Mark of Aggression*, Routledge, London 1994, p. 173 n. 35; C. Rose, 'The Bigger Picture: What Happens after *Thelma and Louise*', *Guardian*, 9 July 1991; J. Smith, 'Road Testing – The Critique', *ibid.* (I am grateful to Lynn Williams for the last two references.)

17 Jack Kerouac, *On the Road*, Penguin, Harmondsworth 1991 [1957], p. 11.

18 The precursor texts which constitute *Thelma and Louise* clearly also include *Bonnie and Clyde* (Arthur Penn, 1967) and *Butch Cassidy and the Sundance Kid* (George Roy Hill, 1969); Cathy Griggers mentions *Sweet Sweetback's Baadasssss Song* (1971), a black urban version of the road movie ('*Thelma and Louise* and the Cultural Generation of the New Butch-Femme', in Collins *et al.*, eds, *Film Theory Goes to the Movies*, p. 130); Carol J. Clover situates the film within a series of rape revenge films (*Men, Women and Chainsaws*, BFI Publishing, London 1993, p. 145). There are brief references to the (male) American frontier tradition within the film: Louise's surname is Sawyer, and both she and Thelma spontaneously cry aloud, 'The call of the wild!' in celebration of Thelma's armed robbery.

19 Quoted by Willis, 'Hardware and Hardbodies', p. 125.

20 Christian Metz, *The Imaginary Signifier*, trs Alfredo Guzzetti *et al.*, Indiana University Press, Bloomington, Indiana 1981, p. 60. Hart repeats this Lacanian vocabulary when discussing the film's ending: 'the canyon is the very image of the relationship between Lacan's "Real" and "reality"' (*Fatal Women*, p. 79); see also Claire Johnston's comment that death, for women in cinema, is 'the location of all impossible signs': here, the canyon must receive the impossible sign of women together evading men (quoted in Mary Ann Doane, 'Film and the Masquerade: Theorizing the Female Spectator', in *Femmes Fatales: Feminism, Film Theory, Psychoanalysis*, Routledge, London 1991, p. 28).

21 Robert Stam, *Reflexivity in Film and Literature, from 'Don Quixote' to Jean-Luc Godard*, UMI Research Press Studies in Cinema, Ann Arbor, Michigan 1985, p. 34.

22 Doane, 'Film and the Masquerade', p. 20.

23 Hart, *Fatal Women*, p. 71.

24 The investigative narrative in *Thelma and Louise* is characterized by its own chronotopic spaces, such as Darrell's living room and the police station; Hal lets himself into Louise's apartment using a credit card, showing the

move from private to public which the women effect in reverse, as he intrudes officially on to her space. These different chronotopes in the same text act dialogically to construct a particular meaning.

25 Stam, *Subversive Pleasures*, p. 187; Michael Gardiner, *The Dialogics of Critique: M. M. Bakhtin and the Theory of Ideology*, Routledge, London 1992, p. 204 n. 6.

26 An interesting comparison here is Muriel Spark's novel *The Driver's Seat* (Penguin, Harmondsworth 1970), in which the contingency and necessity of detective novels are parodied as a disturbed woman tries to grab the steering wheel of the novel in the only way, as a fictional character, she can: by driving to her own death.

27 Griggers emphasizes the signs in the film which place Thelma and Louise at a certain point in the trajectory of their lives; she mentions, for instance, the fact that they are baby boomers without children ('New Butch-Femme', p. 131).

28 See Hart's discussion of the unrepresented rape, *Fatal Women*, pp. 69–72.

29 Griggers, 'New Butch-Femme', p. 130.

30 Willis, 'Hardware and Hardbodies' p. 123; Hart, *Fatal Women*, p. 69.

31 Griggers, 'New Butch-Femme', p. 133. Hart sees the photograph flying away 'into the offscreen space' as a hint at a different, feminine economy: 'the photograph's disappearance allows us to imagine an elsewhere that resists representation' (*Fatal Women*, p. 80).

32 Hart, *Fatal Women*, p. 70; I am grateful to Neil Roberts and Pip Vice for discussing these points.

33 Willis, 'Hardware and Hardbodies', p. 125.

34 Kimberly J. Devlin, 'Pretending in "Penelope": Masquerade, Mimicry, and Molly Bloom', *Novel*, fall 1991, pp. 71–89.

35 Michael Holquist, *Dialogism: Bakhtin and His World*, Methuen, London 1990, p. 113.

36 *Ibid.*, p. 116.

37 Kitty Hart, *Return to Auschwitz*, Granada, London 1983.

38 Ida Fink, *The Journey*, trans. Joanna Wechsler and Francine Prose, Penguin, Harmondsworth 1994; the category given on the Penguin back cover is 'Fiction'.

39 *Ibid.*, pp. 77, 221.

40 *Ibid.*, pp. 179, 22 (where Pola betrays Zosia).

41 *Ibid.*, pp. 45, 224.

42 *Ibid.*, p. 226.

43 *Ibid.*, p. 11.

44 From reviews quoted on the book's back cover, by, respectively, Gabriele Annan in *The Times Literary Supplement*, and Katie Owen in the *Sunday Telegraph*.

45 This is an issue frequently discussed by and on behalf of survivors; in Art Spiegelman's cartoon-book *Maus*, for instance, the narrator, son of an Auschwitz survivor, discusses what made the difference between dying and living in the camps, and says of his father: 'sure, I know there was a lot of luck involved, but he was amazingly present-minded and resourceful', to which his therapist, also a survivor, says: 'But it wasn't the best people

who survived, nor did the best ones die. It was random!' (*Maus II: And Here My Troubles Began*, Pantheon Books, New York 1991, p. 45).

46 *Ibid.*, p. 4.

47 Fink, *The Journey*, p. 6.

48 *Ibid.*, p. 206.

49 *Ibid.*, p. 185.

50 *Ibid.*, p. 241.

51 The narrator of *The Journey* observes of one of her alter egos: 'I would find myself talking like a peasant, like the person I was supposed to be [...] it would occur to me later that I could live just like this: simply and peacefully, without all the things I used to need' (p. 231).

52 *Ibid.*, p. 6.

53 *Ibid.*, p. 57.

54 *Ibid.*, pp. 156, 170.

55 The phrase is used of Martin Amis's *Time's Arrow*, a novel about the Holocaust written not only from the point of view of a perpetrator, but backwards (James Wood, the *Guardian*, quoted on the cover of the Penguin edition, Harmondsworth 1991).

56 See Shlomith Rimmon-Kenan's discussion of narrative order, in *Narrative Fiction: Contemporary Poetics*, Methuen, London 1983, pp. 46–56; she prefers the term 'analepsis' to 'flashback' as it avoids the latter's filmic and psychological connotations (p. 46).

57 Fink, *The Journey*, p. 33.

58 *Ibid.*, p. 62.

59 *Ibid.*, p. 68.

60 See Freud's discussion of the psychological reasons for repeating traumas in one's dreams or behaviour: Sigmund Freud, 'Beyond the Pleasure Principle', *Standard Edition of the Complete Psychological Works*, ed. and trans. James Strachey, The Hogarth Press and the Institute of Psycho-Analysis, London 1953–73, vol. 18.

61 Fink, *The Journey*, p. 247. False summaries are given, predictions uttered very early on, and gaps are not filled in – at the time (in the case of the narrator's lover Marian) or ever (in the case of the fate of a gentile friend Halinka, who was willing to take in the narrator, but not her sister too).

Select bibliography

The Bakhtin circle

Bakhtin, M. M., *Art and Answerability: Early Philosophical Essays*, trs. Vadim Liapunov, ed. Michael Holquist and Vadim Liapunov, University of Texas Press, Austin, Texas 1990

——*The Dialogic Imagination: Four Essays*, trs. Caryl Emerson and Michael Holquist, ed. Michael Holquist, University of Texas Press, Austin, Texas 1981

——*Problems of Dostoevsky's Poetics*, trs. and ed. Caryl Emerson, University of Minnesota Press, Minneapolis, Minnesota 1984

——*Rabelais and His World*, trs. Hélène Iswolsky, Indiana University Press, Bloomington, Indiana 1984

——*Speech Genres and Other Late Essays*, trs. Vern McGee, eds Caryl Emerson and Michael Holquist, University of Texas Press, Austin, Texas 1986

——*Toward a Philosophy of the Act*, trs. Vadim Liapunov, ed. Vadim Liapunov and Michael Holquist, University of Texas Press, Austin, Texas 1993

Bakhtin, M. M./P. N. Medvedev, *The Formal Method in Literary Scholarship: A Critical Introduction to Sociological Poetics*, trs. A. J. Wehrle, Johns Hopkins University Press, Baltimore, Maryland 1978

Volosinov, V. N., *Freudianism*, trs. I. R. Titunik, ed. I. R. Titunik with N. H. Bruss, Indiana University Press, Indianapolis, Indiana 1987

——*Marxism and the Philosophy of Language*, trs. L. Matejka and I. R. Titunik, Harvard University Press, Cambridge, Mass. 1986

Bakhtin circle anthologies

The Bakhtin Reader: Selected Writings of Bakhtin, Medvedev, Voloshinov, ed. Pam Morris, Edward Arnold, London 1994

Bakhtin School Papers, ed. Ann Shukman, Russian Poetics in Translation vol. 10, RPT Publications, Oxford 1983

Bakhtinian Thought: An Introductory Reader, ed. Simon Dentith, Routledge, London 1995

Other primary texts

Atwood, Margaret, *The Edible Woman*, Virago, London 1980 [1969]

Carter, Angela, 'The Kitchen Child', in *Black Venus*, Picador, London 1986

Fink, Ida, *The Journey*, trs. Joanna Wechsler and Francine Prose, Penguin, Harmondsworth 1994 [1992]

Hoffman, Eva, *Lost in Translation: Life in a New Language*, Minerva, London 1991 [1989]

James, Henry, *What Maisie Knew*, Penguin, Harmondsworth 1966 [1897]

Joyce, James, *Ulysses: The Corrected Text*, ed. Hans Walter Gabler *et al.*, Penguin, Harmondsworth 1986 [1922]

Kelman, James, *How Late It Was, How Late*, Minerva, London 1995 [1994]

Lowry, Malcolm, *Under the Volcano*, Picador, London 1990 [1947]

——*The 1940 Under the Volcano*, eds Paul Tiessen and Miguel Mota, MLR Editions, Waterloo, Ontario 1994

Plath, Sylvia, *The Bell Jar*, Faber, London 1966 [1963]

Robertson, James, ed., *A Tongue in Yer Heid*, B&W Publishing, Edinburgh 1994

Roth, Henry, *Call It Sleep*, Bard Books, New York 1963 [1934]

Shute, Jenefer, *Life-size*, Secker and Warburg, London 1992

Zahavi, Helen, *Dirty Weekend*, Flamingo, London 1991

Critical works

Ackerley, Chris, and Lawrence J. Clipper, *A Companion to 'Under the Volcano'*, University of British Columbia Press, Vancouver 1984

Adlam, Carol, 'In the Name of Bakhtin: Russian and Anglo-American Readings of the Literary Writings 1990–1996', in *Exploiting Bakhtin*, eds Renfrew and Roberts

Adlam, Carol, Rachel Falconer, Vitalii Makhlin and Alastair Renfrew, eds, *Face to Face: Bakhtin in Russia and the West*, Sheffield Academic Press, Sheffield 1997

Arac, Jonathan, 'The Form of Carnival in *Under the Volcano*', *PMLA* 92, 1977, pp. 481–9

Ashcroft, Bill, Gareth Griffiths and Helen Tiffin, eds, *The Post-Colonial Studies Reader*, Routledge, London 1995

Barsky, Robert and Michael Holquist, eds, *Discours Social/Social Discourse: Bakhtin and Otherness* 3 (1–2), spring–summer 1990

Bauer, Dale M. and S. Jaret McKinstry, eds, *Feminism, Bakhtin, and the Dialogic*, State University of New York Press, Albany, NY 1991

Bellard-Thompson, Carol, 'Rabelais and Obscenity: A Woman's View', in *The Body and the Text: Hélène Cixous, Reading and Teaching*, eds Helen Wilcox *et al.*, Harvester Wheatsheaf, Hemel Hempstead 1990, pp. 167–74

Bernard-Donals, Michael F., *Mikhail Bakhtin: Between Phenomenology and Marxism*, Cambridge University Press, Cambridge 1994

Blake, Norman, *Non-standard Language in English Literature*, André Deutsch, London 1981

Bocharov, Sergey, 'Conversations with Bakhtin', *PMLA* 109 (5), October 1994, pp. 1009–24

Booth, Wayne, *The Rhetoric of Fiction*, University of Chicago Press, Chicago, Illinois 1961

Caughie, John, 'Adorno's Reproach: Repetition, Difference and Television Genre', *Screen* 32 (2), summer 1991, pp. 139–52

Chatman, Seymour, 'What Novels Can Do That Films Can't (and Vice Versa)', in *Film Theory and Criticism*, eds Gerald Mast, Marshall Cohen and Leo Braudy, Oxford University Press, New York 1992

Craig, Cairns, 'Resisting Arrest: James Kelman', in *The Scottish Novel since the Seventies*, eds Gavin Wallace and Randall Stevenson, Edinburgh University Press, Edinburgh 1993, pp. 99–114

Crawford, Robert, *Identifying Poets: Self and Territory in Twentieth-Century Poetry*, Edinburgh University Press, Edinburgh 1994

Danow, David K., *The Thought of Mikhail Bakhtin: From Word to Culture*, Macmillan, London 1991

Diaz-Diocaretz, Myriam, ed., *The Bakhtin Circle Today: Critical Studies* 1 (2) 1989

Doane, Mary Ann, *Femmes Fatales: Feminism, Film Theory, Psychoanalysis*, Routledge, London 1991

Eagleton, Terry, *Walter Benjamin, or Towards a Revolutionary Criticism*, New Left Books, London 1981

——'Wittgenstein's Friends', *New Left Review* 135, 1982, pp. 64–90

Emerson, Caryl, 'Preface to Mikhail K. Ryklin, "Bodies of Terror"', *New Literary History* 24 (1), winter 1993, pp. 45–9

Erdinast-Vulcan, Daphna, 'Bakhtin's Homesickness: A Late Reply to Julia Kristeva', *Textual Practice* 9 (2), 1995, pp. 223–42

Filipowicz, Halina, 'A Polish Expedition to Baltimore', *Drama Review* 31 (1), spring 1987, pp. 137–65

Fiske, John, *Television Culture*, Routledge, London 1987

Freud, Sigmund, *Standard Edition of the Complete Psychological Works*, ed. and trans. James Strachey, The Hogarth Press and the Institute of Psycho-Analysis, London 1953–73

Gardiner, Michael, *The Dialogics of Critique: M. M. Bakhtin and the Theory of Ideology*, Routledge, London 1992

Griggers, Cathy, '*Thelma and Louise* and the Cultural Generation of the New Butch-Femme', in *Film Theory Goes to the Movies*, eds Jim Collins, Hilary Radner, and Ava Preacher Collins, Routledge, New York 1993, pp. 129–41

Harshav, Benjamin, *The Meaning of Yiddish*, University of California Press, Berkeley and Oxford 1990

Hart, Lynda, *Fatal Women: Lesbian Sexuality and the Mark of Aggression*, Routledge, London 1994

Haynes, D. J., *Bakhtin and the Visual Arts*, Cambridge University Press, Cambridge 1995

Healy, Thomas, *New Latitudes: Theory and English Renaissance Literature*, Edward Arnold, London 1992

Hirschkop, Ken, 'Bakhtin, Discourse and Democracy', *New Left Review* 160, November/December 1986, pp. 92–113

——'Is Dialogue for Real?', *Social Text* 30, 1987, pp. 102–13

Hirschkop, Ken and David Shepherd, eds, *Bakhtin and Cultural Theory*, Manchester University Press, Manchester 1989

Hohne, Karen, and Helen Wussow, eds, *A Dialogue of Voices: Feminist Literary Theory and Bakhtin*, University of Minnesota Press, Minneapolis, Minnesota 1994

Holquist, Michael, *Dialogism: Bakhtin and His World*, Methuen, London 1990

Holquist, Michael and Katerina Clark, *Mikhail Bakhtin*, Harvard University Press, Cambridge, Mass. 1984

Jackson, Peter, 'Street Life: The Politics of Carnival', *Society and Space* 6, 1988, pp. 213–27

Joki, Ilkka, *Mamet, Bakhtin and the Dramatic: The Demotic as a Variable of Addressivity*, Abo Akademy University Press, Abo 1993

Kristeva, Julia, *Powers of Horror: An Essay on Abjection*, trs. Leon S. Roudiez, Columbia University Press, New York 1982

———'Word, Dialogue, and Novel', in *Desire in Language: A Semiotic Approach to Literature and Art*, trans. Leon S. Roudiez, Basil Blackwell, Oxford 1980, pp. 64–91

Leech, Geoffrey and Michael Short, *Style in Fiction*, Longman, London 1982

Lodge, David, *After Bakhtin: Essays on Fiction and Criticism*, Routledge, London 1990

McGuirk, Carol, 'Burns, Bakhtin, and the Opposition of Poetic and Novelistic Discourse: A Response to David Morris', *The Eighteenth Century: Theory and Interpretation* 32 (1), 1991, pp. 58–71

Mandelker, Amy, ed., *Bakhtin in Contexts: Across the Disciplines*, Northwestern University Press, Evanston, Illinois 1995

Miller, Jane, *Seductions: Studies in Reading and Culture*, Virago, London 1990

Moi, Toril, *Sexual/Textual Politics: Feminist Literary Theory*, Methuen, London 1985

Morris, David, 'Burns and Heteroglossia', *The Eighteenth Century: Theory and Interpretation* 28 (1), 1987, pp. 3–27

Morson, Gary Saul, ed., *Bakhtin: Essays and Dialogues on His Work*, University of Chicago Press, Chicago, Illinois 1986

———'Tolstoy's Absolute Language', *Critical Inquiry* 7, 1980–1, pp. 667–85

Morson, Gary Saul and Caryl Emerson, 'Imputations and Amputations: Reply to Wall and Thomson', *Diacritics* 23 (4), winter 1993, pp. 93–9

———*Mikhail Bakhtin: The Creation of a Prosaics*, Stanford University Press, Stanford, California 1990

———eds, *Rethinking Bakhtin: Extensions and Challenges*, Northwestern University Press, Evanston, Illinois 1989

Mulvey, Laura, 'Visual Pleasure and Narrative Cinema', *Screen* 16 (3), 1975, pp. 6–18

Palmer, R. Barton, 'Bakhtinian Translinguistics and Film Criticism: The Dialogical Image?', in *The Cinematic Text: Methods and Approaches*, ed. R. Barton Palmer, AMS Press, New York 1989, pp. 303–41

Pearce, Lynne, *Reading Dialogics*, Edward Arnold, London 1994

Renfrew, Alastair, 'Them and Us? Representation of Speech in Contemporary Scottish Fiction', in *Exploiting Bakhtin*, eds Renfrew and Roberts

Renfrew, Alastair, and Graham Roberts, eds, *Exploiting Bakhtin*, Strathclyde Modern Language Studies, new series, 2, 1997

Rigolot, François, 'Rabelais, Misogyny, and Christian Charity: Biblical Intertextuality and the Renaissance Crisis of Exemplarity', *PMLA* 109 (2), March 1994, pp. 225–37

Rimmon-Kenan, Shlomith, *Narrative Fiction: Contemporary Poetics*, Methuen,

London 1983

Roberts, Diane, *The Myth of Aunt Jemima: Representations of Race and Region*, Routledge, London 1994

Rodger, Liam, 'Tense, Aspect and *The Busconductor Hines* – the Literary Function of Non-Standard Language in the Fiction of James Kelman', Edinburgh Working Papers on Applied Linguistics, 3, 1992, pp. 116–23

Rosten, Leo, *The Joys of Yiddish*, W. H. Allen, London 1970

Russo, Mary, *The Female Grotesque: Risk, Excess, and Modernity*, Routledge, London 1994

Ryklin, Mikhail K., 'Bodies of Terror: Theses Toward a Logic of Violence', *NLH* 24 (1), winter 1993, pp. 51–74

Sage, Lorna, *Angela Carter*, Northcote House Publishing, Plymouth 1994

——ed., *Flesh and the Mirror: Essays on the Art of Angela Carter*, Virago, London 1994

Shepherd, David, ed., *Bakhtin, Carnival and Other Subjects*, Critical Studies 3 (2)–4 (1/2), 1993

Stallybrass, Peter, 'Reading the Body and the Jacobean Theatre of Consumption: *The Revenger's Tragedy* (1606)' in *Staging the Renaissance: Reinterpretations of Elizabethan and Jacobean Drama*, eds David Scott Kastan and Peter Stallybrass, Routledge, London 1991, pp. 210–20

Stallybrass, Peter and Allon White, *The Politics and Poetics of Transgression*, Methuen, London 1986

Stam, Robert, *Reflexivity in Film and Literature, from 'Don Quixote' to Jean-Luc Godard*, UMI Research Press Studies in Cinema, Ann Arbor, Michigan 1985

——*Subversive Pleasures: Bakhtin, Cultural Criticism and Film*, Johns Hopkins University Press, Baltimore, Maryland 1989

Tennenhouse, Leonard, *Power on Display: The Politics of Shakespeare's Genres*, Methuen, London and New York 1986

——'Strategies of State and Political Plays: *A Midsummer Night's Dream, Henry IV, Henry V, Henry VIII'*, in *Political Shakespeare: New Essays in Cultural Materialism*, eds Jonathan Dollimore and Alan Sinfield, Manchester University Press, Manchester 1985

Thomson, Clive, ed., *Mikhail Bakhtin and the Epistemology of Discourse*, Critical Studies 2 (1/2), 1990

Titunik, I.R., 'Bakhtin &/or Volosinov &/or Medvedev: Dialogue &/or Doubletalk?', in *Language and Literary Theory*, eds Benjamin A. Stolz, I. R. Titunik, and Lubomír Dolezel, Papers in Slavic Philology 5, University of Michigan, Ann Arbor, Michigan 1984, pp. 535–64

Todorov, Tzvetan, *Mikhail Bakhtin: The Dialogical Principle*, University of Minnesota Press, Minneapolis, Minnesota 1984

Wall, Anthony and Clive Thomson, 'Cleaning Up Bakhtin's Carnival Act', *Diacritics* 23 (2), summer 1993, pp. 47–70

Wesling, Donald, 'Mikhail Bakhtin and the Social Poetics of Dialect', *Papers in Language and Literature* 29 (3), 1993, pp. 303–220

White, Allon, 'Bakhtin, Sociolinguistics, Deconstruction', in *Carnival, Hysteria and Writing: Collected Essays and an Autobiography*, Oxford University Press, Oxford 1994, pp. 135–59

Williams, Raymond, 'The Road from Vitebsk', *New Left Review* 158, July/August 1986, pp.19–31

Willis, Sharon, 'Hardware and Hardbodies, What Do Women Want?: A Reading of *Thelma and Louise*', in *Film Theory Goes to the Movies*, eds Jim Collins, Hilary Radner, and Ava Preacher Collins, Routledge, New York 1993, pp. 120–8

Index